Wilderness Songs

Wilderness Songs

Justin Anderson

BATSFORD

First published in the United Kingdom
in 2026 by
Batsford
43 Great Ormond Street
London
WC1N 3HZ

An imprint of B. T. Batsford Holdings Limited

ISBN 9781837330669

A CIP catalogue record for this book is available from the British Library.

10 9 8 7 6 5 4 3 2 1

Reproduction by Rival Colour Ltd, UK
Printed in Turkey

This book can be ordered direct from the publisher at www.batsfordbooks.com, or try your local bookshop

Distributed throughout the UK and Europe by Abrams & Chronicle Books, 1st Floor, 22–24 Ely Place, London EC1N 6TE and 57 rue Gaston Tessier, 75166 Paris, France

www.abramsandchronicle.co.uk

info@abramsandchronicle.co.uk

FSC
www.fsc.org
100%
Paper from well-managed forests
FSC® C111584

For Dan

Contents

Prologue

Ghost song

I HEARD SOMETHING. It was enough to pull me from a deep sleep. Entombed in layers of clothing and a warm sleeping bag, it took me a while to free myself. Stepping outside of my tent into the darkness, the crunch of my footsteps and the buzz of the tent zipper seemed amplified against the stillness of the mountains. Just getting out of bed at this high altitude meant I was soon puffing like a train and could feel the blood pumping in my temples. I stood for a while to get my breath back, just listening. It was a beautiful night in the high Himalaya. The mountains were covered in a fresh fall of snow. They glowed under the light of the moon, their ridges extending for miles. Above them, a ceiling of stars looked down over the frozen silence. I pulled off my warm woollen beanie, suffering the cold in order to hear more clearly. Had I imagined it?

Then it came again. My ears pricked. A sound so spectral, it filled me with pure wonder. Echoing around the peaks came the distant song of a snow leopard. Knowing how rare this was to hear, I felt unbelievably lucky and, despite the cold, I stayed listening long after the cat had gone.

I was part of a team that had travelled to the Indian Himalaya to film and record snow leopards for a nature documentary. They are elusive and very well camouflaged, so to see a snow leopard you have to be incredibly fortunate. We were reliant on a wonderful team of local Ladakhi spotters, who barely stopped scanning the mountains with their scopes. Whenever they saw a cat, we all crowded around the telescope and took turns to peer at it through the eyepiece. I remember seeing my first snow leopard like it was yesterday. It was silver-grey with a long luxuriant tail that it had wrapped around its paws as it sat looking down over the valley. It was beautiful. I was so excited that I joined in with our camp cook as he danced a little jig of happiness. The Ladakhi say that when you see a snow leopard, it feels as if your soul is flying.

If seeing a cat is a special and a rare privilege then hearing one sing is on another level. We had come to the mountains at the start of spring, when for just a few short weeks the snow leopards are looking for a mate. Normally these cats are solitary, spending their lives wandering the mountains alone. Across their Himalayan range, snow leopards are few and far between, so finding another snow leopard in the vastness of the mountains is a huge challenge. They do so by first using their sense of smell, marking special 'signpost' rocks with their scent. When a female cat is in heat, males will be able to smell her condition on these marking rocks and, by following their noses, will trail her for days over the mountains. But all this spraying and sniffing is just a first step on the path to finding a mate. The biggest challenge for the snow leopards is actually pinpointing each other in the complex topography of peaks, pinnacles and gorges. They do this by making sound. Both males and females call and it seems they like to climb high up on a ridge top, where the sound of their voices will travel further over the mountains. They take a deep breath and yowl, lifting their heads slightly at the end to embellish each long note. Snow leopards are the only big cats that cannot roar. Their vocal cords lack the layer of fatty elasticated tissue found in lions and other big cats, which vibrates to give the deep rumbling quality of a roar.

So, without this ability, snow leopards yowl instead. The local Ladakhi people often refer to this call as 'singing'. We know so little about exactly what they are saying and whether it's the male or female that calls first. Our remote camera-trap recordings revealed that the cats may have their favourite spots for calling, often a narrow point on a ridge top or a ledge on the edge of a void. Our Ladakhi guides reported seeing the cats call from the same spots on different occasions. Perhaps these favourite vantage points allow them to send their call out further or maybe they are more easily seen by other cats when positioned up high.

Heard close up (for example in a recording from a zoo) the call of a snow leopard sounds like the ugly caterwaul of an alley cat and you might think that I was guilty of over-romanticising things. But this sound is all about the context. When I talk to schoolchildren about snow leopards, I play them this call, but before I do, I always ask them to close their eyes and imagine they are lying in a cold tent, their ears strained against the silence of the frozen mountains. As I press play on the recordings and the kids listen in, broad beaming smiles break out across their faces. The rare call of this most beautiful and mysterious of animals, echoing around the mountains, really is something very special.

Scan to hear the song of a snow leopard.

Introduction

THE STATION ANNOUNCEMENT whistled alarmingly as it blurted out its unwelcome news. The train was late. There was an audible sigh of resignation from the frustrated commuters. We were stuck for another twenty minutes, waiting for an early morning train from south Bristol into the city centre. I looked around for a distraction to fill the time, but the platform was hemmed in by deep walls of brambles and there were no posters to read. So, with nothing to see, I began to listen.

From its perch on the station fence a robin sang, its voice a reminder of long walks in the woods. I could hear two jenny wrens arguing in the bushes, firing staccato notes at each other from one side of the tracks to the other. A beautiful song thrush joined the conversation, its repeated phrases pronounced loud and clear. One moment mellow and fluty and the next metallic and rasping. I found myself thinking it had been a long time since I had heard a thrush here in the city. Its song was a real wake-up call, articulated so fluently that it banished any last remaining memories of sleep with a clarity that made it impossible to ignore.

Even in the centre of our biggest cities there are amazing natural sounds to be heard. All we have to do is tune into them. There were about fifteen other commuters standing there with me on the platform. I looked around at my travel companions, hoping to share a smile or some kind of recognition of the wonderful performance we were being treated to. But everybody else was looking at their phones. Nobody noticed. It was as if the birdsong was simply ambient noise, to be ignored just like the growl of the traffic or the distant roar of a plane overhead. I wondered how we had become so immune to something so wonderful? How is it that we no longer hear it and what does our indifference say about our relationship with the natural world that surrounds us?

In the following chapters I will take you on a global journey from the highest peaks to the bottom of the ocean. As a wildlife filmmaker for over thirty years, I have been lucky enough to visit some of the planet's last true wilderness areas and been face to face with some of the most incredible animals. During this time, I have also experienced some amazing natural sounds and worked hard with my crews to record them. But I have also encountered many new stories and revealing scientific discoveries about natural sound that I am excited to share with you in the following pages.

From blue whales that can converse across oceans to the complexities of birdsong, our planet is alive with incredible sound. There is a buzz on the coral reef, an animal orchestra performs in the rainforest and haunting tones echo around the desert. However, it's only recently that advances in microphones and artificial intelligence have allowed us to listen in and begin to understand the true complexities of these soundscapes. This new generation of technology is helping us to monitor the decline in biodiversity and can play an increasingly important part in saving endangered species. And in a world where human noise is growing ever louder, we will discover how animals have had to adapt their communication to find new ways to be heard.

My adventures and these stories are only a part of the reason for this book. I firmly believe that taking time to listen to our natural world is one of the best ways we can hope to reconnect with nature, and there are now a number of scientific studies that have proved it. Wild sounds act as a reminder of our place in nature and they encourage us to appreciate it and protect it.

As you read each chapter, you will come across a number of QR codes. By scanning these with your mobile phone, you'll be linked to a recording of the sounds that are featured in the story. All you have to do is press play, close your eyes and listen.

The recordings in this book have been captured by dedicated scientists, artists, filmmakers and conservationists. They represent some of the most astonishing sounds in the natural world, from immersive soundscapes, to animal calls beyond the reach of our own hearing. There are sounds sourced from different sonic worlds, from the collapse of a glacier, to the tiny whispering chatter of leafcutter ants. There are sounds to make you laugh and the poignant final recordings of extinct species.

But this book is just the start. Next time you are in the woods, take time to listen to the wind in the trees. Next time you visit the ocean, close your eyes and listen out for the crashing of the waves. When you stand at your kitchen window or at your back door with a coffee before work, listen to the melodious song of your neighbourhood blackbird. It's been scientifically proven to boost your mood and can even improve your health. You may even become part of a growing movement of people seeking to reconnect with nature and build a more sustainable future for us all. Our planet is alive with incredible natural sound. There has never been a better time to listen in to what it is saying.

1. Call of the Wild

WHY NATURAL SOUNDS MATTER

A Brief History of Listening

I AM LUCKY TO have married into an Irish family and most summers we overload the family car with wetsuits, walking boots, snorkels and all kinds of holiday paraphernalia to take the long drive from Bristol to Fishguard for the ferry over to Ireland. We usually end up as guests of my brother-in-law and his wife, staying in their remote rural home among the windswept fields of the coastline of West Cork. Coming from a big city like Bristol it feels good to exchange the soundscapes of the busy city for a place that is noticeably 'quieter'. Upon arrival you experience something of an auditory detox. Without the relentless sounds made by over half a million people this new soundscape can at first feel empty. But after a few days I become aware of my ears adjusting as I begin to hear a whole different set of sounds, timeless and less intrusive than the din from the city but no less prominent – I start to tune into the sounds of nature.

Early on the first morning of one such holidays, I pulled on my trainers and looked out the window. Outside the air was cooler and I could hear the distant waves calling me from down the hill where the road turned towards the sea and gave way to a narrow track leading to a cove and a secluded beach. My run down the lane took me past hedgerows alive with colour. Yellow ragworts and purple tufted vetch fought for space among swaths of orange montbretia and deep pink fuchsias, both non-native but flourishing in the frost free, damp coastal climate. On bowing telegraph wires strung overhead, gangs of fledgling swallows lined up, chattering endlessly among themselves. It was hard not to interpret their lively banter as excitement for the new-found joy of flying and their imminent first adventure down to Africa. I ran past an old tumbledown farmhouse and disturbed a gang of rosy-breasted linnets feeding among rows of freshly cut hay, soon to be baled. They rose up as one and passed overhead, making their sweet twittering call.

I almost stopped in my tracks, when further down the lane I heard the haunting cry of a curlew. Many curlews migrate from Britain and northern Europe to Ireland to overwinter by the coast, so maybe this solitary bird was an early arrival.

In Irish folklore the curlew's call is often thought of as an omen of bad weather and I couldn't help but notice the darkening clouds suddenly rolling in from the sea. Across Britain and Ireland traditional stories once told that the curlew was a member of the 'Seven Whistlers' – a group of mysterious and magical birds that flew together at night. To hear their calls was to receive a warning, predicting anything from an incoming storm to a portent of an untimely death.

The idea that the sound of a bird may come as a warning has long been a common belief among many cultures across the world, and is one that remains widespread today. The Amis people of Taiwan regard owls as guardians of the forest and the carriers of messages between the human and natural worlds. Their hoots are thought to announce news of pregnancies among women in the tribe and the owl's vocalisations can even be interpreted to determine the baby's gender. In Aotearoa New Zealand, the morepork (the country's only native owl species) is an important messenger in Māori culture. Connecting the spiritual and physical worlds, it is known as a spirit guardian or a *kaitiaki.* To hear its distinctive 'more pork' hooting can be seen as a source of comfort or reassurance, but should you hear its sharper 'quee' cry, you should take care as the *kaitiaki* is sending you a warning of things to come. In many cultures, the hooting of an owl is seen as a harbinger of evil and misfortune and it seems that this threat has likely been used for generations to inspire young children to behave well and go to sleep. Among South Africa's Tsonga and Shangaan people, the call of an owl is a curse sent by a witch that could lead to illness or death. In some villages they will even put spikes on their rooftops to discourage any owls from perching there. So, if you happen to hear an owl hooting, you will need to seek out a traditional healer and find out exactly what misfortune the future holds.

These stories remind us that, for most of human history, people have listened closely to the sounds around them – a practice that remains alive in many communities today. The San people (also known as the Bushmen) of the Kalahari region of southern Africa are among the oldest continuous human cultures on Earth. They are expert listeners and can interpret the sounds of animals to help them survive in their desert home. The 'kek kek' alarm of a helmeted guinea fowl is known to flush other species from cover, but approach too quickly and you might get spotted by a go away bird, whose 'go away' alarm call is a warning to be more patient when you are hunting. In the desert water is scarce, so the San have learnt to listen to the animals to lead them to the few precious places to drink. At dawn and again around dusk, flocks of Namaqua sandgrouse make their regular commute out from the bush to find water. As they fly overhead, the birds make a bubbling tremble which the San can follow to find permanent waterholes. If the water in one pan dries up, the croaking chorus of African bullfrogs and the chirping of cicadas can help guide the San to areas where rain has recently fallen. The San believe that these calls are the animals 'speaking' directly to them.

When it comes to natural sounds the San can be considered as deep listeners, as they have the ability to piece together complex natural narratives, revealing an entire ecological conversation from the sounds they can hear. If the guinea fowl are making their alarm call, at the same time as a pair of drongos are screeching and a jackal then barks in the distance, an experienced San hunter might learn that a herd of kudu are on the run and are being chased by a predator. Even the lack of animal sounds could be a clue that there are lions hiding in the thorn bushes close by. Sounds not only provide the San hunter with practical clues, they also carry a spiritual connection as they are all part of a bigger soundscape that they call the 'language of the land'. They have a lot to teach us about the art of listening to nature.

The track narrowed to a grass-covered pathway, and blackberry-laden brambles and wild roses crowded the last short distance to the sea. The secret cove, or *cuan* in Irish, was a rocky horseshoe, open to the Atlantic. Tall cliffs of rust-red and silver rock rose out of the water, enclosing the cove and forcing your eyes to seek out the horizon. I took off my vest and trainers and tiptoed gingerly over the rough shingle and into the water. It was freezing. Stealing myself, I ducked under and immediately leapt up like a salmon, gasping, the breath knocked out of me. Slowly I got used to the cold, my nervous system numbed till the water actually felt comfortable. The swell was gentle and it allowed me to sit down on the seabed, legs and arms outstretched as if cradled in a saltwater armchair. My breathing returning to normal, I closed my eyes and listened.

I could hear the distant waves as they crashed against the arête of sharp rocks that guarded the mouth of the cuan. Having passed this first barrier, each broad and gentle wave would lap along the edge of the cliffs before rolling into a deep black sea cave where they would hit the back of the cavern with a booming slap that echoed back over the beach. I was aware of the 'gloop' from the tide shifting the floating canopy of the kelp, gently tugging on its auburn belts with a satisfying slurp, like the chug of wine poured slowly into a glass. Tuning in, I could just make out an intimate 'plup' from the bubbles sent up by the burrowing of my toes as they gripped into the sand and shingle, holding me in place against the swell. But I could only make out these quieter sounds in the gaps between the impact of the waves. The rise and fall of each swell began with a roar of surging water followed by a crash as the surf hit the beach. This was the loudest sound I could hear. It was predictable and rhythmic, itself like a beating heart. Every collision of water and land was soon followed by the unrolling crackle of the retreating water running over the stones, its rivulets and columns stampeding back to the sea like an army in full retreat. The Irish word for this sound of rushing seawater returning home to the ocean is *stranach*.

With a 7,500km coastline facing the constant tides of the North Atlantic, Ireland is a country rooted in the influence of the sea. It's a land where the great cities and towns along its shores evolved from fishing villages and, as a result, the traditional Irish language was full of references to the ocean – as is the case among other Indigenous languages which have evolved in proximity to the coastline. While many of these words are functional, there is plenty of room for a more poetic, descriptive turn of phrase. In Donegal, *mada doininne* is a dark cloud on the ocean's horizon that translates as 'hounds of the storm', while in Galway *Or bláth bán ar gharraí an iascaire* describes a choppy sea as 'white flowers in the fisherman's garden' and a sarcastic person might be a *tá sé mar a bheadh scadán i dtóin an bharraille* ('like a salted herring from the bottom of the barrel'). But this rich coastal language also has plenty of wonderful words describing the sound of the sea itself. *Tarrantacha* is the sound that comes from the stones being rolled by the current of a retreating spring tide. *Caibleadh* are the faint sounds on the sea breeze, thought to be the whispers of spirits. *Onfais* is the roaring sound of huge plunging waves and *Coel na mara*, literally the 'music of the sea', describes the various melodies and harmonies made by the endlessly shifting ocean.

While there is no evidence that Indigenous languages contain more words that describe nature, it is thought that these languages have historically carried more locally specific nature vocabulary which is used more in everyday speech. The evolution of languages tracks our ecology and livelihoods, so it makes sense if you live a life closer to the sea, or deep in the forest, or high up in the Arctic ice, that you will more commonly use words that describe these worlds, or that the sounds present in them will become imbued with meaning.

The Amazon rainforest is home to as many as 400 different groups of Indigenous peoples. Their complex and varied languages often share an unusually rich system for describing sounds, from bird and insect calls, to the sound of rain and the rustling of leaves. These words are often highly specific and are born from local knowledge of the forest. Many Amazonian languages include words that may evoke a description or even a sensory experience. Words might resemble dripping water by using repeated syllables, follow rhythmic patterns to describe frogs calling at dusk or use sharp consonants for branches snapping in the forest. The Quechua/Kichwa people of the Runa Indigenous communities of the Ecuadorian Amazon have many words that mimic forest sounds from animals, movement, to the flow of water and other environmental phenomena. The word *tandangar* is used for the sound of a woodpecker drumming on a tree. The final 'r' is often trilled to mimic the rapid-fire pecking of the bird. One phrase *tuluk tuluk tuluk* describes the sound and motion of a snake moving inside a hollow stump. The word *bhux* (often strongly aspirated) is spoken to mimic and describe the energetic bursting out of the water by a river dolphin, while *mema* is the sound of a sloth crying and like many of these words is accompanied by visual gestures. Some of these words not only describe the natural sound but associate them with a strong emotional response. *Wiyu yuw* is the sad cry of a sun bittern that can't find any fish to eat, while *shili shili* is the call of a swallow expressing its happiness after the rains. Across the world, words that describe natural sounds speak to a familiarity with the land that's come from listening to it for tens of thousands of years.

Globally, we have a long tradition of listening to natural sounds to inspire art and even science. In the 4th century BCE, the classical Greek philosopher Aristotle wrote his *History of Animals* where he makes several detailed descriptions of animals and their sounds. He was fascinated by cicadas and crickets and described accurately how they make sound through vibration rather than with voices. He also observed the difference between the types of sound made by birds.

> *Some birds utter a cry, others a song; the raven's voice is a cry, the nightingale's a song. Singing birds are for the most part small, and such as are of a lively temperament. Birds with powerful bodies and large in size, like the raven, emit a croak or harsh cry.*

Aristotle even suggested that young birds learn their songs by imitating adult birds, something we now know to be true.

Long before we invented the means to record sound, poets and writers would try to capture its essence in words. A bestiary was an early form of illustrated encyclopaedia that was popular during the 12th to 14th centuries. Their pages contained animals, some real, some gloriously imagined. Today their fragile pages provide a fascinating insight into how we once listened to and interpreted the natural world. Among the collection of the University of Aberdeen's library sits the famous Aberdeen Bestiary. Written sometime in the early 13th century, its pages are made of calfskin vellum and richly illuminated by bright-coloured pigments and sparkling gold leaf. It is thought to have been produced in a monastery or cathedral such as York or Lincoln, both famed for their scriptoriums. This extraordinary 800-year-old book has about 206 pages and contains vivid descriptions of mammals, birds, reptiles, fish, insects, trees, stones and even includes mythical creatures such as the unicorn. The bird section is the largest and there are many examples where the text pays special attention to the sounds they make.

One excerpt about nightingales reads:

The nightingale has a sweet song, and loves to sing. It sings to relieve the tedium as it sits on its nest through the night. At dawn it sings so enthusiastically that it almost dies.

The bestiary goes further and likens the nightingale to a poor mother:

The poor but modest mother, her arm dragging the millstone around, that her children may not lack bread, imitates the nightingale, easing the misery of her poverty with a night-time song … she matches it in her devotion to duty.

Painstakingly handwritten and painted by monks whose names are now long forgotten, bestiaries often give moral or allegorical meanings to the natural sounds they describe. The sweetness of a nightingale's song could symbolise worldly pleasures that lure the soul away from God. The crowing of a cock heralding the dawn was likened to Christ bringing light to the world, and the gentle cooing of a dove represented peace, purity and the Holy Spirit. In these pages birds don't just sing, their voices provide moral guidance.

But not all early written descriptions of natural sound are quite so didactic. Some seem written purely for the pleasure of listening. The 17th-century poet and master of the Japanese haiku, Matsuo Bashō, would commonly use descriptions of natural sounds as a base for his poems. The rain, the chirp of cicadas and the hush of the falling snow all appear in his writing. But perhaps his most famous haiku was born of the joy of listening to the frogs in his small pond outside his simple wooden hut.

an ancient pond
a frog jumps in
the splash of water

Even our own William Wordsworth was constantly inspired by the sounds of nature to fuel his poetic writing. After listening to rushing water he wrote: 'The sounding cataract haunted me like a passion'. He also makes reference to the 'air through budding twigs' to describe the wind moving through the trees. As a poet, Wordsworth was passionate about birds and was clearly thrilled by the delight of birdsong. He tells of the 'airy lay' of the linnet's song and in his poem 'To the Cuckoo', written in 1802, he exalted:

O' blithe New- Comer! I have heard.
I hear thee and rejoice.

The American poet Emily Dickinson took listening to nature to a whole new level. Her home in Amherst, Massachusetts, was surrounded by farms, woods and meadows, and she would often wander through the countryside listening for inspiration. Her poems are so rich in natural sound that they could even be thought of as a series of poetic field recordings. Rather than just describe the sounds, she would use rhythm and punctuation to mimic them, from short staccato words for the quick precise movement of birds …

The humming-bird's quick wing
Beats music in the air,
And all the garden listens close
To hear his tiny snare.

… to the soft dripping of rain on the roof:

The rain is full of ghosts tonight –
Dripping softly on the roof,
Whispers in the darkened grass,
Calling each leaf aloof.

During her lifetime, very few of Dickinson's poems were published. Those that were ended up being altered by editors who changed her punctuation and line breaks and reordered the natural rhythms she had worked so hard to master. Dickinson liked to use dashes rather than the more accepted comma and it may have been that she intended these to signal a longer pause for anyone reading the poem aloud. She used the dashes to mimic the disjointed, irregular movements of the natural world. Dickinson also experimented with rhyme in a way that was seen as unconventional and her editors struggled to grasp her creativity. In one example, her poem about a grass snake titled 'A narrow Fellow in the Grass', the editor added a question mark for grammatical correctness that Dickinson had deliberately omitted and she complained that this change 'defeated' the fluid linking of the lines when read aloud.

Most of her work was discovered after her death in 1886, when her family found over 1,700 poems in boxes of handwritten notebooks. The first collections of Dickinson's poetry were published between 1890 and 1898 but these too were heavily edited to make them more palatable for a conservative audience. It wasn't until 1955 that her work was published unedited with all her off-rhymes and dashes restored, allowing us to fully appreciate her poetry's natural rhythms.

Of course, it's not only poets that have tried to describe natural sounds with words. The great Charles Darwin frequently did so in his writings and often he would link the animal's calls to their behaviour and emotions. He was fascinated by the connection between animal vocalisations and our own human language. Darwin explored the role of sound in telling one species from another and how animals might make sounds to try and attract a mate. On his famous voyage to the Galapagos Islands in 1835, he recorded: 'The frigate-bird utters a loud, harsh cry as it sails; the cormorants, in flocks, have a kind of croaking note, especially when disturbed.'

When describing the sounds he heard, Darwin almost always recorded conclusions about their functional purpose: 'The ground finches are not remarkable for their song; yet one may hear a few shrill notes when the males are contesting their mates or defending their territory.'

And in many cases, he even suggests an emotional context behind the sound. 'The land-iguana, when irritated, hisses loudly and opens its jaws; the sound is not musical, but sufficiently expressive to alarm the timid observer.' And: 'The Galápagos tortoise, in drawing its long breath, emits a low, vibrating hiss, which is heard at some distance. It appears to denote uneasiness more than alarm.'

Reading these notes, it becomes clear that listening to the natural world played a pivotal part in the development of Darwin's theory of evolution and natural selection, which he eventually published as *On the Origin of Species* in 1859.

Up to this point in history, listening to natural sounds could only ever be momentary and the only way to capture them for recollection would be to describe them with words and sometimes in music. But in 1877 Thomas Edison invented the cylinder phonograph and turned 'listening' into 'recording'. His machine mimicked the structure of a human ear, substituting an elastic membrane for an eardrum and a set of levers to act as ear bones. The vibrations picked up were permanently etched in grooves on a tin-foil cylinder, meaning it was then possible to reverse the process and play back the sound. But the tin foil was fragile and could easily tear, so future versions of the machine used cylinders coated in wax. Over the years further refinements led to the cylinders evolving to be a flattened disk with the sounds recorded as a spiral groove becoming the first gramophones and their 'records' made of hard rubber.

Edison is reported to have taken his phonograph into the outside world and attempted to capture the sounds of birds singing around his laboratory. He was keen to demonstrate that even high-pitched, delicate sounds could be captured on his machine. In truth the phonograph wasn't ideally suited to the recordings of nature. The early wax cylinders had a narrow frequency range so, despite Edison's efforts, barely picked up the high-pitched calls of birds and insects. The machine was heavy and delicate so moving it around outdoors was a huge challenge. The clarity of the recording was easily spoiled by ambient noise from wind, rustling leaves or urban noise. The cylinders only allowed for up to four minutes of recording, which limited the sounds you could hope to capture; and even if you did get lucky and capture an amazing sound, the playback sounded muffled and many of the nuances were lost. The early pioneer biologists looking to use Edison's invention to record and study natural sound often brought their subjects inside to make their recordings clearer, and one who did brave the outdoors even went so far as to always set up the phonograph in a tent to find some protection from the spoiling effect of the wind.

It wasn't until the 1920s and 30s that things really changed with the rise of a true pioneer wildlife sound recordist. Born into a wealthy Jewish family living in Frankfurt, Ludwig Koch grew up in a home surrounded by a menagerie of 68 animals. As an eight-year-old he made his first animal sound recordings on an Edison phonograph and a box of wax cylinders that had been a gift from his father. His 1889 recording of the song of his white-rumped shama, a caged Indian bird, is thought to be the oldest surviving recording of birdsong. After World War I, Koch worked for the German government and was commissioned by the German wing of Electrical and Musical Industries (EMI) to start a project working on cultural recordings for the gramophone industry. In 1929 he returned to his childhood passion and started recording animal sounds; he invented the 'sound book' where he combined gramophone records with an illustrated book. In doing so, you could say that he devised the first ever 'multimedia' product.

In 1936, after his recordings won favour with the prominent Nazi Hermann Göring, who as an animal lover was something of a fan, Koch, himself an outspoken critic of Nazi policies, decided to flee to the UK, which he then made his home. Sadly, most of his long catalogue of natural sound recordings remained in Germany and were lost, but he did manage to rescue his first ever boyhood recording of the white-rumped shama. Koch started collecting sounds again and in 1936 released *Songs of Wild Birds* with writer Edward Max Nicholson, which featured recordings of numerous British bird species, including nightingales, cuckoos, skylarks and more. The gramophone disk came with an illustrated book with text that described the birds and the whole thing created a wonderfully immersive experience. The project was a huge hit, remained in print for seventeen years and had eight different impressions. This success brought Koch to the attention of the BBC where soon he had his own radio programme. Koch, in his thick German accent, would tell the story of his quests to record wild sounds and his accounts were full of humour. Then listeners would hear his sound recordings in wonderful uninterrupted detail. It was what the 'wireless' radio was made for.

Koch was incredibly popular with British audiences and became a household name. He appeared on *Children's Hour* and had a regular slot on a show called *Country Magazine*, which at its peak attracted 7 million listeners a week. In the field his innovative recording methods set new standards. Dressed in his oilskins and breeches he would go to extraordinary lengths to make his recordings.

> *I have been trying to recapture the sounds of English birds this spring, it has not been an easy job. You have first of all to watch your bird in its natural surroundings. Sometimes for days on end, before arranging your apparatus, then you set your microphone with a cable trailing through the woods and fields, a mile or so away and sit down and listen from 3 o'clock in the morning till after daybreak. That may sound simple enough, but wild birds, while they are not so well paid as some other performers are temperamental all the same.*

Koch was recording sounds into his eighties and finally passed away in 1974 aged 92. He was in many ways the father of wildlife sound recording and perhaps did more than anyone to bring the sounds of the natural world into people's living rooms. He was really the David Attenborough of the wireless radio age. His recordings are now in the BBC archives and his work directly inspired the development of the 'new' science of studying animals through their vocalisations, known as bioacoustics, the stories of which fill the pages of this book.

The evolution from wax cylinders to shellac disks to magnetic tape changed the opportunities for anyone looking to record natural sounds. And with the mass production of cassettes and vinyl and the proliferation of home stereos, there were new audiences open to listening in. In one famous example, a sound recording of a wild animal even changed the world.

Back in the 1960s a biologist from Massachusetts was listening to the radio when he heard breaking news that would dramatically alter the course of his life. The body of a Cetacean had reportedly washed ashore on a local beach. He made an instant and impulsive decision to drive down and take a look for himself. Roger Payne was a talented scientist with an interest in bioacoustics. At the time, he was busy studying how nocturnal owls made use of sound to catch mice in the darkness of the forest. He had also studied how moths were able to detect the sonar clicks of hunting bats and take evasive manoeuvres. But his visit to the beach would spark a change in direction for his research. After walking along the lonely shore in the darkness, Payne found what he was looking for. He recalled:

'It was a small whale, a porpoise about eight feet long with lovely subtle curves, glistening in the cold rain.'

It had been butchered and someone had cut off the animal's tail flukes. Initials had been cruelly carved into the flesh and, in a final act of wanton disrespect, a cigar had been stuffed in the animal's blow hole. Standing over this sorry scene, with the rain pouring down, Payne couldn't help but be deeply affected. He later wrote:

I removed the cigar and stood there for a long time with feelings I cannot describe. Everybody has some such experience that affects him for life, probably several. That night was one of mine. At some point my flashlight went out, but as the tide came in, I could periodically see the graceful outline of the whale against the white foam cast by the waves. Although its more typical than not of what happens to whales when they encounter man, that experience was somehow the last straw, and I decided to use the first opportunity to learn enough about whales so I might have some effect on their fate.

Payne believed that the disconnect between ourselves and other sentient species, which had led to the desecration of the porpoise, was just the tip of the iceberg. During the 20th century an estimated 3 million great whales were hunted for their oil, meat and to make fertiliser. Whales worldwide were facing extinction from an industrial level of slaughter that had decimated many species. Angered and inspired, Payne switched his research to focus on studying whales. In 1967, having been awed by recordings of whales captured by the Woods Hole Oceanographic Institute, Payne and his wife Katy (herself an eminent scientist in the field of animal communication) travelled to Bermuda to listen in for themselves. They visited Dr Frank Watlington, who had been secretly recording the movements of Soviet submarines with the US Navy's sonar array system of deep-sea listening stations. What he played them would blow the minds of both scientists. In a later interview, Payne recalled that the sounds he heard were 'the most extraordinary, amazing acoustic performances I had ever heard from any animal or have ever heard from any animal since'. They were listening to the songs of humpback whales.

Working alongside whale scientist Scott McVay, the Paynes set out to record and analyse whale song in a way that hadn't been approached before. Their findings, published in the journal *Science*, were a revelation. Not only for what they revealed about the whale's songs but also because of the tone of their writing. They had declared that the sounds of humpback whales were 'beautiful', and the inclusion of such an expressive word in a rigorous scientific study was highly unusual. In 1970 Roger Payne found a way to share the whales' extraordinary voices with a much wider audience. He released a vinyl LP of recordings from Watlington's and his own research called *Songs of the Humpback Whale* that would become a cultural phenomenon. The album sold 125,000 copies very quickly and eventually reached multi-platinum levels of sales. Payne was interviewed on Johnny Carson's *Tonight Show* and *The David Frost Show*. When *National Geographic* became aware of the recordings and decided they wanted to give a free copy to each of their members with their January 1979 magazine issue, they pressed 10.5 million discs for distribution. Even today this holds the record for the largest single print of any recording ever made. There were rumours that Bob Dylan would pause his live gigs to play excerpts from the record. David Bowie's alien character in the movie *The Man Who Fell to Earth* made love to a background track of a singing humpback. Then in 1977, the sounds were loaded onto the *Voyager* probe and sent into outer space as an example of Earthly intelligence to alien life. Whales were now part of pop culture and it was their songs that had made it happen.

It's hard to quantify the effect this had in bringing about an end to industrial whaling, but listening to their songs certainly changed our perception of whales and provided the spark for a huge cultural shift in our relationship with these ocean giants. Before Payne's recordings animals made noises but now it was suddenly clear that they had voices instead. Things began to change quickly. Humpback whales became an icon for a rising environmental awareness. A year after the record's release, Greenpeace and Friends of the Earth were formed. 'Save the Whales' became a slogan and in 1972 the US government introduced the Marine Mammal Protection Act, which banned the killing of whales in US waters. Under increasing global pressure, in 1982 the member states of the International Whaling Commission voted for a moratorium on all commercial whaling.

Even today *Songs of the Humpback Whale* makes for an emotive listening experience. Copies of the original vinyl are hard to find, but the recordings were released on CD, before being now available digitally over the internet. Listening to the tracks I was reminded of a picture of Roger Payne I had seen online. Taken in 1991 somewhere off the Alaskan coast, it shows Payne, in a bright yellow cagoule, rowing what seems to me like a ridiculously small fibreglass boat, listening on his headphones with his eyes focusing on his sound recording device. The whales' voices are extraordinarily moving, particularly when you consider the role these simple sound recordings had in saving the lives of so many whales for future generations.

Roger Payne died of cancer in 2023 at the age of 88. Still consumed with concern about the decline of the natural world, his last public act was to write a final plea in *Time* magazine calling on us to 'Acknowledge the bitter truth' and 'set aside our security – to change all human behaviours that are contributing to the destruction of life, and to change them right down to their deepest roots'.

Since these early recordings, science has learnt much about whale song. You can listen for yourself and find out more about their meaning in future pages of this book. But as I sat at home and played Payne's recordings and the wonderful sounds of whales singing, I became aware that so seldom do we take the time to listen. The sounds of whales reverberating around my kitchen demanded my focus. Their otherworldly calls, rising and falling, transported me from my kitchen table to the open ocean, where I drifted, floating on the ebb and surge of their voices. Roger Payne captured this feeling brilliantly in his sleeve notes for *Song of the Humpback Whale*.

> *As you listen to this recording, I wish only that it conveys to you the pleasant circumstances under which we made it. Through the whole night we listened to the whales, taking turns at the headphones in the cockpit, lulled by the smooth rolling of the boat. Far from land, with a faint breeze and a full moon, we heard these lovely sounds pouring out of the sea.*

In his online tribute to Payne, biologist and writer Tom Mustill recalls asking his friend, 'How do you listen?' and Payne's reply: 'Attentively – you should listen silently. You should listen with nothing else to distract you. With a completely open mind. That's the way to listen.'

The world has changed much since Payne sat in his tiny boat, hydrophone trailing in the water and headphones sat snugly on his ears. The digital revolution has further upgraded our opportunities to record the natural world. Biologists can now capture sounds with greater detail, over greater distances and for longer. Microphones are more sensitive and can be as small as a grain of rice. We can record sounds that our own ears cannot even pick up and interpret the tiny vibrations of insects to listen to their hidden chatter. We have bugged the deepest canyons of the sea with hydrophones and can listen in remotely on life in the forest canopy. But despite this revolution in recording, for most of us, listening to the natural world is no longer a common experience.

Modern lives leave us with less time to tune in and our own human-generated noise (called anthrophony by sound ecologists) is getting louder in our ears. Human activity is also leading directly to a sharp decline in biodiversity. With less nature out there making noise comes less opportunity to tune in and, in many ways, we have forgotten how to even listen.

'Nature connectedness' refers to the relationship we all have with the natural world, including how we think, feel and experience it. A recent study indicates that the British are among the 'least' connected to nature, ranking a lowly fifty-fifth out of sixty-one countries. Researchers from the University of Derby discovered that our connection to nature has fallen by about 60 per cent in the last 200 years, while a study in Sheffield used people's smartphones to track how much time they spent in green spaces each day and found that the median time was just 4 minutes and 36 seconds. Perhaps the most worrying trend is that younger generations now relate less to nature than older ones.

Sadly, this shift is even reflected in the very language we use. Despite the vibrancy of the Irish language, those beautiful words used to describe the sea, mada doininne, caibleadh, stranach are now almost entirely forgotten. In 1603 English colonists defeated Ireland's last chieftains and so began a slow cultural repression and decline of the traditional language. In 1973, Ireland's entry into the EU and a subsequent collapse in Ireland's fishing industry hastened the loss of the traditional language and its words of the sea. Language evolves and changes but you have to wonder if the loss of these particular words is down to more than the influence of history and politics. When words cease to be useful to us for the modern lives we live, they can often become lost.

This 'disappearance' of natural words is by no means limited to Indigenous language. One study published in 2012 looked at the use of words related to nature – the names of birds, trees and flowers – found in fiction books published in America between 1900 and 2000. The study found that in some cases the use of these words had declined by over 30 per cent, and they were also disappearing from our film scripts and song lyrics, suggesting that nature plays a smaller part in our everyday lives. As nature becomes less embedded in our popular culture it may become easier to stop caring about its future.

Psychologists have found that people who feel connected to nature are likely to do more to protect it. So, with the natural world under increasing threat, our declining relationship with nature is a huge concern.

In 2024 the World Wide Fund for Nature (WWF) and the Zoological Society of London published their 'Living Planet Report', which tracks nearly 35,000 populations of 5,495 different species of mammals, birds, fish, reptiles and amphibians. The report's findings were devastating. Global wildlife populations have crashed by an average of 73 per cent in the last 50 years.

We are caught in a spiral of decline as plummeting wildlife numbers further limit meaningful interactions with nature, eroding our familiarity and attachment. Conservationists are calling it an 'extinction of experience'. How can you care about something when you have no understanding of it? Our relationship with the natural world is failing, but listening to natural sounds can play an important part in fixing our broken connection with nature.

The sharp 'chee-ow' calls of a pair of chatty, red-billed choughs brought me back from the ocean and I opened my eyes. It began to rain. A gentle mist at first, its soothing touch 'fizzed' as it fell on the sea. Soon the rain fell more heavily and as the approaching curtain of falling water swept in off the ocean, the rising rhythm of the drops grew from distinct impacts into a mess of white noise, sizzling like a fire as the surface of the ocean danced. It looked as if the curlew's warning had come to pass.

Why natural sounds matter

Natural sounds are of course vitally important to the animals that make them. Many species rely on sound for social communication, mating, finding food, territory defence, navigation and survival. We've read how the sounds of nature have been integral to our own human traditions, storytelling, art, science and spirituality, but why else might they be important to us?

Natural sounds allow us to monitor the environmental and the ecological processes that sustain us. The soundscapes of natural habitats, the animals and birds, the insects, the water and the wind can be a measure of biodiversity and the general health of a balanced ecosystem. Changes in these natural soundscapes, for example the disappearance of a bird call or the drying up of a tumbling stream, can be a sign of habitat degradation. By tuning in to natural sounds, we can pick up early warning signals that ecosystems are struggling or that particular species are in decline. The soundscape of a wilderness is in many ways its heartbeat.

It might seem obvious that sound would be directly linked to the health of wild habitats, but it will perhaps be a surprise to many that natural sound has a strong influence on our own health and wellbeing. In 2024 the University of Oxford performed a 'real world' test on the effects that listening to nature had on the stress levels of commuters travelling on South Western Railway.

The researchers played the sounds of flowing rivers, storms and birdsong to commuters on a forty-seven-minute journey to London's Waterloo station. Passengers also had access to their own audio experiences in the form of their regular preferred music or podcasts. The forty-six passengers that were part of the study filled in mood-assessment surveys before departing and then at fifteen-minute intervals throughout their journey. The researchers found that those who listened to nature reported being 35 per cent less stressed and 32 per cent less nervous. In comparison, the passengers tuning in to music or podcasts only registered an 11 per cent reduction in stress.

In a much larger study conducted in 2022, Exeter and Bristol University teamed up with the BBC to look at the therapeutic effects of listening to natural sounds. Drawing on data collected from over 7,500 people, the participants listened to recordings from a range of forests across the world, from English woodlands to the jungles of Papua New Guinea. They were also played the sounds of breaking waves and falling rain. The study found that participants listening to the natural world felt less stress and had reduced mental fatigue. It was also discovered that animal sounds in particular were important, as without them the positive psychological benefits were reduced. Interestingly, after listening, participants reported an increased motivation to protect the world's ecosystems.

One study from Brighton University in 2017 revealed that listening to natural sounds can improve cognitive function and boost our mood, suggesting that these sounds don't just calm the mind but can also sharpen our focus and make us more productive.

As far back as 2015, we have known that the experience of listening to a natural soundscape can help us to sleep. A Korean study looked at how different types of sound might help us nod off. White noise is understood to have properties that help induce sleep. Ask any parent that has played a detuned radio to their wakeful baby and you'll find it does seem to work. Pink noise (a similar 'fuzz' track to white noise but at a lower frequency) is known to have the same sleep-enhancing properties. The Korean scientists played both pink and white noise to people as they tried to sleep. They also played the sounds of the forest and discovered that these natural sounds were even more effective than pink and white noise in helping a good night's sleep.

Elsewhere research has found that exposure to natural sounds can lower your heart rate and reduce muscle tension, effects that weren't seen even when participants listened to music or to silence. Surgical patients exposed to natural sounds in the operating theatre showed lower levels of alpha-amylase, a well-known biomarker of stress, in their saliva.

There is today a growing body of evidence that supports the theory that listening to natural sounds, even in our own homes, on a train or in an operating theatre, can reduce stress, making us both physically and mentally healthier. But there is one benefit of listening to natural sounds that could have a bearing beyond our own health and wellbeing. It may even have a part to play in helping us save the planet.

Become a deep listener

Sometimes it can feel like the endless distractions of modern life can leave our senses deadened. Before we continue on our exploration of natural sound, here are some simple exercises to help you sharpen your listening skills and reawaken your ability to tune in. They are a kind of listening practice if you like, designed to warm up your ears and heighten your perception.

If you can, make some space and time to properly tune in to

the recordings. Find somewhere quiet with no distractions. Use headphones if you have them and think about sitting or lying down and closing your eyes just after you press play. These recordings are longer than some in the book and can therefore give you a deeper sense of immersion into the wilderness.

Before you listen to the first soundscape, bear these questions in mind. How many separate sources of sound can you pick out? Can you identify what type of animals are calling? Does the sound feel close or far away and does that give you any clues to what type of habitat you might be in? Is the overall feeling one of endless space or more claustrophobic? When you have finished listening, read on.

How does listening to this sound make you feel? Its it threatening or does it make you smile?

Scan to listen to soundscape 1.

The sound you have just been listening to is the extraordinary singing of indris in a Madagascan forest. One of the island's largest lemur species, indris live in small family groups that are known to sing together about seven times a day. Their startling chorus acts to strengthen their family bond as well as being a good way to announce their presence and defend their territory from rival groups.

Now prepare to listen to the second soundscape. See if you can notice how much space there is compared to the first. You might feel that just by listening you can tell what kind of landscape it has been recorded in – whether it's a cold northern or warm tropical soundscape? Do you see a picture of the landscape in your head when you listen? What colours do you see? You'll hear an animal calling. You may already know what it is – but if you don't recognise it, listen closely and see what kind of animal your senses tell you it might be. When you have finished listening, read on.

Scan to listen to soundscape 2.

You have just been listening to the sound of a great northern diver, also known as a loon, calling from a stretch of water in Sweden's Svartälven or Black River region of forests and wetlands. Did you notice that the call seems like a two-way conversation, where one loon calls, 'Where are you?' and its distant partner answers as if to say, 'I am here'. For the third sound, try and guess whether the source of the sound is big or small. Do you think the microphone is close to the source or far away?

Scan to listen to soundscape 3.

This sound was recorded in the Kalahari Desert of southern Africa and the various delightful chirps and whimpers are being made by meercat pups. These small members of the mongoose family are highly social, living in groups of up to thirty individuals, and they are almost always chatting among themselves. Studies have identified up to twelve different combinations of sounds that they make to communicate anything from care for their young to warning each other when there is a predator around. The meercat group in the recording is well studied and used to human visitors, so the sound recordist was able to get the microphone closer than you normally would for a wild animal. The meercat pup you can hear was busy wrestling with the body of a dead scorpion ready to eat it.

Hopefully by now your ears are 'warmed up' and you have feel engaged with taking time to listen. Our wild sonic journey can now begin, and the first adventure takes us to a special place that is one of the most evocative soundscapes on the planet.

2. Hidden Conversations

CRACKING THE CODE OF ANIMAL COMMUNICATIONS

Grunts, grumbles, hoots and honks

THE CAMPFIRE CRACKED and the damp wood popped, sending clouds of orange sparks up to dance among the stars. Nightjars tumbled through the sky, chasing flickering swarms of insects. Rising up from the water of the swamp was a constant resonant conversation. Our campsite on an island, surrounded by the seasonal floods of Botswana's Okavango Delta, was the perfect place to listen in. We could hear the rumbling explosions of bubbles, strange and oddly human shouts, and the deep bass laughter of a malevolent fairy-tale giant. Our mission was to film and record the vocalisations of hippos and, based on the hubbub coming from the swamp water, we had come to the right place.

If there was ever a film-maker's list of challenging and dangerous animals to film, hippos would have to sit right at the top. An adult male can measure 3.5 metres long and weigh as much 3,200 kilograms. They are fiercely territorial and will aggressively defend their home pool or channel.

In the water they can hold their breath for about five minutes, making them hard to spot and easy to surprise. If disturbed they can propel themselves through the water, bouncing along the bottom, at speeds of 8 kilometres per hour, fast enough to overtake a boat. Encounter a hippo on land and it can charge you at speeds of 30 kilometres per hour. They have huge jaws with large lower canine 'tusks' that can grow to 50 centimetres long and they are more than happy to use them.

So, filming these 'swamp tanks' takes careful planning, experienced guidance and an ability to read the signs to avoid getting too close. Sharing stories after dark around a campfire is usually a wonderful experience, but that night the talk among our team was making me jumpy. We discussed our approach to filming the hippos, what the risks were and what we should look out for. We had to watch out for the big males. As dominant members of the pod, they would likely be the ones to become aggressive. We needed to stay a respectful distance away and not ever corner them. But occasionally hippos can come out of nowhere. They are a common sight when travelling around by boat, and sharing the maze of flooded channels and lagoons with hippos is one of the everyday challenges of navigating life in the delta. So sometimes a hippo can take you by surprise.

One of our guides recounted the story of a hippo encounter that I will never forget. Earlier that year, a group of three locals out fishing in the delta had been charged at by an angry hippo. It came out of nowhere and flipped their small metal boat, sending all three into the water. The water was shallow enough that they managed to regroup, getting behind the boat and using it as a shield against the hippo. The enraged animal attacked again and again, its huge canines puncturing holes clean through the boat's metal hull with every charge. By the time the hippo was done, it had made fifty holes in the hull and one of the fishermen had broken wrists from holding the boat in place to take the impact of the hippo's charges. When the hippo finally moved on, the group had to wade back to their camp through the water, but, knowing the channels were full of hippos, they were fearful of further attack so decided to hang on to the crumpled and punctured remains of their boat, carrying it over their heads and shuffling along the riverbed like an armoured beetle.

Hearing stories about the hippo's determined aggression, it came as no surprise that they kill an estimated 500 people every year in Africa, making them perhaps the deadliest large land mammal on the continent.

I asked our camera operator, who had experience filming hippos, what we should do if the hippo 'flipped' our boat. His instruction was to swim down and along the bottom and head for the shore. I have never been a great swimmer and my rear end seems blessed with a natural buoyancy so, worried about my chances of diving down to the bottom, I asked what would happen if you were to swim away on the surface?

'Chomp,' he said. For the hippos it would be 'just like apple-bobbing'. Feeling more than a little nervous, I drained my beer can and retreated into my tent. But it was hard to get to sleep. I lay there worrying and thinking about the challenge that we faced, all the while listening to the calls of the hippos, ringing like laughter in the darkness.

The next morning, we were out on the water shortly after sunrise. Our vessel was a shallow metal-hulled rectangle with a canopy for shade. At the front we had rigged a specialised gyro-stabilised camera with a powerful zoom lens. I sat with my camera operator on a bench under the canopy and our experienced skipper steered the boat from a small column right at the rear.

It was a beautiful day in the delta. We followed a channel of rum-coloured water where flotillas of lily pads sat atop spiralling columns of stalks. The surface was dotted with white and occasionally blue lily flowers, like a carpet of fallen stars. There were birds everywhere: vibrant malachite and pied kingfishers buzzed back and forth over the water. The banks were stalked by hamerkops and herons and the tall reedbeds were dotted with foraging carmine bee-eaters and vivid electric-blue swamphen. There were jacanas – lily trotters – everywhere, almost too many to count, their long toes allowing them to seemingly walk on the water. We spotted herds of lechwe and families of elephants. African fish eagles sat atop the tallest trees and, throwing back their heads, would give their evocative piercing yodel, 'we-oh-oo', sometimes called 'the sound of Africa'.

The maze of lagoons and narrow channels was as complex as it was beguiling, and I wasn't sure how our skipper managed to navigate us in the right direction. But it wasn't long before we entered a palm-fringed lagoon that was known to be home to a pod of hippos. We slowed almost to a halt and parked up at the entrance to the lagoon. On the far shore we could see a raft of great pink and grey bodies seeming to float on the surface. About halfway between us and the pod a large head rose up flat in the water. It was the dominant male. He snorted air from his nostrils, waggled his ears and watched us. We sat still and silent with our engines off and waited.

After a while the male lost interest in us and, using a long pole, we gently punted our way closer to the pod, silently inching our way along the bank to get to a position where we could film the hippos. I watched them through my binoculars. All I could see were the tops of their heads, the flicking of their ears and their nostrils, sitting atop their own little island above the surface. They were clearly very at home in the water, but hippos are creatures of two worlds. At night they use the cover of darkness to wander up onto the banks, sometimes travelling far from the water to graze on the grass or chomp on sausage fruits, fallen from the trees. Then before morning they return to the water, where during the day they spend most of their time resting. It's a safe place to slowly and efficiently digest their grassy supper from the night before.

Unusually for such an aquatic lifestyle, hippos cannot swim, at least not in the way that we would describe as swimming. Their bulbous body shape and huge heads don't help for streamlining and there is no webbing to be found between their four toes (although their west African relative the pygmy hippo does have webbing). They have no natural buoyancy so in deeper water they must 'jump', propelling themselves on their stumpy legs to reach the surface. They run along the bottom and for this reason they don't like water that is too deep or fast flowing. But they do have some clever adaptations for their aquatic life. Their nostrils sit high on the tops of their snouts, allowing them to keep a low profile in the water and breathe easily. They also have skin that is covered with glands that exude a red fluid which is thought may act as a waterproof varnish, a protective sunscreen and antiseptic cream, or even a kind of social perfume.

Our skipper spotted that one of the female hippos had a small calf. It was tiny and must have been pretty new to the world. We laughed as this pink, wriggly sausage fought valiantly to climb up onto its mum's back before slipping and falling into the water again. Finally, it struggled on top and secured a good spot in the sun. There it dozed for a while until a commotion in the pod led Mum to shift position and the calf was unceremoniously dumped back in the water. Perhaps it would be a good opportunity for the calf to feed – our skipper told us that hippos can suckle underwater using their toughened lips and folding tongues to make a watertight clamp around Mum's nipple. Watching the baby hippo's antics through my binoculars it was hard to equate these animals with some of the stories we had shared around the campfire.

There was a constant grumbling, honking, snorting and heavy sighing coming from the pod. They really did make some extraordinary sounds. We started to deploy some remote sound recording devices, sinking them on weighted poles in the water.

Our project was working alongside researchers at the University of Touro in California, who were at the scientific forefront of decoding hippo vocalisations. Our hope was to share our recordings with them to help their research and help us interpret the hippos' constant chatter. As part of our efforts, we even released a floating sound recorder in a waterproof case that gently bobbed its way towards the pod. This device had mics that recorded both above and below the water at the same time.

The reason for this was that hippos, sitting with the top of their heads just out of the water, can make vocalisations in two different worlds. Known as 'amphibious communication', the hippos can produce sounds from their nostrils above the water that travel through the air, and at the same time make sounds from their larynx that are transmitted through the fat in their necks and through their bottom jaw, which send sound waves through the water. Researchers studying hippos in Ruaha National Park in Tanzania were able to look at how hippos responded to these two different signals that together they called 'Simultaneous Amphibious Signals' or SAS. By picking up signals from above and below the water, they suggested that female hippos may be able to monitor the croaks of a creche of calves underwater while simultaneously watching and listening to what was going on above the water. Alpha males can keep tabs on the underwater social interactions of his pod while keeping their eyes and ears out for predators or rival males on the surface.

So far everything had remained pretty calm, but it wasn't long until the hippos showed us the other side to their personality and just why they had such a fearsome reputation. A new hippo wandered out of the bushes. We could see he was a male, a big boy and covered with pock marks and scars. He furtively slid into the water at the far end of the lagoon, and at first there was no reaction from the pod. But as the interloper started to get closer to the others, the resident male set out straight for him, cutting a V-shaped wake through the water. The two males reared up, mouths agape, resting their lower jaws against the other's. Their impressive dentistry was there for all to see with the incisors in their upper jaws horribly spiked and those in the lower jaw set as daggers pointed forward for stabbing. Their huge lower canines, sharp and curving, looked like they could do a lot of damage and suddenly the interloper's scars began to make sense. They growled at each other and the sound reverberated up through the boat and into my chest. Pandemonium broke out among the pod with the females diving and surfacing with lots of snorting. But there was to be no fight today and, unable to match the bigger resident male, the newcomer backed away; after a short chase, he kept his distance at the far end of the lagoon.

The victorious male yawned in threat and, as if to announce that the pool was his, he 'dung showered' to mark his territory, by swinging his tail vigorously from side to side, while defecating so that he sent excrement flying everywhere like a muck spreader. This display might spread his scent but, in the water where scent is less reliable, it also makes a dramatic visual signal. And with his tail swings making a soggy slapping like the clapping of hands wearing wet rubber gloves, there could even be a sonic element to his signal.

The researchers from Touro have been working with hippos in captivity to crack the code of hippo vocalisations. By recording the sounds the hippos made and matching them to behaviours recorded on video cameras, they were able to interpret them. They've managed to discover at least eleven different sounds that hippos produce in three different ways. The first is through bursts of air. These calls include 'chuffs', 'snorts' and 'blowing bubbles', and tend to be social in context and often submissive. The second types of hippo sound are tonal and include 'grunts', 'groans', 'screams' and 'whines', and these calls are most often associated with social dominance and different levels of aggression. But perhaps the most well-known hippo call is the 'wheeze honk', a deep, laughing 'hoh, hoh, hoh'.

Researchers working in Mozambique found it was the most

commonly made hippo call and the loudest, travelling as far as a kilometre in distance. They theorised that the calls might contain information about the identity of the individual caller, helping the hippos maintain their social relationships. The researchers broadcast the wheeze honk call from speakers set up on the shore of a lake and watched to see how the hippos responded. They discovered that they could tell apart friends from strangers just from their voices. The hippos reacted immediately to the broadcast calls, and showed more aggression when played the calls of hippo 'strangers', responding with more intensive calling of their own and territorial bouts of dung spraying. The study even suggested that hippos may have a knowledge of all the voices of other individual hippos around them, allowing them to tell friend from foe.

Alongside making tonal sounds and sounds from 'bursts of air', hippos also make 'pulsed' sounds. These can include 'croaks' and aggressive 'growls' but they are also known to 'click'.

The researchers from California call these streams of clicking sounds 'click trains' and discovered that in captivity male hippos were recorded making click trains when they were alone and searching for food within their underwater pens. This would suggest that these calls don't have a social function and it's been theorised that they may even be a rudimentary form of echolocation. Hippos often live in murky water and being able to use sound to find their way, just like dolphins and whales, might be useful.

Scan to hear the varied vocalisations of hippos.

To me, the final hour before sunset always showed the Okavango at its most beautiful. The breeze had dropped and the sky reflected in the glassy water turned it into mercury. A million buzzing insects rose up in clouds, golden against the reed heads. We passed a tiny kingfisher, perched on a bulrush, its eyes fixed on the surface. A group of elephants played in the water, their bodies turning black with the falling light.

Steering our boat through the main channel on our way back to camp, ahead of us a big hippo charged off the bank and dived into the water. We slowed down but, suddenly, an ominous trail of bubbles was coming straight for our boat. It burst out of the water right next to us, huge mouth gaping, before diving beneath us with a great splash. Suddenly the boat lurched and we jolted with a sickening bump. The trail of bubbles headed away but then turned and came towards us again. Afraid we might get flipped over, our skipper hit the gas and we looked back just in time to see the hippo's enormous head pop up on the surface as it chased us off with a threatening yawn. It had been a close call. Hippos, with their unusual lifestyle and extraordinary vocalisations, will always inspire fear and fascination in equal parts.

Nature bugged

We live in a golden age of discoveries when it comes to listening in on the natural world. We now have tiny microphones, the size of a grain of rice, remote recording devices that can bug the wild and computers that can analyse sounds to find patterns that help uncover their meaning.

Some of these discoveries are revealing the most surprising of natural secrets. About twenty-five years ago a Spanish biologist discovered bird feathers in the droppings of Europe's largest bat species, the greater noctule. It remained unexplained, as everyone thought it absurd that a bat would be able to catch and eat a bird.

That was until 2025, when the latest listening technology provided evidence of a grizzly new behaviour. Scientists from the Doñana Biological Station, Seville, took individual greater noctule bats and fitted them with tiny surveillance 'backpacks'. These contained instrumentation that could record the bat's altitude, speed and – crucially – a tiny microphone for recording sound.

What they discovered was truly extraordinary. These bats were hunting, killing and eating robins on the wing. The backpack recorded a bat climbing to 1,200 metres before diving down to pursue its prey. Attacking at speed from above and in the darkness of night, the bat hunted like a stealth fighter jet, leaving the birds with no warning. The robins, unable to hear the bat's echolocation, were at a huge disadvantage. The instruments recorded that as the bat got closer, it may have alerted the bird – either with its moving shadow or from the sound of its beating wings – sending the robin into a spiralling escape dive. The bat then gave chase, following the bird for over a kilometre, during which the onboard microphone recorded twenty-one distress calls from the robin. As the chase came close to the ground, the robin gave a small final shriek that was followed by twenty-three minutes of continuous chewing noises from the bat as it devoured its victim mid-flight. A robin weighs about half as much as a greater noctule and one of the scientists compared it to 'me eating a 35-kilogram animal while out jogging'.

The researchers even discovered severed bird wings underneath the bats' favourite hunting area; when they looked closely, it appeared that the bats were biting off the robin's wings, perhaps to reduce the weight and drag as they carried their prize through the air. Greater noctules are a very rare species and are protected across most of Europe. Their future is threatened by wildfires and drought, so while this predation may seem savage to us, it could be key to the bats' ongoing survival. One thing is for sure: without the new generation of miniature microphones, we would have no idea that this extraordinary behaviour even existed.

Wild conversation

Scientists have long wondered whether animal vocalisations have meaning. In 1872, Charles Darwin noted in his book *The Expression of the Emotions in Man and Animals* that vocal sounds reflect an animal's emotional state, speculating that they may experience fear, pain, pleasure or anger.

He wrote: 'The sounds uttered by animals serve as their chief means of communication with each other, and express their various states of mind.' Darwin observed how a dog's 'growl' expresses anger and may serve to warn others, while a dog's 'whine' could express 'affection' or 'submission'.

But what if we could do more than interpret simple emotions from animal sounds and unravel the hidden complexities of what they are really communicating? New technologies are now allowing us to 'break the code' of animal communication. Species that are very familiar to us and have been historically well studied are suddenly being revealed to have a huge level of sophistication in their vocalisations.

Botswana is home to an estimated 130,000 elephants, more than any other country in Africa. On our travels around the Okavango Delta, they were everywhere. Seeing such a well-known and instantly recognisable animal lends a sense of familiarity to any encounter with them. We are so used to seeing their image that it's easy to take elephants for granted, but after just a morning watching them up close in the delta, I was soon completely awestruck in their presence. No picture book or video clip can prepare you for seeing a 'real' elephant. Navigating the channels of the delta would bring us incredibly close to these wonderful animals. We drifted by a huge lone bull elephant, submerged in the swamp, feeding in the long grass. He seemed to tolerate us until the channel led us close by him and he voiced his irritation with a loud trumpet, flashed us with his ears and gave a dramatic head shake, throwing his trunk in our direction. As he moved, clouds of dust rose from his broad back. His sheer size, the depth of his rumbling voice and the ear-shredding volume of his trumpeting left such an impression on me that it was like discovering a brand-new animal. He watched us closely as we moved on, his wild eyes simultaneously fierce and full of wisdom.

We have known for many years that elephants live in highly social groups and that they show a sophisticated level of communication. The basic unit of elephant society is the herd and these are made up of groups of related females, including a mother, her young and her grown-up daughters with their offspring. Males leave the maternal herd when they reach adolescence and they will alternate between spending time alone or joining bachelor herds, grouping with other males.

Elephants generate sounds through the larynx just like we do, but their voices are modified as the sound passes through their trunks. Packed with 150,000 muscle fibres, the elephant's famous 'nose hose' has a near endless capacity to change shape and this hugely expands the variety of calls that the elephant can make. 'Trumpeting' is perhaps the most well known of elephant sounds. It's produced by the animal blowing air hard through its nostrils with enough force to make the trunk resonate. By either holding their trunk to face straight down or curving it, an elephant can change its trumpet from a short blast, like that given when startled, to a much longer cry of rage. Elephants also trumpet when they are sounding the alarm for help if they are attacked by lions, and during their greeting ceremonies when familiar elephants meet up after time spent apart.

Scan to listen to the dramatic sounds of elephants trumpeting at night.

We regularly encountered female herds of elephants feeding. They would space out over the swamp and spend hours pulling up great clumps of grass with their trunks to chew like contented cows. The soundtrack to all this digestion was a sporadic deep rumbling. Research has suggested that these rumbles could be a way of staying in touch, reassuring each elephant that the others were close by. Sometimes called 'baroo-rumbles', they seem to play an important role in greetings and social cohesion. Other elephant sounds include screaming or squealing when distressed, growling, roaring and bellowing.

New research published in 2024 has even postulated that elephants use 'names'. Scientists from Colorado State University followed elephants across Kenya's Samburu National Reserve and Amboseli National Park, recording their vocalisations. They used machine learning (a form of artificial intelligence) to confirm that the elephants' rumbling calls contained some form of 'name-like' component that helped identify the intended recipient of the call. When the researchers played back the 'name' calls to an elephant, it was seen to respond affirmatively to calls that addressed it directly by replying or approaching the speaker. When the elephant was played calls that were meant for other elephants, they would show less of a reaction.

For the elephants to tell one individual from another by using names, they have to learn to produce new sounds – a rare ability among animals. These kinds of sounds are known to biologists as 'arbitrary communication', which mean when a sound represents an idea but doesn't imitate it. For example, in the English language the word 'cat' has no inherent link to the description of the animal itself. The meaning of the word 'cat' is based entirely on the social agreement among those of us who speak English.

This ability to make noises that don't just sound like what we are talking about hugely expands our vocabulary and the complexity of our language. And to some degree it could be the same with elephants. The study also found that the elephants, just like us, don't always address each other by name in everyday conversation. The use of individual names was more commonly seen in long-distance communication or when talking to young calves. There is a lot more research to be done to isolate the 'named' elements of the individual calls, but the use of machine learning to help us translate the meaning of elephant vocalisations is hugely exciting. Having a conversation with an elephant is still a fantasy, but perhaps one day it could become reality. There would be so much to learn and, in a world of increased human–animal conflict, being able to 'talk elephant' might be a way to reduce the tension and keep both humans and elephants safe.

Spend any time with elephants and you are likely to hear their trumpets, baroo-rumbles, whooshes and growls. But many elephant vocalisations are made at frequencies beyond our own hearing and new research has been able to listen in on this secret language. Elephants can produce infrasonic sounds at frequencies lower than 20 hertz (the range of human hearing is 20–20,000 hertz, while the African elephant's voices occur from 15–35 hertz).

Lower-frequency sounds travel further than higher-frequency ones because longer wavelengths aren't so easily blocked or absorbed. It's thought these infrasonic calls allow members of an elephant herd to communicate over vast distances – possibly as far as 10 kilometres. Studies at Amboseli National Park have identified several different types of infrasonic messages made by elephants that can be used to communicate across a wide range of circumstances. From the 'greeting rumbles' made by adult females when reuniting with family, to the 'musth rumble', a low-frequency pulsed rumble made by males in musth (the time when their testosterone surges ready for breeding), elephants are making plenty of sound, even when they may appear silent to us.

Returning to our Okavango camp one evening, we crossed a large, still lagoon, that so perfectly reflected the orange sky it was hard to tell whether we were in a boat or sailing through the clouds. A bachelor group of elephants came out of the swamp and started to wade across the lagoon in front of us. At one point the water became so deep that only their trunks poked up like snorkels. As they slowly waded up into the shallower water on the far bank, two of the younger males stopped and started to play and, with their trunks intwined, they wrestled, trying to tip each other over.

The sound of their playful trumpeting and low growls was wonderful and it was hard not to interpret their calls as expressions of joy. One of the males ended up on his back, prone and with his legs sticking up out of the water like tree trunks in a flood. A larger male came across the water, his enormous head forcing an impressive bow wave as he waded. Once on the far shore, he trumpeted at the youngsters and they stopped their exuberance and followed him out of the water and onwards into the bush.

These male elephant bachelor herds are often loose assemblies of largely unrelated individuals. Males, especially young ones who have been forced out of their maternal herds, will wander far and wide and often spend a lot of time alone. But they will team up with other males to form bachelor herds and some of these can see as many as 114 members get together. Past research indicated that vocal communication in these male groups doesn't match the sophistication seen in the more social female herds. But a new study published in 2024 challenges this idea.

Observing bachelor herds in Etosha National Park in Namibia, researchers from Stanford University recorded dominant male elephants making a 'let's go' rumble, a deep infrasonic rumble that signals to the rest of the group it's time to depart. For twenty years, the research team bugged a waterhole with night-vision cameras and buried microphones in order to capture the infrasonic calls of the male elephants and match them with the behaviour seen on the video. When the dominant male rumbles, it's soon followed by the next individual's rumble and so on until each male has added his own voice. It's a bit like the harmonies in a barbershop quartet and is a behaviour that is highly ritualised. The fact that dominant male elephants initiate the 'let's go' instruction adds further credence to the idea that within these bachelor herds, older male elephants will 'mentor' the younger ones, taking them under their wing and helping them survive. The males likely learn this ritual when they are part of the maternal herd, as the matriarch will also give 'let's go' rumbles. The exciting prospect for biologists is that if elephants are communicating with verbs (let's go) and nouns (by using names), and if they were ever recorded using both together, it would be an example of syntax and could properly be considered as 'language'.

But the incredible vocalisations of elephants aren't the only way they use sound. Elephants are also known to use 'seismic' communication by sending and receiving vibrations directly through the ground. Research with Asian elephants showed how they lean forward, putting more weight on their larger front feet and make a posture called 'freezing' that allows their legs and shoulder bones to transmit seismic signals to their middle ear. The elephants' cushioned feet contain nodules of cartilaginous tissue that may have sound-transmitting properties. They also possess a unique muscle sphincter around their ear canal that can contract, constricting the passageway and dampening any airborne signals, allowing the elephant to more easily hear vibrations coming through the ground. The elephants can pick up sound waves from both vocalisations and movements, as they travel through the ground. The footsteps of running elephants are known to create these seismic signals. One study showed that the seismic waveforms made by elephants walking and running could travel distances of up to 32 kilometres. So, elephants can pick up the footsteps of other elephants even when they can't see them.

Scan to hear the extraordinary vocalisations of African elephants.

It's not just the big, familiar animals that are at the forefront of this new age of bioacoustics research. By turning the microphones onto some of the smallest animals, scientists are hearing a whole new surprising soundscape.

Perhaps the most sophisticated sets of sounds we have discovered from this miniature world are made by spiders. Researchers listened in on the tiny red-faced jumping spider of North America and were amazed at what they heard. At around 4–8 millimetres, red-faced jumpers are on the small side, but what they lack in size they make up for in enthusiasm, especially when it comes to male spiders impressing a female. Upon finding a potential mate, the males will channel their inner disco king and approach the female, showing off with a series of highly complex dance moves, including 'bounces', 'foreleg flicks' and 'body shakes'. Scientists from Berkeley spent hours filming the spiders with high-speed video, but wondered if there might be a sonic element to the spider's displays. Spiders don't have vocal cords to make sound and don't have ears to hear. Instead, they communicate by sending signals through surfaces. Biologists call this 'substrate-borne signalling'. By moving, rubbing and tapping parts of their bodies together, the spiders can send vibrations down their legs and into the ground. The female spiders will feel these vibrations through sensory organs in their legs (called 'sensilla'). By recording these vibrations with sensitive laser instruments, the researchers could match them with the spider's dance moves to unlock the spider's performance.

What they discovered was nothing short of astonishing. The male spider's display proved to be a highly complex signalling method, with twenty different elements making up their vibratory songs. Combined with the male's dance moves, these sounds formed a series of functional 'motifs' that grew in complexity as the courtship progressed.

As each male approaches a female to dance, he turns to face her directly and stands just a short distance away. Then the show begins. His performance is broken down into seven motifs or movements. The first is his 'Intro', with elements of leg flicks and bouncing and high-intensity 'thumps'. But this is just a warm-up. The male then enters the 'Tik-Rev' motif where he revs like a motorcycle. In the 'Third Leg' motif the scientists recorded a wide variety of dance moves from 'leg switches' to 'leg slides', 'body shakes' and even 'body pops', where the spider lifts his legs and makes a loud 'popping' sound. Other motifs included low hums and a high but intense buzzing. Some of the motifs had intermissions with 'bridge' elements, where the spider would make a short but intense two-part 'thump'. The whole display ends with the 'Pre-mount' motif, the grand finale just before attempted copulation, with the male arching his forelegs to point the tips towards the female while making a constant high-frequency buzzing.

But what are the spiders saying to each other with their funky skills? Male jumping spiders don't take care of their offspring, so the female isn't judging his performance in order to pick a good father. They also don't hold territories, so the female won't be rating his disco moves as a measure of a good dinner. So, it's likely that by performing his routine well, the male is showing himself to be a healthy genetic specimen and well worth mating with. The scientists found that these tiny dancers had one of the most complex communication systems ever seen in arthropods and, incredibly, all of it beyond the scope of human hearing.

Scan to hear the body-popping performance of a red-faced jumping spider.

There is one group of animals that takes sonic communication to a whole new level: the primates and, in particular, the apes. Their calls aren't just for simple recognition – they hint at something deeper, more complex and surprisingly close to our own way of communicating. Take a wander at dawn through the forests of north-east India, Bangladesh or south-east Asia and you might be lucky enough to hear voices that can't fail to make you smile. One of the most wonderful of all natural sounds has to be the morning duet of a pair of gibbons. There are twenty species of these so-called 'lesser apes', known for their incredible ability to swing through the trees at breakneck speeds of 55 kilometres per hour. Gibbons mate for life, although they don't always remain monogamous and separations occasionally do occur. The long loud hooting duet between a mated pair is an advert for their relationship, the strength of their bond and a marker of their territory. The largest gibbon species is the siamang, found in Sumatra, the Malay Peninsula and parts of Thailand. Their morning chorus consists of a duet where the males make a two-tone scream and the females a long bark. The pair each have a large throat sac that helps amplify their calls, making them the loudest of all the gibbons. The sound of their songs can be heard echoing through the forest from three kilometres away.

But these loud and iconic calls aren't the only sounds that gibbons make. Researchers from Durham University spent four months recording the calls of lar gibbons in the forests of Khao Yai National Park, north-east Thailand. They decided to focus on the quieter, more 'whispered' calls that gibbons make – which they named 'hoo' calls. In contrast to their deafening duets, which are broadcast to the whole forest, these hoo calls are more of an intimate, covert way of communicating between the gibbons themselves. You could say it's their own secret language. Some of these whispers are so quiet to be inaudible to our human ears. The study analysed 450 hoo-call recordings and were able to link them to a wide variety of different contexts, including during feeding, when separated, encountering predators and interacting with neighbours.

The hoo calls related to predators were often the quietest and produced at frequencies well below the hearing thresholds of eagles and other birds of prey. Raptors hear best in the 1–4 hertz range and the gibbons' hoos were recorded to be below 1 kilohertz. This would seem to suggest that these quiet alarm calls were a way of alerting nearby gibbons to a predator's presence without alerting the predator itself. The gibbons also had a distinct warning call for 'big cats', including leopards and tigers.

A team from the University of Wisconsin-Madison further analysed the Thai gibbon recordings, using computer algorithms, to form a sort of gibbon dictionary. Incredibly, they discovered a further nineteen different types of gibbon call, on top of the seven identified in the original research. The warning for a clouded leopard sounded like 'waoo-hoo-hoo-hoo-wa-wa', while the threat of a snake would elicit a 'waoo-hoo-hoo-hoo-hoo-hoo'. They also found that there might be more to these calls than simple warnings. They found instances where an extra element was added by the gibbons on the end of their alarm call. An example of this was when the predator was observed to be stationary.

The researchers have speculated that these added extras could be akin to 'adjectives' added to the warning, giving context to the threat, for example, 'Clouded leopard, standing still!' Groups of gibbons are led by dominant females and the researchers noticed that these leaders often had more to say than other members of the group. One particular alpha female used eight extra sound elements that no other gibbon used. Although the scientists don't yet know what these might be saying, they have theorised that it could be the female giving specific instructions to the rest of the group. They may even contain advice on how to get out of danger: 'Clouded leopard, climb higher.'

Scan to hear the morning calls of Bornean gibbons, Danum Valley, Borneo.

Gibbons are among the smallest of the ape species, but what about the big guys? Scientists from the Max Planck Institute for Ornithology in Leipzig, Germany, observed two groups of western lowland gorillas that lived in the forests of the Republic of the Congo. They discovered that the gorillas made 'happy' songs that they would hum during meal times. The gorillas would 'hum' with a steady, low-frequency tone that sounded a little like a deep, contented sigh. Some would also 'sing' with a series of quiet, short notes of varying pitch, just as we would hum a tune. The gorillas don't sing the same songs again and again, rather they compose new ditties with each meal. It seems that singing may be a way that gorillas express contentment with their meal and it could also be a way of signalling to others in the group that it's dinner time.

Observations from gorillas in zoos report that if given their favourite food the gorillas will sing louder, while the researchers in the Congo found that it was generally only the dominant male silverback that sang and hummed while he ate. This means that beyond just expressing a gorilla's sense of pleasure from eating, the silverback might be telling his group that 'it's time to eat and it isn't yet time to move on', his calls perhaps playing an important role in group cohesion.

Scan to hear the sound of a silverback gorilla feeding.

It's thought that in gorillas, only the dominant male silverback makes these subtle feeding calls because he is responsible for looking after all the females in his group. But in chimpanzee society, which is much more fluid, everyone gets to talk at the dinner table.

Recent research has discovered that chimp vocalisations are more complex than previously thought and may even question the idea that humans are the only species on Earth to use 'language'. When we combine sounds into words, then words into sentences, we are able to communicate an infinite number of meanings. Take two simple words, 'cut' and 'short'. Both those words have their own meaning but can be combined to make a whole new concept: 'cut short'. But this can also be reversed to make yet another meaning: 'short cut'. Syntax is the name given to how we combine words and how their order can affect their meaning. While we have discovered that both elephants and gibbons may show elements of syntax in their vocalisations, what about our nearest relative, the chimpanzee?

Research by scientists at the Max Planck Institute looked at thousands of hours of recorded vocalisations from three groups of chimpanzees that live in the Tai Forest National Park in west Africa's Ivory Coast. The study found that chimps can change combinations of calls in four different ways, resulting in sixteen different two-call combinations. This is the first time such complex 'word' building has been seen outside of our own species.

The chimps were able to combine two sounds to get a third 'new' meaning. They could also add sounds that would modify the meaning of other sounds, in the same way that we use a suffix or a prefix. (As humans, we add the suffix 'ness' to the adjective 'kind' to make a new noun: 'kindness'.) In the same way, the chimps could swap the order of calls to make entirely new meanings: for example, a 'hoo + grunt' is usually associated with the chimps feeding or resting, but a 'grunt + hoo' was a call made mostly during travelling or when two chimp groups came together. We have observed other animals combining sounds, but only in very specific situations, such as the alarm calls of gibbons. But it seems that chimpanzees can go way beyond this limited scope to give much more varied and detailed messages. Some of these recorded combinations are incredibly specific, for example the joining of 'hoo + pant' seems to have a very precise meaning and is the signal given before making a nest up in a tree, safely away from predators, rather than sleeping on the ground. It seems that chimps have the building blocks of a complex language. This gives us clues as to how language evolved to flourish among our ape ancestors, becoming the infinite combinations and meanings that we see in our own speech today.

Chimpanzees make all kinds of wonderful sounds. When they are relaxed and sitting as a group eating fallen fruit, they softly chatter. When grooming, they may smack their lips and blow gentle raspberries. But things can get considerably louder when the chimps 'pant-hoot'. This is a complex sequence of calls, starting with an introduction of soft 'hoo' sounds, building up to include a series of in-out panting increasing in speed. The whole show climaxes with loud, ear-splitting screams, before slowing down and gently fading out. Pant-hoots are made in a variety of situations, from discovering a new food source to encountering a rival group. The call can be used to keep in touch with other chimps over a long distance, helping groups maintain their spatial awareness. They can be an expression of excitement or can even be made to impart information on the caller's social status. High-ranking males tend to pant-hoot more often and it's thought that they are communicating social dominance and sending a warning to would-be rivals.

Chimpanzees aren't just vocalists, they are also pretty adept at percussion. Male chimps will thrash around in the foliage and 'drum' on buttress roots of trees, slapping them with their hands, as part of their dominance displays. A new study by scientists from Vienna University has discovered that each chimpanzee has their own unique drumming style. The drumming also shows elements of musicality, with evenly spaced timings. By comparing the drumming of chimps in different locations, the study was able to observe that west African chimps drum with beats at equal intervals whereas east African chimps drum by alternating shorter and longer intervals between hits. The western chimps also produced more drumming hits and drummed at a faster tempo while including their drumming earlier in their pant-hoot calls. The research team speculated that such drumming may have been present in our shared common ancestor. Perhaps the sounds of our ancestor's fists and palms beating a rhythm on a tree could be the foundation of our own human musicality.

Scan to hear the pant-hoot of an alpha male chimpanzee in the forests of Gabon.

King of the beasts

In the African bush, trying to get a good night's kip is a bit like living one floor below a student party. Sleep is a lovely idea, but you'll be lucky to make it through to morning without a host of rude interruptions. Our camp was nestled on an island deep in the heart of the Okavango Delta and my tent was right on the edge of the swamp. Here I was, lying on my bedroll, eyes wide open, unable to sleep again. The last few nights I had been kept awake by an unsettling snuffling and the delicate scratching of claws, as a beast unknown had skittered around in the low branches of the jackalberry tree that formed a natural ceiling above my tent. I had even heard a dainty 'sniffing'. Once my ears were tuned in to the activity, there was little chance of dropping off. Increasingly keen to identify my midnight sniffer, I had set up a camera trap on a branch to see what might come by. The morning had revealed the camera had triggered on an empty frame, all except for the blurred fuzz of a long black and white striped tail, exiting the scene of the crime. It was enough to identify my night-time visitor was a genet and, judging by the strange fox-like vocalisations coming from above my head, tonight he had brought a genet friend.

The genet wasn't the only one making a racket. As I had turned in, the island's baboon troop had experienced an almighty disagreement. Branches cracked and a big male barked 'RAAAR' with such force that I could imagine his angry frown and threatening canines. It was followed by the pathetic screech of a whimpering youngster, no doubt being disciplined by the bigger monkey. Next up were the hippos, blowing bubbles in the swamp and belching their grumbling laughs, 'hoh, hoh, hoh'. Being so close to the water, I was nervous about the hippos. At night they like to wander out onto the island and crop the greenery. On more than one occasion I was convinced that I could hear the soft pad of their footsteps through the grass, passing just outside my tent.

But the loudest animal of all to resound across the night was was the elephant. A constant noise of the shredding and chewing of the grass rose from out in the swamp, punctuated by the occasional trumpets and seismic rumblings of their vocalisations. Partway through the night they came out of the water meadows and up onto the island to dine. I could hear the giants shaking the trees, pushing their huge foreheads and long trunks against the tall palms so that their crowns shook and rattled like maracas. Then a few moments later came the 'thud, thud, thud' as the falling palm nuts hit the floor. It sounded like one elephant was trying to push a tree all the way over. First there was the sound of sharp cracks, then splintering wood and a huge crashing of vegetation, as the tree finally succumbed.

The absurdity of trying to sleep through the sound of the world's largest land animal using its brute force to tear a tree limb from limb made me giggle and I gave in to the madness. After all, it's not every night you are exposed to such an entertaining soundscape. Accepting my insomnia, I tuned in and began to relish every rumble, snort and crash that the bush's night orchestra threw at me. Alongside the regular performers, I could sometimes pick out strange distant noises from far out over the water. The chuckle of a hyena, the hoot of an owl, it was hard to tell. As the night passed into the early hours of morning, the party seemed to settle down. Now all I could hear was a gentler soundtrack, provided by the crickets chirping, the vibrant snoring of guttural toads and a few chirpy 'pips' from the tiny reed frogs clinging to the flooded grass stems. There was an odd watery slurping sound that our guide later told me was the gloopy writhing of shoals of catfish, wriggling through the shallows. No doubt comforted by the continuous underscore, I finally nodded off in the wee small hours.

But just before dawn, in the grey half-light, I was woken abruptly by a roaring lion. The sound was unmistakable and my reaction to it was immediate. Adrenaline sharpened my senses and I sat bolt upright. I suddenly remembered where I was. I was instantly afraid and tried to rationalise how far away the sound was and whether my tent would provide any meagre protection from the attack of a hungry predator. I focused on remaining quiet and staying still, all ears, just like a gazelle.

A study by bioacoustics scientists from North Carolina has proposed that when prey species hear the roar of a large predator like a lion or tiger, they may actually experience fear paralysis. They theorised that the low frequency and the loudness of the roar could have a chilling effect on humans too. This may go some way to explaining my terrified reaction while lying in my tent in Botswana.

Both male and female lions can roar, usually performing in the time between dusk and dawn when the sound travels further in the cold, still air, so it can be heard from up to 8 kilometres. The roaring takes the form of a series of vocalisations delivered in distinct bouts, usually lasting thirty to sixty seconds. It starts with several soft introductory moans, then escalates to a series of full-throated roars before finishing with a sequence of staccato grunts. The sound seems to have many functions. It's a way to stay in touch with companions, pride members and coalition males. It strengthens the bond between pride members, and it's also a dramatic territorial threat to intimidate rivals. The secret to making such a deep and vibrating sound is that lions have very large and very loose vocal cords that vibrate irregularly, so the sound created has a quivering roughness.

Lions can discriminate between the roars of pride members and those of rivals. They have been shown to be sensitive to the number of those rivals, being able to tell the difference between the roars of large and small groups. Scientists at the University of Oxford used data loggers and pattern recognition software to study a lion's roar in detail. They discovered that they could identify individual lions from their roar. A lion's roar is made up of elements across a range of different frequencies. The research found patterns within the lowest-frequency elements that were unique to the individual lion. So, it seems likely that one lion can recognise another individual just by listening to the unique patterns hidden in their roar. The roars of male lions are lower pitched than those of females, and males will only tend to roar in their own territories. It's been shown that roaring is a good way to defend your territory and avoid costly fights. In fact, lions with a good territory, rich in prey and females, roar more regularly to defend it. Males that roar while in the territories of rivals would expect things to escalate quickly and the rival males to respond with an attack. Roaring on your rival's turf is sending out a serious challenge that says you are ready for a fight. We know that female lions with cubs become agitated and will retreat when they hear the roars of unfamiliar males, but that they will stay relaxed when they hear their own resident male's roaring. Sometimes females will roar in chorus and this is thought to be a warning to deter the approach of rival males who may be a threat to their cubs.

Whether it inspires fear or wonder, the roar of a lion certainly has to be one of the most thrilling sounds in the natural world. As I lay there in my tent, my waking brain slowly deciphered the sound and I realised that, although the roar sounded close, it was far enough away that there wasn't a hungry lion on the other side of the tent door, trying to work out the zipper. At that point my sense of excitement took over, until I was actually willing the sound to get louder and the lion to come ever closer into our camp. Letting the exhilaration wash over me, I lay back down on my pillow to listen.

Scan to listen to lions roaring at night in Botswana.

Chasing shadows

Sometimes nature just doesn't play ball. We were into our fourth day trying to film leopards in the delta. We had driven around the bush and back again, followed tracks, staked out kill sites and chased leads, but – so far – the cats had proved elusive. The hard thing about leopards is if they don't want to be seen, they can just melt into the landscape. We had been scanning every tree and under every bush in hope. On the first day, I spotted the silhouette of a leopard, ears pricked and sitting upright beneath a bush. Hearts quickening, we investigated, grabbing our binoculars and slowly driving closer, but embarrassingly, my big cat was nothing more than a leopard-shaped tree stump. We would see the arch of a leopard's back and it would turn out to be a twist in a fallen branch. Picking out a patch of spots in the dark bows of an acacia, we'd be disappointed to find it was the sun dapples falling over orange lichen. The golden yellow of a leopard's coat would end up being just an old weaver bird's nest. That lazy tail hanging from a tree? Nothing more than a branch snapped by the elephants.

It was October and the dry season in the delta. Away from the swamps, we were focusing our search for leopards in the dry thorny scrub around our camp. It was swelteringly hot and dust devils spiralled through the twisted black skeletons of the mopane trees. Out over the pans, bone white and cracked like dropped china, lines of elephant footprints told of a desperate quest for water. But our camp lodge had a small but permanent waterhole, kept filled for the thirsty wildlife. Throughout the day, nervous giraffe, groups of impala and a near constant procession of elephants all stopped by to drink. Our hope was that all these thirsty animals might make this the perfect spot for a hunting leopard, but so far we had been chasing ghosts.

Our trackers had picked up the pugmarks (footprints) of a big male, but the trail led us into thorn scrub so thick that even our four-wheel drive Land Cruiser couldn't follow. Back at camp, one of the team had spotted a female leopard and we followed her tracks around the water-hole where I set up a small camera trap on a pole we sank into the water.

The next day, we downloaded the shots and overnight we had captured lots of elephants. In fact, one had repositioned the camera with its trunk. We even caught the local pack of wild dogs lined up to take a drink. But oddly the waterhole at night seemed a pretty quiet place. Perhaps its fringes were stalked by a predator that forced the impala to drink during the day, when they could better keep watch against an ambush. Towards the end of the night, a cat did come down to drink, but it was a small African wildcat, not much bigger than a domestic moggy. As the cat finished drinking and slinked out of shot, a few seconds passed on the recording and then suddenly, the leopard crept into frame. Her shoulders rose and fell like well-oiled pistons as she stalked along the edge of the water. She was hunting the wildcat and she sprang after it, her chase taking her out of frame. Because the camera was fixed and running remotely, we couldn't hope to follow the action, but the wildcat must have escaped as the leopard returned a few minutes later to squat down and drink at the water's edge. She was beautiful and her form was mirrored perfectly as a silvery reflection in the dark black water. She even sat in the shallows, perhaps trying to keep cool, until she was eventually chased away by a rumbling herd of elephants, who weren't up for sharing their drinking spot. But these few grainy black-and-white moments on a cheap camera trap weren't good enough quality for our project, so were only a taster of what we had hoped to film.

Each morning, we would follow her tracks from the night before and she would remain impossible to find. Her footprints even led around our dining shelter and into the toilet, where it looked as if she was drinking from the water in the toilet bowl. We spent one day following her footprints all over and around the camp only to give up exhausted by the heat and with daylight fading. We had sat around a campfire overlooking the waterhole, cursing our luck, when our guide picked out the female leopard sitting watching us in the beam of his torch. One of our trackers even tried to keep up with her movements at night in the hope that we could find her first thing after sunrise and finally earn the right to film her with our daylight cameras. But she would always give us the slip. Just where she went during the day became a real mystery, but it felt like she was teasing us. One of our guides, laughing at our efforts, told us it was nothing personal, 'Just leopards being leopards!'

Having scouted in the trees and bushes, set up camera traps and followed pugmarks in the sand, we were still no closer to filming a leopard. But our luck changed on our last morning at the camp and it did so thanks to the 'bush telegraph' – the natural soundscape of the bush.

Listening in on the sounds of the bush is one of the key skills of any good tracker. The 'chrrr' of an oxpecker can lead you to rhino. The cracking of branches is a sure signal that elephants are feeding in the trees. The sounds of alarm calls can give away the presence of a predator. And so it was when one of our trackers reported over the radio that they were investigating an alarm call from a black-backed jackal. These jackals will give a repeated call, part yelp, part plaintive cry, should they pick up the scent of – or directly spot – a predator.

Scan to hear the call of a black-backed jackal.

Then the radio crackled into life again: 'Visual, repeat, I have a visual!' and we drove over to our spotter's position brimming with nervous excitement. At last, we had eyes on a leopard. But this wasn't the shy, elusive and graceful female we had been tracking around camp. This leopard was a brute. A huge male. He was walking through the bush without a care for who might see him, placing his big paws with a deliberate rhythm. His basketball head was huge and he had 'dewlaps' – loose folds of skin on his throat, hanging like jowls – a sign he was a mature male. His shoulders were a sloping pyramid of muscle and he moved with the swagger of a super-middleweight prize-fighter. Every so often he would stop, sniff at a bush and turn and scent-mark, sending a pungent signal to other leopards that he was in the area. As he walked, his tail was raised behind him, its white tip flicking. Leopards are often seen walking past herds of gazelle, tail aloft, in this way. It's been theorised that the cat is signalling its intention not to hunt and they will often show this behaviour just after a failed chase. While actively hunting, the cat keeps a much lower profile and tries hard to remain unseen, so by raising 'the white flag' on the end of their tails, they are thought to be communicating that they are no threat. This could save the leopard energy on unnecessary chases and signal to the prey that, this time, they don't need to run.

Watching our big boy stroll through the mopane, I wasn't sure that the rest of the bush were buying his signal of disinterest. For every step our male leopard made he was being watched. Alarm signals rose up from every corner of the bush as he passed through. The prehistoric-looking helmeted guinea fowl would let out a dirge of squeaky chittering everywhere the leopard went. In the end, taking a big yawn, he settled down in the shade of a termite mound for a nap. We were able to approach him slowly and zoom right in on our camera for a closer look. In the monitor I could see the incredible details of his scarred face and the cracks in the pads on his huge paws. I smiled as I wondered if these were the same pads that had created one of the many leopard tracks we had followed so fruitlessly over the last long week.

Listening to the constant terrified blather of the guinea fowl, I couldn't help but feel sorry for the poor cat as he tried to sleep. It had been a long night hunting and he could barely keep his beautiful pale-yellow eyes open. With so many look-outs in the bush, life is not always easy for predators. There are at least twelve animals known to have alarm calls specifically for leopards alone. Amazingly, among the animal members of this 'neighbourhood watch', it's been discovered that there is a hidden complextity to the animals' signals and a clear hierarchy where not all alarm calls are treated as seriously as others.

Lechwe are the leopard's favourite prey and they make for a good target as they never seem to sound the alarm until a predator is actually spotted. It also means their alarm signal is a reliable one, so is often enough to make other species flee. This isn't always the case and some animals seem more ready to alarm at the merest hint of danger, making their signals less reliable. When it comes to giving an alarm you can trust, it turns out that impalas are the 'drama queens' of the African bush. It's been discovered that they will give their short-barked alarm, pushing air rapidly through their flared nostrils, at the drop of a hat. It's even been discovered that when an impala alarm snorts, there is a 25 per cent chance they will have been scared by nothing more than the wind blowing in the grass. This means other animals such as wildebeest and zebra will often simply ignore the bark of a nervous impala as the signal tends to be a false alarm. Even the impalas themselves, are more likely to react to the alarms of zebra than they do to those of another impala.

Some animals seem to respond only to alarm calls of animals that are the same size or bigger than them. Vervet monkeys have acoustically different alarm calls for different types of predators, making a sharp 'chirp' call when they see a leopard. They can often be heard giving this call at dawn and dusk, perhaps to deter hungry leopards from approaching their sleeping sites. On hearing the alarm, members of the vervet troop will rush up into the branches of the nearest tree. It's known that impalas and baboons will also respond to the monkeys' chirps and, despite being such alarmists, impala are listened to by baboons, who will respond to their snorting. The impalas too have some ability to recognise the baboon's specific leopard alarm. Both species are of similar size and both are very much on the menu for hunting leopards, so it pays for one to keep an ear out for the other.

Kudu, being one of the largest antelope, only alarm-call for the biggest predators. They make a low-frequency hooting sound that can travel long distances through the bush and is the loudest vocalisation of any antelope. But there is one animal's alarm call that everyone is listening out for and everyone takes seriously. Zebra can weigh up to 450 kilograms and are big enough to attract the attention of lions, the largest predator in the delta. They give a 'bra-ha-ha' braying call that elicits alarm among the whole neighbourhood. When a zebra says run, it's time to run. It's not just prey species that are listening out. Spotted hyena are known to be drawn to some alarm calls as it might lead them to a kill they could attempt to steal.

When it comes to reporting leopards, the alarm call heard most frequently comes from the African tree squirrel. With the guinea fowl gone, our big male leopard's hard-won sleep was now disturbed by a high-pitched chittering. It grated my ears like the laughter of one of those creepy mechanical clown toys you often see in horror films. Tree squirrels only make up around 0.5 per cent of a leopard's diet, so their persistent alarming of leopards they encounter is either working really well for them, or verging on outright harassment! Upon spotting a leopard, the squirrel's alarm will alert all members of the family group and they will mob the cat, surrounding it from safe vantage points in the trees above. They will berate it with a constant chorus of their maddening alarm, each laughing phrase accompanied by a vexatious waggling of their tails. But, a bit like the impalas, the squirrels do seem to alarm-call at anything that moves, even other squirrels, so their alarm is often a false one. Larger animals hear it so frequently they will simply ignore it. However, the squirrels do have their own leopard-specific alarm and other animals have come to recognise this. If the squirrels give their 'leopard' alarm and deliver it with enough dedication, other animals are then more inclined to take it seriously.

We watched our cat try and sleep, his eyelids heavy. At one point he got to his feet and stretched. His movement was enough to set off another round of sonic bullying from the watchful squirrels. The leopard even slumped down in the shade of a bush right next to our vehicle and tried to sleep again. He was close enough now that I could even hear the deep panting from his breathing and the occasional low growl as he looked up in irritation at the squirrels. Ambush predators such as leopards aren't well known for their vocalisations and are often portrayed as silent assassins. But leopards themselves have fourteen different recorded vocalisations made in different circumstances of submission, aggression, play, nursing and mating. One night in camp, one of our guides had reported hearing a leopard giving its distinctive call that sounds just like wood being cut with a saw. Used both for territorial defence and to attract a mate, it could have been our camp female, or our sleeping male, or just as likely another cat altogether.

In a brand-new study, scientists from the University of Exeter have been working to find out more about this distinctive vocalisation. Working in Nyerere National Park in Tanzania, the team paired up infra-red camera traps with microphones so they could capture both images and vocalisations of animals at night. They were able to extract the bouts where leopards were 'sawing' from the audio and match it to the exact cats that appeared in the video. They discovered that each cat had a uniquely distinctive roar and it was possible to identify individual leopards from their recordings with a 93.1 per cent accuracy.

By listening in on leopards remotely and identifying individual cats, the researchers hope to learn more about how leopards use the landscape. Their recordings could go on to help us understand how leopards interact. As our crew had discovered, these elusive cats are often hard to find and to follow, making studying their behaviour challenging. By listening in remotely, there is now the opportunity to learn more about these shadows in the bush. It's hoped that the study could also help in conserving leopards by giving more accurate counts of their populations and by providing an early warning for villages that leopards in the region are mating. This is a time when the cats are thought to be more aggressive and more likely to attack people. Avoiding conflict between predators and local communities is an important conservation goal and by listening to leopards, there is a chance to help big cats and people coexist more peacefully.

As the day grew older, our big male leopard finally got up and moved on. We tried to follow him at a distance, but after a while he headed into a thick patch of thorn scrub and we let him go. I watched through my binoculars in the fading light until all I could see was his tail, raised like a white flag, its tip dancing, until it disappeared in the long grass. He was a beautiful cat.

On the drive back to camp, lightning flickered across the taupe sky. Huge clouds were forming on the horizon and it looked as if the rain was finally coming. Back around the campfire, one of the camp staff came over to us and told us they had seen the female leopard again. They had followed her footprints as she walked here and there among the camp buildings and then the tracks had led them to our tents or, more exactly, right to my tent. Our sleeping shelters were pitched on a raised platform of wooden floorboards and it seemed that the leopard had been spending her days sleeping in the shade beneath. The mystery of our disappearing leopard had been solved. All this time I had been sharing my tent with a big cat!

Scan to hear the 'sawing' call of an African leopard.

3. The Forest Orchestra

LISTENING IN ON THE RAINFOREST

When the Jungle Roars

THE BOAT CHUGGED along the brown lazy river. After several hours on the water, the once broad expanse of low islands and sand bars had reduced to a narrow channel, hemmed in by misty jungle. It felt as if we were tiny visitors to a world of giants. Huge trees lined the banks, their lofty crowns draped with jumbled lianas; they seemed to lean over the water. It was hard to shake the feeling that we were being watched. A few years ago, a British photographer had rounded a bend in this river and come face to face with a pure black jaguar. I'm not sure this adds much – the sentiment is a bit confused + the next sentence also ends in imagination so this avoids the repetition. As the cat stepped out from behind the dark cloak of the forest, the photographer captured an image that had become seared into my imagination. With its sultry black fur and piercing golden eyes, the forest had revealed one of its most beautiful secrets. As we passed along the same stretch of water, I was ready, eyes peeled to see what surprises the forest might reveal to us on our own journey.

I was in Ecuador, travelling with a film crew to the world-renowned Tiputini Biodiversity Station, deep inside the Amazon rainforest. The world was still recovering from the Covid pandemic but we had been given special permission to travel and would be the only outside visitors allowed to come this way for many months. Our mission was to set up remote camera traps to try and capture film of the jaguar, the forest's apex predator, but we were also charged with recording the incredible soundscapes of the jungle.

After recent heavy rains, the water in the river was very high and our skipper had to cautiously steer the bow around the branches of submerged trees and dangerous floating logs. As we passed one dead branch emerging out of the water, we disturbed a small roost of daylight-loving proboscis bats, with their haughty upturned noses and stripy forearms. They took to the air in a flurry of wingbeats before settling on another branch further downstream.

Our guide signalled the skipper to pull over to a huge tree, fallen on the bank. He leant low over the side of the boat, looking carefully into the water. Apparently, it was a spot where the biggest anaconda he had ever seen liked to bask out. Sadly, this serpent's sunbed was empty today, but as we travelled on I got the growing sense that the forest was becoming more 'alive' with every passing moment. A puff of air like a punctured tyre led to excited voices and fingers pointing at the water, as our guide spotted a river dolphin. It passed by again and I could see the shiny pink skin on its domed head and its tiny black dot of an eye, just before it dived into the murk. I was learning that in the forest you almost always hear something before you see it and the crashing of branches low over the water revealed the slender frame of a spider monkey that had come down to the river to drink, a baby dangling from its chest. But then we heard an altogether more ominous sound coming from the trees ahead.

To anyone visiting a tropical forest for the first time the soundscape is overwhelming. You experience a biophonic overload, leaving you 'ear-struck' by a living surround sound. The air around us was alive with the strange calls of birds and insects. It was a soundscape richer and more colourful than anything I had experienced before. But with every moment's progress down the river, the ominous sound was growing. A low growling that echoed around the tree-tops, almost lost in the mist. Deeper than a tiger's roar and more menacing than any bear, it was more than a little scary and for a moment I wondered what kind of threatening creature could create such a noise.

Rounding the next bend in the river we saw them. The distinctive golden-orange fur and unmistakable loudness of a troop of howler monkeys. If ever there was a sound designed to intimidate, it's the roar of a howler monkey. When I first heard this sound close up, I was blown away by just how noisy it was. At 140 decibels, it's louder than a pneumatic drill and is the loudest sound made by any land animal. The secret to the howler's remarkable call is hidden in its throat sac. Here there is a bone called the hyoid, which in humans is a small U-shaped bone that sits at the top of your neck, just under your jaw. In howler monkeys, the hyoid has evolved into a hollow sphere about the size of an orange. It's effectively an echo chamber, resonating and amplifying the howler's call, making it louder and deeper. It's the perfect tool for long-distance communication, as deeper sounds travel further across the forest, meaning a howler's call can be heard from up to 5 kilometres away.

Scan to hear the loudest sound of any land animal – the howler monkey.

Both male and female howlers call but the hyoid bone is larger in males, making their voices the loudest. They'll commonly call first before sunrise when the still, cold air means that their voices can travel the furthest. Being woken up by this distant early-morning chorus is the most exciting alarm clock I know. These so-called 'long calls' have been interpreted by scientists as an announcement, where the male howler, on behalf of his troop, is proclaiming their location. It's a gentle reminder to other howler troops in the area that says, 'We are here and this feeding tree is ours.'

The reason why howlers have evolved such a dramatic signal is all about their access to food. Howler troops (typically made up of one to four adult males and two to four adult females) do not hold distinct territories, so in any given area they will be sharing space with other troops. Within these areas there are certain favourite feeding trees, with the tastiest leaves, ripest fruits or seed pods, which each troop will want to access. With lots of howler troops sharing the same space and wanting to visit the feeding trees, howlers needed a way to resolve daily conflicts without having to resort to physical fights. These monkeys survive on a low-calorie diet of greenery, so howling may seem like an obvious waste of their energy, but it's still more efficient than resorting to a scrap.

Scientists have recorded a second distinct type of howl made by males when other troops come too close. These more aggressive encounters, occurring over shorter distances, include more staccato 'barks', as the males try to intimidate each other. Compared to the gentler message of the 'long calls', these barks are saying, 'Stay away, unless you want a fight.'

Often the rest of the troop will join in, adding their voices to the dominant male's, but only if he is calling and not ever on their own. It's thought these extra voices may help tip the balance, raising the volume enough to win the acoustic battle. It's also been suggested that if things ended in violence between rival troop males, the winning male may take over the loser's troop and potentially kill any existing offspring so he can mate with the females. So, it could be in the females' interest to join the chorus and help defend their young. By settling their disagreements through shouting at their neighbours, howler monkeys can defend their feeding trees and keep their families safe. And by listening to the calls of the competition, the weaker troops can save energy and avoid dangerous fights.

There is a direct link between a male howler monkey's strength and size, and how loud and long he can call for. If a male is better at defending space and his group of females, it would make sense that the loudness of his call would somehow have an effect on his breeding success. But interestingly, it's not that simple.

In one particularly quirky piece of research, it's been discovered, rather surprisingly, that the males with the biggest hyoid bones and the deepest, loudest voices also have the smallest testicles. Males with larger hyoids and smaller testicles tend to be the only male in the troop, monopolising a group of females. Males with smaller hyoids and bigger testicles tend to live in groups alongside both other males and females. The small-testicled, louder males have exclusive access to their group of females, while the big-testicled, quieter males have more competition and cannot hope to win females with their calls alone. So, these males need to make the most of their breeding opportunities and therefore come equipped with the sperm-producing hardware to make things count when called into action!

Having left the monkeys roaring behind us, the skipper steered the boat around one more bend in the river and cut the engines. We glided alongside a wooden pontoon that emerged from the forest sticking out over the water. It was the first sign of human activity we had seen in hours. We hauled all our gear up a steep wooden staircase and found ourselves swallowed up by the forest. Here and there we could make out buildings dotted among the trees. We had finally arrived at the research station. With the forest all around us, I experienced a sudden sensory overload, but with all the dense growth it was hard to see very far, so my ears were working overtime. A feeding troop of woolly monkeys argued above us, the fruit they dropped crashing through the foliage before splattering on the floor. Hidden among the trees, strange birds called. Insects, like some ecological tinnitus, hissed without pause. From the forest soundscape alone, I could tell this forest was more alive than any other place I had ever visited.

Conducting the forest orchestra

TIPUTINI IS PART of a huge area of protected forest that borders the world-famous Yasuni National Park. An area covering about 10,000 square kilometres, it's five times the size of London. Within this area there are 596 species of birds, 150 species of frogs and over 200 mammals – including five different cats. There are twenty species of frog, nineteen species of bird and four species of mammal that are found nowhere else on Earth. In just one hectare of forest, researchers found 100,000 different insect species. An average hectare of forest in Tiputini contains more than 655 tree species. That's more than are found in the entire continental space of the United States and Canada. If you increase that area to a 25-hectare sample, the number of tree species found rises to over 1,100.

Within Yasuni's borders there are more species of animals and plants than can be found anywhere else on Earth. It's been called the 'centre' for life on our planet and a 'biologist's Disneyland'. E. O. Wilson, the renowned naturalist and former professor of entomology at Havard, once suggested that Yasuni may even harbour the highest number of species that have ever existed at any time in our planet's long history. As one guide at the research centre told me over a cold beer, this means that Yasuni is not just the centre of life on Earth but is also home to more life than 'anywhere in the known solar system'. With my sense of reality widened, I sat listening to all the outlandish and unfamiliar sounds coming out of the forest. It certainly sounded like there was a vast array of lifeforms on the research station's doorstep.

The soundscape was so overwhelming it induced a kind of temporary auditory confusion, a bit like listening to an unsophisticated heavy-metal band at a festival. Each musician appeared to be doing their own thing regardless of the other band members and were hellbent on playing their own solo over the top of everyone else. But as the days went by and we headed out on our sound-recording trips into the forest, my ears started to adjust to things and I found that the forest soundscape had its own distinct pattern and rhythm to learn.

The thick green jumble of the Amazon rainforest can be almost totally impenetrable, making it hard to see very far. Visual cues become largely redundant and in this living maze it's only sound that provides any sense of distance and orientation. Sound becomes the best way to communicate, find a mate and defend your territory. But with so much noisy life here, competition for the airwaves is fierce. How on earth do you make yourself heard above the din? One way is to become louder – just like a howler monkey. But many animals making sound in the rainforest use a higher degree of sophistication. Across the forest, light, temperature and humidity change throughout the day and this alters the conditions for the propagation of sound. It creates a series of sound-making opportunities that scientists call 'acoustic niches'. Like DJs on a radio station, across the course of a day there is a performance schedule with slots for each animal to take the mic. In the Amazon each animal sound is made at exactly the same time and frequency – in the same broadcast slot on any given day. And in many cases they have been performing to this schedule for thousands of years.

There are four obvious periods in the forest's sound cycle: late night to early morning (11 pm to 8 am); daytime (9 am to 7 pm); evening

(6 pm to 7 pm); and night (7 pm to 11 pm). The sonic day starts in the early morning when the growing heat of the sun warms the air in the treetops, creating a temperature inversion that traps cooler air just below the canopy. Sound travels further in the cool air, so this is the perfect time to broadcast long-distance vocalisations and the best time to hear monkeys calling. This is true in rainforests across the world. In south-east Asia, early morning is exactly the time to hear other primates such as gibbons and siamang calling. The dawn chorus of birds usually consists of short, high-intensity calls, and as the morning builds to become daytime you can continue to hear their calls. Some bird species are known to time their calls to reduce overlap with other bird species. But by midday, when the overhead sun reaches down into the forest and the temperature is at its highest, the bird calls lessen and the predominant sound is that of buzzing insects. At this time the soundscape is dominated by cicadas. As it's the hottest time of day, birds and mammals stay quiet to conserve their energy and avoid overheating. Insects such as cicadas are cold-blooded so thrive in the hot humid conditions under the midday sun. Most birds also avoid overlapping their calls with loud cicadas. They will reduce and even stop their own singing with the onset of a cicada call if it occurs in the same sonic range. Many forest birds have evolved to call at frequencies that don't overlap with the much higher amplitude of a cicada's signalling.

Scan to hear cicadas in the daytime forest.

As the afternoon stretches on and it gets cooler again, you'll hear the bird calls build up, once more reaching a crescendo just before dusk. This is also the time that grasshoppers and crickets start to sing. At Tiputini the final rays of the sun were often accompanied by the haunting cry of a great tinamou bird, almost like a military bugler signalling the end of the day. It's at this time, in the rainforests of Borneo, that the six o'clock cicada sings its song, while on the Malaysian Peninsula the slightly larger seven o'clock cicada sings an hour later. The male cicadas are the ones singing to try and attract females. They do so by contracting and relaxing a special ribbed membrane on their underside called a tymbal. The sounds they make can be incredibly loud, with the record for the loudest insect on Earth being set by an Australian species, known as the double drummer cicada, which makes a high-pitched whine that can reach 120 decibels. With nightfall a new cast of performers dominates the airwaves. Out of the sun and less vulnerable to predators, this is the time you'll hear amphibian voices, as frogs and toads form the night shift. They are supported by the continuing chirps and buzzes of crickets and katydids, the signature sound of nighttime in the forest.

But the sonic world of the Amazon isn't just divided by time, it is also separated by physical space. On the forest floor any sound made will soon get weaker as it becomes obstructed by fallen leaves. Sound also reflects off the ground itself, weakening the message further. But travel vertically just a metre above the ground to make your call and things get easier, with the effect of any obstruction reducing. In the middle layer of the vertical forest, you find the understorey. It's often a dimly lit, humid world dominated by small trees and shrubs. Because only between 2–15 per cent of sunlight reaches the understorey, the trees here often have large leaves to capture any available light, and all this dense foliage can act as a physical barrier to sound. Sound is also reflected off tree trunks so that it can only travel short distances and there is a subtle reverberation here, almost like you would expect to find in an indoor space. Songs that contain shorter notes, repeated after long intervals, travel more efficiently through this dense vegetation.

Climb above the understorey and you reach the forest canopy. With more open space, there is less reflection and weakening of any sound waves, meaning animal calls can travel further. Animals will change the height at which they vocalise to make the best of the conditions and send their signal further. The difference between singing from the ground and singing from the canopy could increase their communication distance by five times. In the high forest canopy sound comes from every direction, with birds and monkeys calling above you and the sound of frogs and insects coming up from below. Up in the canopy the soundscape of the forest seems at its loudest and this is likely due to the fact that sound travels further up here, but it could also be that the canopy is the most biodiverse layer, with an estimated 70–90 per cent of all rainforest species living in the treetops.

So, my initial impression of a soundscape akin to an unruly thrash-metal band, all screaming at once to be heard, couldn't have been more wrong. The rainforest is in fact more like a disciplined classical orchestra, where every player has their own physical space to perform and also knows exactly when to play. By inhabiting subtly different acoustic niches, animals here give themselves the best chance to be heard above the competition. And with so much life here, the soundscape at Tiputini could just be the richest and most complicated 'biophony' on the planet.

I woke with a feeling of unsettling anxiety. The ghostly shapes of the trees in the half-light and the distant roars of the howler monkeys were like an ominous warning. The night had been full of strange noises, which – combined with the humidity – meant I had struggled to sleep. In the small hours I had drifted off, only to be jolted awake by an extraordinary animal sound that was just like the sirens of two police cars having an argument. With morning the forest slowly became less troubling and my imaginings condensed into reality with the growing light. After a hearty breakfast we headed out into the forest to set up the first of our remote camera traps, with the aim of capturing shots of jaguars.

We followed a narrow path through the forest, slowly climbing a sharp ridge. From ahead of us came an angry 'chuc chuc' sound. It was the alarm call of two golden-mantled tamarins. They were sitting at just above our eye-level in the understorey and, judging by their irritation, we had clearly disturbed their breakfast. With their white cheeks, slate-grey heads and coppery ruff, these pretty monkeys are endemic to the forests of the Yasuni region, so it was a rare treat to watch them, watching us.

Further on through the forest we came across a wonderful sight, a huge column of leafcutter ants crossing the path. These ants form some of the largest and most complex animal societies on the planet. Lying on my belly, I took a closer look. An endless stream of worker ants passed by, each carrying a large piece of leaf. They looked like a procession of bizarre miniature windsurfers. I could see the tiny 'minima', the smallest of the ants' castes, riding the leaf sails, their front limbs raised to ward off parasitic flies that like to ambush the column and lay their eggs on the workers. I had to watch myself, as lining the edge of the endless procession stood a protective guard of massive soldier ants with their huge heart-shaped heads and sharp curved mandibles. Leafcutters can live in colonies of up to 10 million individuals. They do not eat the leaves they forage for, but return them to their massive nests and feed them to their fungus gardens. The fungus then provides the ants with the food they need to feed their own larvae.

We remembered that in the sound-recording kit we had a couple of 'contact' microphones – flattened to a disk and perfect for recording sound through direct contact on a vibrating surface, rather than directly through the air. They're the ideal device for picking up sounds close to the ground. As we set up the mics and listened in on the headphones, we tuned in on the ants' 'conversations'. Leafcutters can produce vibrations, called 'stridulations', by rubbing a specialised structure found on their abdomens against a ridged scraper on their thorax. The vibrations are transmitted through the ground and picked up by other ants.

Research has discovered that they make this sound in several different situations and it seems the ants can change the pattern and frequency of the vibrations to communicate different messages. The ants can signal an alarm call, if they are buried or trapped and need the help of others to free them. They also stridulate when they are cutting leaves and this may attract nearby nest mates to point them towards new sources of foliage and work that needs to be done. It can sometimes be a request for help, in the instance that the ant cutting the leaf has bitten off more than it can carry. Amazingly, the vibrations produced during the cutting of the leaf might act to stiffen the leaf's tissues, making it easier for the ant's jaws to saw through. There are probably many other messages the ants could be sending with their vibrations, but listening in on them was joyous. Their high-pitched chatter felt oddly like they were talking, the incomprehensible squeaking of a miniature marching army.

Scan to hear the stridulations of leafcutter ants.

As the morning wore on the insects seemed to get louder and louder, their ceaseless stridulations dominating the airwaves. But there were still other sounds that rose up from the forest. Branches cracked and fell from above. It was as if the trees themselves were adding their own punctuating percussion. And the Amazon is home to some very noisy trees. The cannonball tree grows clusters of spherical fruit on short branches close to its central trunk. Each fruit typically holds up to sixty-five seeds and there can be as many as 150 fruit growing on the tree at any one time. These fruits can take up to eighteen months to ripen, but when they do it can rain fruit down onto the forest floor. Each one can weigh up to a kilogram, so it's not wise to loiter too long under the tree. They fall with enough force to create a heavy 'thud' on landing and their impact is enough to split the woody fruit apart, exposing the seeds inside, which are a favourite food for peccaries.

The sandbox tree, also known as the dynamite tree, makes a loud bang as its ripe seed pods explode, sending the precious seeds far and wide. The drying seed pod (which looks like a small brown pumpkin) shrinks, causing a growing tension in its structural fibres. When the tension gets too much, the pod explodes. Seeds are flung out in all directions, travelling at 250 kilometres per hour, and the sound, which has been likened to a gunshot, can be heard up to 45 metres away. The sandbox's trunk is covered with an armour of sharp spines, it has poisonous sap and its fruit contain toxins that will make you sick if ingested. No wonder it's been called 'the tree that wants you dead'.

If we were going to find jaguars, our best hope was to visit a clay lick or *saladero* or *collpa*. Because rainforest fruits are often low in sodium, many of the Amazon's birds and mammals have to get their salts and other essential minerals from a different source. They might also need these natural supplements to aid digestion if they regularly encounter plant toxins as part of their diets. So, they must visit clay licks to get the minerals they need. In a few secret, special places in the forest, outcrops of mineral-rich soils are exposed at the surface, to form these clay licks. These can draw in large numbers of species, looking to consume the soil or drink from the water that often pools there. One study discovered that up to fifteen different birds and twenty-three different mammal species regularly visit these hotspots. However, all these animals in one place can draw the attention of predators. Jaguars are rarely recorded at clay licks, but they can be seen following the forest trails that lead to them and often set their ambush for deer or peccaries that are busy coming and going to the lick.

The large animals that visit the licks, from tapirs to monkeys to deer, are often cautious and remain incredibly quiet. Monkeys especially take their time to approach and stay ever watchful. Climbing down to the ground leaves them vulnerable and they tread lightly, fearful to make a sound, not wanting to attract any unnecessary attention. In camp on the previous evening, our guide had shared with us one of his old camera-trap shots. It showed a pair of big male howler monkeys in a physical dispute over a patch of earth at a clay lick. In this extraordinary clip, the battling monkeys were so scared of attracting predators that their whole dispute took place in complete silence. Quite something for the loudest land animal on the planet. At one of the licks we visited that morning, we were joined by a small group of spider monkeys that were coming down from the trees to drink from the shallow muddy water when they spotted us. They shook the branches in mock threat and barked their rasping alarm call, but even though we sat silently they would not come down until after we had moved on.

At one of the largest clay licks, we struggled through deep sticky mud, trying to line up the camera trap's infra-red beams so they would break and start the camera should an animal choose to visit the lick and trigger the sensors. Occasional surges of pulsating whirring would rush past us where we stood. If we turned our heads quickly enough, we were sometimes lucky to catch a glimpse of a blur of beating wings and a burst of dazzling colour. The clay lick seemed to be a magnet for passing hummingbirds, their names – blue-tailed emerald, golden-tailed sapphire and fiery topaz – as exotic as their brilliant plumage. Tiputini is home to about nineteen species of these tiny, jewelled marvels, coming in a vivid array of pulsating colours that flash and fade as they buzz through the shafts of sunlight.

The clay lick was a great place to spot birds. Sometimes Amazon birds are known to form mixed flocks of up to seventy different species. These super-flocks move through the mid-layer of the rainforest understorey and can persist for over twenty years. Being part of a big group can improve your opportunities, as you have a better chance of discovering good feeding locations and can exploit a wider range of food from the forest. Having many eyes in the flock also means there are more look-outs for predators, giving improved odds for escaping should one attack. In the Amazon, two birds are typically leaders of these super-flocks. The dusky-throated antshrike and the cinereous antshrike almost always seem to be the ones who determine the direction and rate of movement for the whole flock. Both birds have a wide array of vocalisations that play a role in maintaining the cohesion of the flock. They also act as a neighbourhood watch for the other birds, as their high-pitched 'cheeping' alarm calls create a safe zone, protecting their flock mates from predators. These small birds can be said to have become 'keystone' species, having a huge effect on the survival of lots of other birds in the forest.

With all the angles at the clay lick covered by camera traps, we headed deeper into the forest. After crossing a small stream by balancing on a precarious fallen log, we entered an area of rolling hills covered by palms. Our guide had had lots of success camera-trapping this part of the forest before and told us proudly that there was probably a higher density of jaguars here than anywhere else in the world. We set up numerous cameras on the path and even rigged one high in a tree, looking down onto the forest below, hoping to film a jaguar passing beneath. Every now and then I would pause from working and my gaze would drift out into the trees and far into the forest. I wondered if there was a black jaguar out there somewhere, watching us as we worked. Just as our task was nearly done it began to rain. A few spots at first, but soon a drenching downpour. We hurried to set the last cameras, shutting them closed, desperate not to let the rain get inside and short-circuit the electrics. Slipping and sliding in the mud, we gathered the scattered boxes and bags and piled them up under a tarpaulin. We sat in a miserable heap under a smaller and wholly inadequate tarp and waited out the rainstorm. From under our shelter, I started to listen to the forest. Without me really noticing at first, the forest's rich and relentless soundscape had now changed beyond all recognition. As the rain fell it created a wall of noise. The impact of each falling raindrop, each a different size, hitting different-shaped leaves at different heights in the forest, created a diverse spectrum of frequencies. The combination of all these impacts was like the endless rhythm of a samba band with many drums. It's been estimated that there are trillions of raindrops that fall in in a typical tropical rainstorm, so together that's enough to make a sound akin to white noise. Alongside the drumming, the falling water itself acts as a physical barrier to any travelling sound waves, meaning any animal calls are deadened and don't travel so far. So, any deluge brings a temporary truce to the forest's constant competition for the airwaves. It's not worth the energy calling when nothing is likely to hear you.

As I sat there shivering in the dampness, I couldn't hear any birds and the insects too seemed to have all gone quiet. There were just one or two 'waterproof' cicadas still buzzing away, but otherwise the forest was silent. As the storm passed and we emerged, wet through from our derisory shelter, the forest soundscape quickly came back to life: first the insects and then the birds, until everything had returned to normal.

Scan to hear the sounds of the forest orchestra awakening after an Amazon rainstorm.

We packed up and began the long walk back to base. As we crossed the log and headed down the muddy trail, our guide spotted something on the path and we all crowded around, excited to get a look. It was the perfect paw print of a large big cat.

Wonders of the rainforest

THERE ARE SOME animal sounds that are very familiar. We have all heard a wolf's howl or a lion's roar, if only on the television. But not many among us can claim to have heard the call of a sloth. Who even knows what these strange and secretive animals sound like? With their lives of deliberate slowness, how can we know for sure that they make any noise at all?

Well, they do, and when they do, they do it with some gusto! Female sloths 'scream'. Coming from such a low-key, seemingly laid-back animal, the sound comes as a complete and utter surprise. But it's a sound that is very much a result of the sloth's unique low-energy lifestyle.

It's easy to characterise sloths as slow and lacking in

intelligence, but theirs is a winning, if very unusual, evolutionary formula. Sloths have been around in one shape or another for about 60 million years so they must be doing something right. The word 'sloth' is often used to describe laziness, but in truth these animals only sleep for eight to ten hours a day, which is two hours less than a cheetah (and nobody calls a cheetah lazy). Most of the time, three-fingered sloths only eat leaves. They are so slow at digesting that it can take them a whole month to process a single leaf and to do so they have a four-chambered stomach. With all this digestion going on and surviving on such a low-calorie diet, sloths don't have the energy for a high-octane lifestyle. For them it's a life in the slow lane, with a top speed of about 2.4 kilometres per hour, meaning sloths are the slowest of all mammals.

Being so committed to a life stuck in first gear means that sloths are vulnerable to predators. They are definitely high on the menu for harpy eagles and jaguars, and they have no chance of outrunning either should they be caught out. But by taking it slow and remaining quiet, their winning strategy is not to draw any attention to themselves. They've been likened to a mobile compost heap because their fur provides a habitat for algae to grow, making them the only green-coloured mammal, and it's the perfect camouflage for the forest. Furthermore, it's been claimed that you could fire a gun next to a sloth's head and it wouldn't react. Not because it's in any way stupid – more that it's an evolutionary survival skill: never to move fast or do anything that could attract attention. There is, however, one time when sloths have to risk being noticed.

Once every month when a female sloth comes into heat, she will scream for a mate. It's an extraordinary sound coming from such a seemingly gentle animal. When calling, the female will open her mouth wide, close her eyes and let out a note of near operatic purity, so alarmingly high-pitched it could make your eyes water.

Scan to hear the love scream of a female sloth.

Most rainforest animals call pretty much like clockwork. But the sloth doesn't stick to a timetable. A female sloth looking to attract a male will call at any time of day or night. At the start of her cycle, she'll call maybe once a day. Her irregular calls might mean it's harder for predators to find her. If she sat calling again and again from the same place, it would be like ringing a dinner bell for any hungry harpy eagle. Amazingly, the cycles of female sloths in the same area don't follow the same pattern. Each will have their own unique monthly cycle. In this way female sloths become even more unpredictable in their calling and this may make it even harder for predators to know where to look.

But what of the male? To our ears the female's scream isn't the prettiest, but for a male it's the voice of an angel. Woken up by her call, he'll climb down his tree and head in her general direction. With jaguars about, it's dangerous for him on the forest floor, but it's often the most direct route to find her. High-pitched calls (like our female's scream) don't travel so far through the forest. They tend to bounce off all the leaves. But there is some research into birds that suggests high-pitched calls are easier to triangulate. Perhaps the high pitch of our female's scream helps the male pinpoint exactly where she is? As her hormones peak, the female will start to risk calling more regularly, increasing her screams to as many as once every fifteen to twenty minutes, and this peak of performance might last for a day or two. The male by now should be well on his way to her tree and he won't be alone. It's not unusual for several males to fight over access to a calling female.

By screaming to an irregular timetable, the female sloth may avoid the attention of predators and win herself a mate. Their coupling usually takes place safely up off the ground and the whole thing lasts less than a minute. It's one of the very few things sloths manage to do quickly!

In the cloud forests of Ecuador lives a small bird that has a unique way of making itself heard above the competition. The male club-winged manakin is a pretty, rusty-coloured bird with black wings and a bright red skull cap. But it lives in forest so thick with lianas and mossy epiphytes that in the dense undergrowth its bright feathers can be hard to spot. Most male birds sing to attract a mate, but the club-winged manakin goes a step further by using his wings as a musical instrument.

For around eight months of the year male club-wings will gather a loose aggregation called a lek. This is an 'assembly area' where the birds come to complete their courtship. Each male will display on his own but within hearing distance of rival males. All the noise will draw in the green-coloured female manakins, who will tour the lek listening out for the best performer. When the lek activity is at its peak, the forest rings out with strange beeps and mechanical pulses. Each displaying male will find a thin horizontal branch that will act as his stage. With a female nearby he will begin his display. Bowing his head down, he dips forwards and lifts his wings behind him. In a blur of feathers, he makes a sound so unusual that it's like no other bird in the forest. It's a high-pitched, almost electronic 'bleeep' that only lasts a brief second or two, but is loud enough to come as quite a surprise.

But how is the bird making these bizarre sounds? Slow-motion filming has revealed that the male manakin bends its wings back into a position no other bird is known to do, holding them high above the head, and that the top of the wings beat together. But feathers are soft, so how could beating them together make any kind of sound, let alone one so dramatic? The answer lies in the specialist structure of the manakin's feathers. Taking a closer look at the manakin's secondary wing feathers revealed that in the sixth and the seventh secondary feathers, the rachis (the long central shaft of the feather) broaden out at the end to become enlarged. This club-like rachis on the sixth feather has ridges across its surface. The fifth feather is also modified. It is slender but bends at a 45-degree angle so that it slides over the ridges on the sixth feather, creating a stridulation. It's just like running the end of a pencil over a comb, with every movement of the pencil bumping the teeth of the comb, causing a short sound, that when combined in one big movement creates stridulation. The outer 'clubbed' feathers bumping together don't actually make the sound, but their collision does push the other feathers to slide over each other, and it's this that makes the 'bleeep'. In real time, the manakin beats its wings together 107 times a second, so all you see is a blur and all the stridulations combine to become an extended note.

This mechanical creation of sound in animals by stridulation is called 'sonation' and is common in insects. It's a way of making sound that is much less common in vertebrates. Puffer fish can make a sound by rubbing their teeth together and some saw-scaled vipers in the north African desert can rub their coils together to make a sizzling sound. Among mammals, the lowland streaked tenrec of Madagascar can make a high-pitched squealing noise by rubbing its spiny quills together, but the club-winged manakin is thought to be the only bird that does it.

Female manakins must be incredibly picky, as the performing males have a wide variety of smooth moves to impress them. The 'wing flash' is the males' favourite and most frequently used display behaviour. The wings are flicked, creating a short stridulation described by scientists as a 'tick', before the male bows his head, lifts his wings behind him and, feathers whirring, creates a longer stridulating 'ting'. It's been suggested by scientists that the short 'tick' might be something of a warm-up, like a musician tuning up, just before performing the main event.

Another element to this delightful forest cabaret is the backwards wing flash, where the male manakin bows, legs extended, feathers sleek against his body, and hops backwards on the perch. After six hops he will pause dramatically, produce two mechanical 'tings', hop backwards once more and add a final double-ting to end. These charming little entertainers will also throw in 'lateral springs', 'crouching calls' and 'bow' with their wings open. But my favourite part of their entertaining medley is the 'jump turn', which has to be the manakin's 'killer move' on the dancefloor. It starts with a rapid wing flick and a stridulating tick before the bird leaps in the air, legs dangling, and rotates 180 degrees, before landing facing the opposite direction. Each male works hard to impress any potential mate. One male, observed for one hour, performed ten crouching calls, twelve backwards wing flashes, twenty-one lateral springs, twenty jump turns and – most frequently – 180 wing flashes, including the incredible stridulating 'tick-ting' sonation. Another male was even recorded making sixty-five of these calls in a ten-minute period. Up to fifteen male birds can perform across an extended lek and when things are kicking off, the forest, with its beeps, ticks and outlandish electronical tones, sounds just like an old-school computer arcade.

Scan to hear the sonation of a club-winged manakin.

The rainforest's unceasing cacophony has led to some ingenious and surprising ways of making your voice heard above the noise. Spix's disk-winged bat is a tiny bat weighing only four grams. It has a foxy red back and a cute fluffy white belly and lives in small family roosts of up to six bats. It's named after the disk-like suckers that can be found on its thumbs and hind feet. These suction cups allow it to cling to smooth surfaces, a bit like a plush toy suckered to a car window.

The bats spend the daylight hours huddled together in the most unusual of roosting sites. The fleshy new leaves of rainforest plants called heliconia and calathea slowly open up, providing a funnel-shaped tube that the bats like to shelter in. They will sleep there during the day, each bat stuck to the leaf surface with its suckers. At night the bats wake up and leave their shelter to forage, gleaning low over the forest floor for insect food. But the new leaves they use for shelter open fully after just a day or two, meaning that the bats must regularly look for a new home. Before the sun rises again, the bats must search their patch of forest for a newly emerging leaf to roost in. But if one bat gets lucky and finds a good opening leaf, they need a way to call in the other bats, and they do this by making an infinitesimally puny high-pitched squeak, known as a 'social' call. Bats flying around the forest looking for their roost mates send out a specific 'enquiry call' and any bat lucky enough to have found a leaf will send out a response in order to guide the others to their new home.

But scientists from the University of Costa Rica studying the bat's vocalisations discovered that the heliconia leaf itself can dramatically change the strength of the bat's signals. According to their research, the calls from the bats outside the leaf were channelled and compressed down the funnel-shaped leaf, boosting the call's volume by 10 decibels. This might lengthen the reach of the call by over 10 metres. It would seem the bat's leafy shelter acts just like an old-fashioned ear trumpet, a hearing aid for the bats that helps them find each other in the noisy forest. However, the leaf's shape doesn't only make the calls louder, it also distorts the incoming calls, meaning it's harder for the bat already in the leaf to discriminate friends from strangers. To get around this, the bat in the leaf calls again with a more complex 'group call' made of twenty-five different sounds. This call is likely unique to the individual roosting colony and recognised by the other bats, which can then home in on their new shelter for the night. The researchers are hoping to look into how the properties of the leaf – the differences in species, size and shape – may affect the sound transmission and whether the bats ever consider these things when looking for the perfect roost.

On rare occasions, recordings can change our perception of how animals use sound and can reveal a whole new spectrum of communication. As humans we are most used to hearing sound that travels through the air, but there are many animals that send and receive messages in an entirely different way. Among the insects there is one group that makes sounds so bizarre, they wouldn't feel out of place in a science fiction movie. Welcome to the strange world of treehoppers and thorn bugs. Members of the insect family known as Membracidae, they are most closely related to cicadas and leafhoppers, and they can be found on every continent with the exception of Antarctica (where it's just too cold!).

There are about 3,200 species of treehopper worldwide that we know of. However, more are being discovered all the time and in the Amazon the variety of their shapes and colours is astounding. Some have bodies that look just like thorns to act as camouflage. Others are painted with bright eyewatering patterns and some have such crazy appendages that they look like a lifeform from a different universe. Treehoppers live on plants and suck at the sap with specialised piercing mouth parts. If you spot one in the undergrowth, sitting quietly on a leaf, it would be easy to assume that not a lot is going on. But out of range of our own hearing, there is a near constant chatter.

Treehoppers don't use sound as we know it, as they have no voices and they don't have ears. Just like the jumping spiders in Chapter 2, they communicate by using vibrations they make with their bodies. They stand firm with their legs stiff and locked and then they quiver their abdomens, a bit like a wobbly jelly. These vibrations spread down the calling treehopper's legs and into the plant they are resting on. Then the wave of tremors will travel along their host plant's stem, to be picked up by other treehoppers through sensory nerves in their own legs. It's like the plant stem has become a telephone line, connecting the treehoppers' conversations.

In 2018 biologists first recorded this covert alien soundscape by using a cool piece of tech called a laser vibrometer – an instrument that uses a laser beam to detect tiny vibrations. The laser is bounced off the treehopper's plant stem and picks up the frequency and amplitude of any vibration signals, which, when played back, are translated into a sound we can actually hear. Scientists discovered that the variety of these sounds is as diverse and wonderful as the treehoppers themselves. Playing back these recordings is like eavesdropping on a convention of extra-terrestrials, with each alien species more bizarre and ridiculous than the last.

But what are these tiny insects saying? Scientists now think that they make vibrations when they're foraging for food, which may help alert others to the location of a good food plant. They also call to attract mates, with males and females 'duetting' to find love and competitive male suitors 'jamming' each other's romantic signals in the hope of finding the female first. Treehoppers also call to alert others to predators. One particular species, the green treehopper, from the Amazon, takes these alarm calls to a remarkable level of complexity. Unusually for insects, female green treehoppers will provide maternal care, staying with their nursery of nymphs to look after them. The nymphs are a favourite food of birds and other insects and are covered in huge spikes and bright warning colours in an effort to deter unwanted attention. But should a predatory bug or another threat come close by, the cluster of nymphs will vibrate their alarm call, the ripple of sound travelling away from the approaching predator like a Mexican wave. Amazingly, their mum can detect from the direction of this vibrating alarm just where the threat is coming from and she'll leap into action to defend her brood with her wings buzzing. If this aggressive show isn't enough to put the predator off, she'll kick out with those amazing legs that are just as good at kick-boxing as they are at transmitting and receiving vibration signals. With the danger passed, Mum will 'purr' at her young constantly in what could be an attempt to soothe them. Some scientists think that with all these calls, treehopper communication may be at least as complex as that seen in some backboned animals.

And it's not just the treehoppers. With over 190,000 different species of insect known to communicate through vibration, we can now eavesdrop on a whole soundscape that, until recently, we didn't even know existed. A secret world of sound, hidden in the forest.

Scan to hear the alien sounds of treehoppers.

Moonlit chorus

By far the most exciting time to explore a rainforest is at night. During daylight hours, as you wander through the tangle, it seems as if the place is just about tolerating your presence, but take a walk at night and the forest can start to feel openly hostile. You never see any further than beyond the light of your head torch and the darkness is truly impenetrable. Your sense of hearing comes to the fore and every strange animal call, each twitch in the undergrowth or drip falling from the canopy above, suddenly becomes more immediate. Night is the loudest time in the rainforest. Fuelled by this overwhelming soundscape and without the comforting certainty of vision, your imagination starts to fill in the blanks.

The dry season was well under way and over the last few days the Tiputini River had started to shrink. The water level had fallen by at least two metres and, along the banks, new areas of once submerged forest had been revealed. The river's drop had been so sudden that the leaves of the understorey were still painted with a layer of brown silt left behind by the falling waters. We were keen to explore the virgin forest of this former flood plain and record its soundscape after dark. Despite the oppressive humidity, we donned our long-sleeved shirts and trousers to ward off the worst of the mosquitos and pulled on our wellies to give us some protection against the snakes. Sticking close to our guide, we left the research station and followed a path into the darkness. We were yet to enter the forest, when a shriek went up. It was our fixer from Lima. We crowded around to see what she had spotted. In the beam of her head torch, just sitting there on the wall of a wooden shed, was a huge 10 centimetre wandering spider. Perhaps the most dangerous spider in South America, they use their venom to hunt for treefrogs but their bite can also be deadly to humans. Not being a big fan of spiders, our fixer made her excuses and retreated back to her cabin. The team was a player down and we hadn't even made it past the first tree!

We left the spider and headed deeper into the forest. Our guide walked slowly and deliberately, scanning the ground and the branches above with deliberate sweeps of his torch beam. During the day we had spotted birds and monkeys in the forest, but at night the place was truly alive. A brightly banded coral snake slid through the leaf litter. Black tree scorpions scuttled along low branches and a colony of funnel wasps stood guard over their nest, hanging like an icicle from the underside of a leaf. Huge moths battered into us, drawn in by our head torches. Fuzzy-legged tarantulas wandered over the forest floor and a cricket the length of my hand perched on a leaf, the biggest bug I think I have ever seen. But for all the variety revealed in our torchlight it was the compilation of sounds that left the biggest impression. The chirping of countless crickets and katydids made for a perpetual underscore that seemed to physically enclose us in sound. Occasional night-calling cicadas added their buzz track and, from far away, a deep low hooting boomed across the forest. It sounded like the call of a very huge and very sleepy monkey, but I was surprised to learn it was the song of a bird. Salvin's curassow is a large black bird with a broad red beak that often sings on clear but moonless nights, in order to attract a mate. They sing from the cover of the mid-canopy level, meaning their booming can be heard all across the forest. But by far my favourite singers in the all-night line-up were the frogs and toads.

Ever since I was a boy, I have been fascinated by all things amphibian. I think it started with a sequence in David Attenborough's *Life on Earth* where shots of different tropical frogs calling were cut together, the edits getting faster and faster and the frogs odder and ever more colourful, their quirky calls building to a comic crescendo. No matter where my travels took me, I would never miss the chance to go on a 'frog hunt', torch in hand.

The forests of Yasuni are home to a record-setting 150 species of amphibians, so a frog hunt here had the potential to be my best one yet, and soon into our night walk I was in herpetology heaven.

On the forest floor was a whole squad of robust-looking toads, from the warty cane toad to the mitred forest toad with its strange, crested head, its stridulating call sounding just like a South American percussionist playing the guiro. My favourite Tiputini toad had to be the smooth-sided toad. A rather bland name for such a mighty character, females of this huge toad can grow to around 20 centimetres long. I was lucky enough to have one of these solid individuals sit outside my forest cabin, using the lamps there to hunt for bugs. They are famous for being able to squirt jets of poison from two swollen parotid glands that sit just behind their eyes. This toxin has been known to cause heart failure in humans if ingested, so I always kept my mouth firmly shut when photographing this brute.

Their calls are equally impressive, a loud pulsing klaxon that somehow reminded me of Sigourney Weaver trying to escape the Alien, as the alarm on her spaceship counted down to self-destruction. From somewhere in the forest, we could hear the excited 'whoop!' of a smoky jungle frog, another large amphibian of the forest floor with huge amber eyes that reflect a menacing red in your torchlight. These powerful hunters can devour small rodents and lizards and have even been reported to eat bats. Their enthusiastic rising whoop is repeated every five to ten seconds and, once they have found a mate, the female will lay about a thousand eggs into a nest the male has made of foam whipped up from skin secretions and whisked into a perfect meringue with his legs.

Off the ground and extending up into the canopy was a whole other set of wonderful frogs. Sitting calling from a leaf still covered with mud from the retreating river was a beautiful vivid lime-green and lemon-yellow treefrog, known as a Demerara Falls treefrog. It blinked its orange eyelids in the torch beam and stopped its vocalising, but when we moved on it resumed its call of several short squeaky notes, a little like a twittering bird.

By far the most numerous of all the amphibian voices in the forest belonged to a rather dull-coloured tree climber called a tan-faced spiny-backed frog, or the Napo River slender-legged treefrog, depending on your herpetologist. Its call is just like a staccato quacking duck, but occasionally it throws in a longer croak-quack, which starts with a reverberating note that ends as a fully formed quack. These frogs like to live in bromeliads commonly over six metres off the forest floor. Perhaps with the retreating river the forest was damp enough to draw them down, as they seemed to be calling from everywhere – even just a few feet above our heads. Surrounded by this choir of indomitable ducks, we decided to stop and record some sound. But by stopping still in the forest our head torches were soon attracting squadrons of flying insects and their buzzing and bumping against the mic was enough to ruin the recording. So, we decided to turn our torches off.

We were plunged into the soundscape like never before. The crickets, the booming curassow, an occasional 'waa' of an unknown treefrog in the canopy and too many quacking frogs to count, all came together in an exuberant chorus. In the darkness, it was as if the sound gave a scale and dimension to the forest that our eyes couldn't register. Sound was coming from below us, and far above us, from near at hand and out in the far distance, lost in the trees. Just as we were getting swept up in the wonder of it all there suddenly came a new sound, this time too close for comfort. The buzzing of swarms of blood-hungry mosquitos.

Scan to hear the quacking of slender-legged treefrogs.

The first insects appeared about 400 million years ago. In the beginning they were silent and deaf to sound, but with the evolution of crickets and grasshoppers about 300 million years ago the world began to change and our forests came alive with buzzing and chirping. Fossils of katydids, dating back 160 million years, have been found that have primitive tympanal ears, suggesting they used sound for communication. Insect hearing has evolved multiple times with different types of insects, developing different structures for receiving sound. Insects also make sounds in a variety of ways, from rubbing limbs together to vibrating wing membranes and even by ejecting out fluids. But then, about 100–200 million years ago, amphibians started making sounds of their own. Standing in the forest and listening to the frogs calling, I was reminded that amphibian voices were the first of any vertebrate to echo over the land, which had until then only ever heard the chirps of insects.

Everyone knows that frogs 'croak', but in truth they make a huge variety of sounds from barks to clicks, beeps, whoops and screams. My absolute favourite is the menwig frog that populates flooded grasslands and roadside ditches across South America. Their call is just like a zooming racing car, so that a group of these frogs calling together sounds exactly like a Formula One race!

Scan to hear the 'racing car' frog.

Some of the sounds made by frogs can reach 100 decibels and rank among the loudest made by any land animal. The calls of Australia's bleating treefrog are loud enough to be almost be painful to listen to!

The main organ responsible for sound production in frogs is the larynx, also called 'voice box'. In a frog, this is a small sac supported by rings of cartilage that contains elastic folds called vocal cords. To make calls, a frog contracts the muscles surrounding its lungs, which pushes air through the larynx. This incoming air vibrates its vocal cords and the larynx itself before the air enters the frog's mouth and, in calling males, often passes through a pair of slits to inflate a vocal sac. This is the balloon-like structure on the frog's throat that blows up when the frog calls. This sac acts as a resonating chamber, amplifying the sounds from the larynx and making the frog's call louder so that it travels further. It also allows the calling frog to recycle the air without the constant need to freshly inflate its lungs, meaning the frog can call more frequently and for longer durations. It's a little like the 'circular breathing' of a trumpet player.

Amphibian vocal sacs come in all different shapes and sizes but belong to one of three basic types: a single sac in the middle of the throat, paired sacs either side of the throat, or paired lateral sacs that sit on the side of the head just behind the angle of the jaw. In some ground-living species, the vocal sac has even been found to transmit vibrations through the ground and it may play a role in keeping the calling frog cool by increasing its surface area for skin evaporation. These bombastic balloons also add a strong visual element to the frogs' call, which may further help in attracting a female frog.

Listening in to the frog cacophony at Tiputini, it was hard to imagine that this was just an average performance. On some rare nights – when rainfall, temperature and humidity create the perfect conditions for laying their eggs – the forests' frogs will take part in a mass spawning. Then multiple species will gather together and call for mates in an explosive breeding event that will only last one or two nights. When male frogs like to advertise for a mate, they tend to sit in one place and call repeatedly. Listening in on the frogs on this, a 'quiet' night, I wondered just how any female frog could pinpoint a mate when all the other frogs in the area were busy singing for just the same reason.

The answer is that female frogs may come equipped with something akin to a built-in pair of 'noise cancelling headphones'. In 2021, researchers from the University of Minnesota studying female American green treefrogs discovered that when female frogs inflated their lungs, it reduced the sensitivity of their eardrums to environmental noise. All frogs have a unique pathway that transmits sound from their inflated lungs to their air-filled middle ears through the mouth cavity, the glottis (the valve between the lungs and mouth) and their Eustachian tubes (a tube that connects the middle ear to the throat). But the purpose of this link between the lungs and the ears had always remained unknown. By measuring the resonance of the frog's inflated lungs with a laser vibrometer (the same tech used to study treehoppers) the scientists discovered that when the organs were inflated it selectively reduced the eardrum's sensitivity to the frequencies outside of those made by calling male green treefrogs. So, during explosive breeding, when forest airwaves are overwhelmed with thousands of frog species all calling for a mate, female green treefrogs can cut through the noise and just listen in on the voices of their own males.

A female frog listening to a chorus to choose a mate may be drawn to deeper, louder voices that could indicate a larger, healthier male. But this is not the case in all frog species. Researchers from Australia's Griffith University studying the orange-thighed treefrog in the coastal forests north of Sydney discovered that for females of this particular frog, size doesn't matter. Smaller males can make higher-pitched calls that require less energy to make. This means they have the stamina to call for longer, making them more attractive to the females. Larger males with their energy-sapping, deeper, lower-frequency calls might just tire out more quickly. So, females were more attracted to a male's vocal stamina and not his depth or strength.

We often think of frog calls as being simple and unrefined, but evolution has led to a surprising degree of sophistication. There was one frog that sat at the top of my wish list on any Amazonian night-time frog hunt. Much to my disappointment I didn't get to see one during my stay at Tiputini, but I did get lucky a few months later on a trip to Peru's Tambopata Reserve. Not only does the gladiator frog have a great name, it's also just an all-round amphibian bad-ass.

One particular species of this huge treefrog, the Rosenberg's gladiator, can measure 7–9 centimetres long, making it one of the world's largest treefrogs. Often a pale tan colour, they sometimes have beautiful dark patterning, making their skin look a little like marble. They have partly webbed fingers and fully webbed toes, characteristics that give a clue to their mixed use of habitat. These frogs clamber around the branches of the canopy, but during the few months of their breeding season they'll descend to the forest floor and seek out standing water. At the edge of a pond or a slow-running stream the male frog will shape a round, low-walled and water-filled enclosure made of mud, sculpting it smooth with his broad spatula-like fingers. It's a tiny pond in which he can raise a family. But first he needs to attract a female, and he isn't the only one as other gladiators have also climbed down and built their mud nests, with around ten to fifteen found on just a six-metre stretch of waterfront. To attract female frogs out of the trees, the males will sing their advertisement call with a guttural three-note 'gronk gronk gronk'.

Using playback experiments, scientists from the University of Wisconsin discovered that the presence of other males and the distance to the nearest calling male was enough to influence the male frogs' rate of calling. They found that the male frogs quickly noticed any changes to their acoustic environment and reacted to those changes. As competition increased in the soundscape, with more gladiator rivals calling, the males would increase their own calling rate; as the competition reduced and things became quieter, the males would respond in turn and call less. Perhaps it makes sense to save your energy for the main event when the competition for female attention hots up.

Scan to hear the call of the Rosenberg's gladiator frog.

If a female likes a male gladiator's call, she will climb into his mud nest and swim around inspecting it. The male might then switch, ceasing his advertising call for a longer 'courtship' call. Then the pair will join together, the male mounting the female's back and clasping her with his arms in what herpetologists call 'amplexus'.

This can last for up to ten minutes and by the end the female's fertilised eggs are spread floating across the surface of the miniature pond. If all goes well, the pond will be a safe place for the eggs to develop and the tadpoles to grow. The male frogs will often stay for a couple of days to protect the eggs from rival males looking to make use of the nest rather than build their own. There is lots of competition for females and only a minority of males will get to mate. It seems that persistent singing pays off, with one study finding that the most successful males were usually the ones that spent the most nights participating in the calling chorus.

Male gladiators were also recorded making a different 'territorial' call loosely directed at rival males, warning them to stay away. But with competition so fierce things can sometimes get violent. On occasion males will invade another's nest and try and steal a female and it can turn nasty. They will charge and chase each other and will wrestle, trying to drive the other away. During these violent encounters they emit yet more vocalisations, growling, mewing and hissing at each other. Each male comes armed with a pair of deadly prepollical spines. These are sharp, scythe-shaped spines that the frogs can extend from a fleshy sheath on each hand where we would have a thumb. The gladiators use these spines to stab at each other repeatedly, aiming for the eyes and eardrums. Damaging a rival's senses will seriously impair his ability to attract a female and thus remove that rival from the competition. On some occasions fights between gladiators have even resulted in death. Should the protagonists survive and the fight break apart, allowing one frog to retreat, the rivals will call with a 'bark' as a concluding gesture. Who would have thought it, frogs with flick knives.

So, frogs such as the gladiator show us that amphibians aren't just simple automatons calling without regard. They can adjust their calls in the face of competition, have different calls to communicate different messages and can also adapt their calling in the face of subtle changes in their environments.

Frogs and toads can also use the sounds of their environment to their own advantage. In the rainforests of the Guianas in the northern Amazon, tread carefully across the forest floor and you might be lucky enough to spot a dyeing or 'voiceless' poison frog. These colourful forest sprites are the largest of all poison-dart frog species at about 5 centimetres long. They come in thirty known colour morphs, including a startling bright blue specimen from the forests of Suriname. The name 'voiceless' isn't entirely accurate as they do make tiny sounds. Their call is a low intense buzzing that often lasts less than a second. Researchers have struggled to record their calls and report having to be within a metre of a vocalising frog to have any chance of hearing its diminutive voice. These frogs are unusual in that they don't vocalise to attract a mate; the male dyeing frogs do not have the advertisement calls seen in so many other frogs and toads, only raising their voices during direct courtship or in aggressive encounters between males. So how on earth do these discreet and speechless frogs attract a mate? Researchers from the University of Vienna counted the population of dyeing frogs they found in a forest area of French Guiana between 2009 and 2017. They discovered that the frogs were frequently sighted in the gaps left in the forest made by falling trees; 140 frogs were found in nine treefall gaps within the first three days of the gap appearing. And most of these frogs appeared in the gaps within twenty-four hours of a tree first falling.

Trees in the Amazon rainforest are always falling down. They will die, weakened by disease, and be blown down by strong winds that can rip through the forest like a tornado. A large tree falling can create quite a sound, sometimes more than 100 decibels. The subsequent cracking and crashing of branches splitting on impact prolongs the racket and sends shockwaves out from the tree through both the air and the ground. The researchers in Guiana have speculated that these 'voiceless' frogs may be picking up on the sound and the low-frequency seismic impact of a tree falling. By listening out for falling trees and following the sound to its origin, these quiet frogs could have found a way to come together in the same space. So far, there is little evidence that the frogs are gathering to breed and it might be that heading to the treefall gaps just give them an attractive feeding opportunity. More observations are needed, but it does show how sound in the forest is very important – even for the inhabitants that don't shout the loudest.

There is one tiny South American frog whose calls present a real acoustic oddity. For animal vocalisation to work, there has to be a communicator and a receiver. But the diminutive pumpkin toadlet only appears to satisfy the first half of this rule. Just the length of your fingernail and bright orange, at first glance they look more like a baked bean than a frog. These frogs are found among the leaf litter of Brazil's rapidly disappearing Atlantic rainforests. Their call is a repeated chirping sound, a little like a cricket. But it's a sound that none of them can ever hear, not even the frog making the call. In fact, it's likely been millions of years since their ancestors last heard their own voices.

The ears of the pumpkin toadlet are underdeveloped when compared to other frogs. The *basilla papillae* – the part of the ear responsible for detecting sound waves – are much simpler and smaller than in other frogs, meaning the pumpkin toadlet can't hear high-frequency sounds. And that, oddly enough, includes their own calling. Researchers think the expanded vocal sacs seen in calling males could, in the absence of sound, be giving the female frogs a visual cue telling her the male is looking for love. It's thought that the frogs may have become just too small for their ears to function normally and that they have now become vestigial, evolutionary remnants of a long-lost function, something akin to the wings on a flightless bird or our own tailbone.

The pumpkin toadlets' poorly developed ears cause them problems beyond their lack of hearing. They also have the smallest ever recorded semi-circular canals of any vertebrate. Semi-circular canals are three fluid-filled loops in the inner ear responsible for balance and stabilisation. Filled with fluid, when an animal moves, tiny hairs pick up the directional flow of the fluid and translate this to help orientation. Having such tiny canals means the pumpkin toadlet's vestibular system – the one responsible for balance and spatial orientation – isn't fit for purpose. There simply isn't enough space inside their canals for the fluid to move sufficiently and tell the frog where it is, which way is up, how fast they are travelling or how to judge a landing. This means that when the frog jumps it may nail the take-off but, without any sense of orientation, it soon loses its bearings and cartwheels through the air, often landing flat on its back with an uncoordinated crash. Pumpkin toadlets are perhaps the world's clumsiest vertebrate or, more positively, nature's tiniest stunt person. Using molecular analysis, scientists can estimate when these frogs first appeared, and it seems that their genus diversified and miniaturised roughly 5–20 million years ago. So, despite challenges in hearing and movement, these frogs have managed to survive, successfully, for a very, very long time.

Standing in the dark and listening to the bizarre soundtrack of the forest at night was magical, but it couldn't last forever. Pumping out clouds of exhaled carbon dioxide, our team presented an irresistible feast of blood for huge numbers of mosquitos. We could hear their buzzing ever louder and I began to feel the irritation as they brushed against my skin. We had managed to stay silent for the sound recording of the frogs quacking but our work was now being punctuated by the slapping of hands, swatting violently to squash the bugs, and the muffled whines of our growing discomfort. It was time to retreat. We stopped recording and turned on our head torches. I pulled up my shirt and already my skin had the pattern of polka dots, pin-cushioned with angry red bites.

Making our way back through the forest, our guide suddenly shouted, 'Run!' and broke into a sprint, leaping along the path. Panic set in and we followed without question or reason. Heart pounding, I paused for breath before noticing the area of ground under my head torch was swarming with countless tiny, stinging fire ants. They were hunting as a super-swarm all over the forest. Having suffered more than enough insect bites for one night, I ran on and soon we were back at the research station, puffed out and shaken up but lucky not to have been stung. As we turned in to our cabins I spotted my friendly neighbourhood smooth-sided toad, sitting grumpily in the lamplight. Feeling my mozzie bites starting to itch, I found myself speculating that without frogs and toads, the forest would be swarming with insect infestations to a whole different level. A moth fluttered into the light. As if to prove my point, the toad sprang to life, launching to gulp the moth with a dramatic 'whump' before landing, its huge bulbous eyes sinking down into the roof of its mouth to help swallow down its prize.

The magnificent frog chorus of this forest is, sadly, now under threat. And it all started with a single road. In 1990, Texas-based fossil fuel company Maxus Energy was given permission to build a road into the heart of Yasuni National Park. Their plan was to explore the region and open it up for potential extraction of the oil and gas reserves known to exist beneath the forest. The bulldozers cut a dirty red scar 140 kilometres into the trees. It triggered a cascade of environmental, ecological and social changes, including altering the Indigenous Waorani people's traditional nomadic lifestyle, allowing them to settle along the road, where they had access to markets for the wild meat they hunt. This led to the commercialisation of bush meat hunted from the forest and local extinctions of many of the forest's mammals. The road and its construction has led to a rise in pollution, deforestation and fragmentation of the forest habitat. But it also changed the forest's soundscape.

The Yasuni rain frog lives in bromeliads high up in the forest canopy. Related to the 'quacking' slender-legged treefrog, the rain frog makes a series of squeaking notes that sounds oddly musical. It spends much of its life hanging out in the water collected inside bromeliads. Each plant can contain around four litres of standing water, so for the frogs they represent a safe and comfortable home. A high-rise apartment, complete with luxury swimming pool. But life is very different for the rain frogs and other frog species that found themselves living in trees close to the Maxus Road.

Researchers from Texas State University found that frog populations that lived inside bromeliads were incredibly sensitive to any impact. They collected ninety-five frogs representing ten different species from 160 bromeliads in thirty-two trees and then compared the numbers of frogs collected from along the oil-access road with trees located adjacent to pathways in undisturbed forest. They discovered that the number of bromeliad frogs present in forest locations disturbed by roads were only half the number of those found in the untouched forests. Despite the promises of the oil company that the road would have little impact on the surrounding forest, the researchers were surprised that even this narrow roadway, with primary forest right up to its edge, was disturbed enough to significantly reduce the number of frogs that survived there.

A changing climate can also influence the nightly chorus of frogs. In the forests of Puerto Rico, scientists have discovered that the mating calls of common coqui frogs have led to higher-pitched and shorter calls. Rising temperatures have caused the frogs to shrink in size, changing the characteristics of their voices. The frogs have also begun to move uphill to escape the heat, meaning that their choruses are being heard at higher altitudes. The calls of frogs have been a part of nature's soundtrack for millions of years.

With amphibians increasingly under threat, the loss of frog voices is just one way the rainforest soundscape is changing.

Scan to hear the peak chorus of coqui frogs in the rainforests of Puerto Rico.

Echoes of Impact

ON ONE OF our last walks into the rainforest we got up early and followed a long path out to one of the clay licks. The camera trap hadn't triggered and it looked as if the brutal humidity was frying the internal circuitry. We fixed things the best we could and started to walk back through the forest. Suddenly, a strange call burst out from the dense foliage. Our guide excitedly identified it as a pair of titi monkeys. These small red-coloured monkeys live in family groups, often in the thick vegetation of the understorey. They can sometimes be spotted sitting with their long tails entwined. They look impossibly cute, but I couldn't square that image with the racket coming from the bushes before us.

Pairs of male and female titi monkeys sing an early morning duet made up of extraordinary bellows, pants, honks, moans and 'pumps'. These duets may play a role in territorial encounters with neighbouring pairs of titis or they might just be a simple 'we are here' announcement, declaring the monkeys' location. Both male and females sing identical sequences of calls but alternate, taking turns to sing each part of the song as they cycle through the different parts. We were being treated to a performance by the rainforest's premier vocal double act. Beginning with a series of low moans, a pair of titis will launch into a cycle of loud bellows. The male will bellow first while the female pants and then they swap, the female taking the lead to bellow while her duetting partner does the panting. This is followed by a series of rapid 'pumping' notes sung by both monkeys, before the duet ends with a bout of excited honking.

Scan to hear the duet of a pair of titi monkeys.

As I put on the headphones to listen to the duetting monkeys over the recording device, I could hear another sound. A background hum, so pervasive that I thought there was something wrong with the recorder and started to fiddle with the various knobs to see if I could fix it. Then our guide told us it wasn't an imagined sound or a recorder malfunction, the hum was real. It was coming from the distant oilfields, just 13 kilometres to the north-east. As the hum got louder, we no longer needed the headphones to hear it. It was as if a dark blanket had been laid over the forest and we all just stood there, numbed. Like a hellish mechanical imitation of the monkey's duet, another sound rose up in answer, getting louder and louder. Suddenly a helicopter buzzed low over the canopy, circled and headed away again. It was prospectors from the oil company, out searching the forest for possible drilling sites. I had been told by the research staff that at night, from atop the observation tower, it was possible to see the glow of the gas flares from the distant oilfields. There was a tangible sense that this special place was surrounded by the activities of oil and gas companies. But as an outsider, to hear the sound of those activities so far into the protected area of the forest felt like a real shock.

Yasuni's ITT block (named after its constituent areas of Ishpingo, Tambococha and Tiputini) is known to contain untapped reserves of crude oil amounting to about 850 million barrels. The government of Ecuador and various oil companies have been prospecting in the adjacent area since the 1940s and have long had their eye on the riches found beneath the forest. But, aware of the ecological importance of the ITT, in 2007 the then-president of Ecuador, Rafael Correa, offered to leave the oil in the ground indefinitely if the world compensated the country for half of what it would make in exploiting the resource. Back in 2007 this amounted to $3.6 billion (roughly equivalent to $5.1 billion today). Correa planned that the money raised would be put into clean-energy alternatives and used to fund community development.

At the time, the idea that we should pay developing countries to protect their globally significant forests was an exciting one. But by 2012, the global community had only come up with about $200 million towards the required figure. Correa started to issue angry ultimatums and some critical observers felt the project seemed a little like blackmail. Without receiving the necessary support, Correa went on record to say he felt he had no choice but to 'exploit the oil' and, slowly but surely, a creeping network of roads and infrastructure appeared around the fringes of the forest.

We sat at dinner that night watching hordes of insects buzz around the lights and got talking with the research team. I couldn't believe that the governments of the world couldn't find the money to protect this incredible forest for future generations. After all, if we can't save the 'centre of life' in the known solar system, what are we good for? We started to speculate if commercial corporations – often richer than many governments – couldn't take up the slack. One of the locals with us pondered, 'Why can't Amazon help pay for the Amazon?' It's an interesting idea. At the end of 2025, Amazon (the company – not the forest) announced an annual turnover of $716.9 billion, with the year's profits reaching a staggering $77.7 billion. When you consider that the company is seeing an average increase in profits of about 15 per cent every single year, it would seem the $5.1 billion needed to save the world's most amazing forest could be easily affordable. I guess the challenge is convincing corporate CEOs that their vast profits are better spent preserving the biodiversity of life on Earth, rather than hiring all of Venice for a celebrity wedding or sending pop stars into space.

On Sunday, 20 August 2023, the people of Ecuador voted in a remarkable referendum, where 58 per cent of the country's population voted for the state to permanently stop drilling for oil in the ITT forest. It was a historic moment for 'people power' and a game-changing result for conservation efforts in the Amazon. The legally binding result gave the government and their petroleum companies one year to halt activities and dismantle their practices across the area. Sadly, by 2025, the country's government hadn't made much progress, besides setting up a commission. In January 2024, the new president, Daniel Noboa, told local press that the current level of debt, economic hardship and outbreaks of political violence in Ecuador meant he would issue a 'moratorium' on the referendum results. Correspondence with my Tiputini guide has confirmed to me that, today, the drilling continues and the threat to the forest is still real. As I write this, the country's current government are attempting to bypass the referendum by shifting the opportunity to exploit the oil reserves from government-run to private companies. On 14 June 2025, President Noboa proposed new legislation that aimed to put the country's protected areas in the hands of private companies, allowing them to legally exploit resources as part of the government's economic recovery plan. Despite Ecuador's protected areas being home to ten different Indigenous nationalities, not a single community was consulted or even mentioned in the proposed legislation. Yasuni borders the territory of the Waorani people and the introduction of roads from mining exploration has already done much to change their traditional way of life. In the southern fringes of Yasuni is the 'Terra Intangible', the forbidden area set aside to protect the uncontacted Tagaeri and Taromenane tribes. So Yasuni is much more than a biodiversity hotspot, it's also where Indigenous people call the forest home. These Indigenous groups and conservationists are now part of an ongoing fight against the government to ensure it respects the will of the people to save their forests.

Perhaps the most shocking truth behind the struggle to save Yasuni is that the entire oil reserves beneath the forest would only ever be enough to power the United States for forty days. It would appear that our lust for fossil fuels is such that we would gladly destroy the 'zenith' of all life on Earth, just to maintain a month or so of our modern lifestyles.

Back in the UK, I swapped the limitless wonders of the rainforest for ten days of Covid quarantine in a cramped and airless hotel room at Heathrow. The days would drag slowly but when I pulled on my headphones and sat listening to the sound recordings from our visit, I was transported straight back into the forest.

Several months after our return we finally started to receive footage from our camera traps. The images were extraordinary, but it was the sounds that we had captured that were really something special. Cicadas hissed as colourful butterflies flitted over a forest path bathed in sunshine. An urgent chatter of squawking announced the arrival of a flock of grey-winged trumpeters, who paraded through the undergrowth with the stiff movements of their pale stilt-like legs. At the clay lick, a pair of watchful tapirs whistled gently to each other. And a huge herd of white-lipped peccaries splodged through the thick mud, noses to the ground, slurping from the pools of water. You could hear their teeth clattering as the herd kept in contact. With big herds of over a hundred peccaries, this noise can be so loud that it's been confused for the sound of an approaching forest fire. Then at last we got our first jaguar. A big male, his golden coat printed with shadowy rosettes, walking confidently down the narrow path as if out for a Sunday stroll. From the trees above a watchful bird offered up an alarm call. The jaguar didn't seem to care and came ever closer with his tail lifted. As he passed, brushing the camera, you could hear the soft pad of his paws on the wet leaf litter and the gentle huff of his breathing.

A while later, after our filming project had ended, I got a message from our guide at Tiputini. Their camera traps were still working and had captured something even more remarkable. I sat at my kitchen table in Bristol and opened the file. There, standing in the frame, I could see a big cat, but this one was even more special. This time there were no rosettes painted onto its skin. I could see a pair of golden eyes set into a shadowy dark form. It was a magnificent black jaguar.

4. From Earth and Beyond

THE SOUNDS OF OUR PLANET AND ITS ATMOSPHERE

The big bang

THE RHYTHMIC WHEEZING rose and fell, coming up in waves from the bunk below mine. I shuffled deeper into my sleeping bag hoping to shut out the din. The Arctic winter storm blowing outside had driven the temperature down to –20 degrees Celsius but in our tiny wooden hut, with the heater on, it was toasty. It was far too dark to see anything, but – unable to sleep – my other senses came to the fore. With four grown men and a ton of kit, squished into a space little bigger than a deluxe garden shed, the whole place had a rich smell of pine resin, strong coffee, pasta sauce and socks. When I listened, all I could hear was the wind buffeting the tiny ill-fitting window, the patter of the snow falling on the roof and of course the constant snoring of my colleague – our Arctic guide, sleeping in the bottom bunk below.

Our small crew had travelled through the darkness, riding snow machines for 120 kilometres over mountains, glaciers and frozen fjords to arrive at our new home. The hunters' hut sat close to the shoreline in the bay of Kvalvagen, on the east coast of Spitsbergen Island, up in the Norwegian Arctic's archipelago of Svalbard.

We had come to film the northern lights and to try and capture the first sunrise of the year. The sun had last set over the mountains at the end of October and since the middle of November the island had been deep in the darkness of the continuous polar night. It was now early February and a few days before the sun had been scheduled to make its return, rising for the first time in months to peep its face over the frozen sea ice that stretched all the way to the horizon.

The first polar sunrise is thought to be a magnificent sight, the weak orange light painting the blank white canvas of snow and ice with soft pastel brushstrokes. But instead, the whole eastern coast had been stuck under a blanket of thick, low cloud. There had been no sunrise to be seen, let alone to film. The pattern of the days was already getting repetitive. The alarm would wake us early, giving us plenty of time to get ready to head out to film the dawn. I would jump down in my socks onto the cold floorboards of the hut and wipe away the frost from the window. Hoping we might get lucky with a beautiful sunrise, I would peer outside to see if the clouds had lifted. But each morning it was the same. More thick cloud with no hope of clear skies. We'd had the same fortune trying to film the northern lights. We would get up throughout the night and check outside. In the beam of my torch, the endless snowflakes whizzing past, it looked a bit like the hut was travelling through outer space. But there was never much hope of seeing any real stars.

I was worried that we had come all this way and we might not even get to see the northern lights – let alone film them – and my sleep was suffering as a consequence. Our guide's snoring was loud enough that I could feel its vibrations rise up through the bed frame, wobbling my top bunk. I sighed in deep frustration at the disturbance. If anything, the noise seemed to be getting stronger. More of a rumble than a snore. It grew in power and felt as if we had woken up in the path of an oncoming freight train. It was a sound that I will never forget. Suddenly the whole hut started to shake violently. The frying pan fell from its nail on the wall onto the floor with a clatter, followed by a stack of tin plates. A box of candles was thrown from the top shelf, the sound of each hitting the deck like a rolling snare drum. The wooden structure of the hut began to creek and crack and a series of loud bangs came from the doorframe. It was as if the whole building was being shaken. The others woke in an instant, the nervous twitch of their torch beams scanning the darkness. Our guide leapt up and shuffled over to the shelf, towards his rifle. My heart was racing. A polar bear was trying to break into the hut. We had seen signs of their footprints in the snow, and when we arrived the door of the hut had needed some major repairs from where a bear had torn its lower panel apart to get inside. No doubt the curious animal had been drawn in by the residual smell of humans and food.

When we were back in town at the start of the trip, our guide had told us the colourful story of a Norwegian man sleeping in a similar Arctic hut, who had woken to find a polar bear had crashed through the small window, grabbed his sleeping bag and was trying to haul him outside 'like it would haul a seal from an ice hole'. In sheer panic the man had reached out and snatched a cast-iron skillet hanging on the wall above his bed and proceeded to whack the bear repeatedly on the nose until it finally let go and ran off into the night. Polar bears were a real danger here and we had learnt to always be watchful when we stepped outside to pee. Our hut was surrounded by a safety cordon of firecrackers strung on a low wire, which were supposed to explode and scare away any large furry visitors that tripped the wire. That night, it seems like the early warning system had failed.

We stood braced for the bear to claw its way through the front door. But as suddenly as the attack had begun, everything went quiet. The shaking stopped. The hut fell silent and outside the deep rumbling faded into the distance. We took a breath and fired up the gas lamp. The bear must have run off. Our guide was worried that it might have been dining instead on the leather and foam of one of our snow-machine seats. Apparently, they were something of a favourite delicacy among the local bears. But crowding in the doorway to shine our torches into the night, there was no bear to be seen. Scanning the snow around the hut, we couldn't find any footprints and there were no gashes or marks on the door from a bear's claws. It was then that we realised we had experienced an earthquake.

It wasn't until a few days later that we received an update on our adventure through a message on the satellite phone. At 3:46 am the earthquake had struck. It was recorded at a depth of 12 kilometres below the sea floor and its epicentre was about 50 kilometres away from our hut, out at sea. It's highly likely that we had been the closest humans to the quake's centre. While earthquakes of this size are extremely rare in the region, Svalbard sits within 100 kilometres of the geologically active COT (Continent Ocean Transition) of the Mid-Atlantic Ridge. In Svalbard's capital of Longyearbyen over 145 kilometres away, the quake was enough to shake people in their beds and rattle the glasses on the shelf above the local bar. A senior researcher at Norway's seismic institute was quoted as saying it could have been a 'catastrophic disaster' if the epicentre had occurred closer to a populated area.

The quake measured 6.2 on the Richter scale – releasing 8.9×10^{13} joules or 24.8 gigawatt hours of power. That's equivalent to 21,301 tons of TNT exploding, or the force of 1.3 atomic bombs. It wasn't a polar bear that woke us early that morning, it was the largest earthquake ever recorded in Norwegian territory and one of the biggest ever felt in northern Europe. While having front-row seats (or beds) to the planet's awesome geological power was pretty alarming, it was probably a better outcome than having a large hungry polar bear gatecrash your accommodation, and it did at least interrupt my friend's incessant snoring!

Making sound isn't just the preserve of living organisms. The Earth itself creates plenty of its own. Scientists call these earthly sounds 'geophony'. By far the most dramatic of these sounds, those made by rockfall, avalanche, flash flood, earthquake and volcano, are known as 'abrupt geophony' (as opposed to the sounds of wind, tide and river, which are continuous or ephemeral geophony). The British Geological Survey defines an earthquake as 'the sudden release of strain energy in the Earth's crust, resulting in waves that radiate out from the earthquake's source'. The Earth's crust is made up of continental 'tectonic' plates that move anything up to 10 centimetres a year. This movement puts the rocks of the Earth's crust under tremendous strain and when the stresses in the crust exceed the strength of the rocks, it breaks and the energy is released as an earthquake. The one thing I remember from my experience in Svalbard is hearing rumbling a few short seconds before the shaking started. I recall being a bit concerned that it was an avalanche roaring down the hill from the mountain behind our cabin. This low, ominous rumble is often heard preceding an earthquake.

At 5:12 am on 18 April 1906, the Pacific coast of California was struck by a huge quake with a magnitude of 7.9. In San Francisco more than 3,000 people died and over 80 per cent of the city was destroyed. After the disaster there was a real desire to understand what had happened and one Canadian geologist was at the forefront of the investigations. In 1908 Andrew Lawson published his report into the San Francisco earthquake. His work established the role of the San Andreas Fault as a source for earthquakes and he mapped its length and details. He outlined what's known as the 'elastic rebound theory', which describes how the energy stored in rocks as they deform is released as a sudden rupture during an earthquake. Lawson also studied seismograph readings and uncovered the link between the intensity of the shaking during a quake and the local geology, showing that softer, grainier, marshy soils were the areas with the greatest damage.

But Lawson's ground-breaking study didn't just look at the geology. The report took an innovative and wide-ranging approach to studying the quake and even included the collection of eyewitness reports from those on the ground who had experienced and survived the disaster. One section of the report is titled 'Sounds connected with the Earthquake' and has many colourful accounts from 'earwitnesses' who describe the quake as a 'rumbling, roaring sound', 'a heavy wind', 'a rushing noise', 'an approaching train' or 'a team (of horses) crossing a bridge'. More recently, in April 2015, people in Nepal's Kathmandu Valley reported hearing a 'tremendous rumble' before the magnitude 7.9 earthquake struck that would go on to kill 8,962 people and damage or destroy over 600,000 buildings.

One study by Italian geologists in 2012 looked in detail at our perception of earthquake sound. They surveyed 77,000 people who had experienced earthquakes in Italy, originating from a depth shallower than 20 kilometres and occurring between 2007 and 2011. The study found that in some instances 50 per cent of the population reported hearing a sound from the quake when they were within 8 kilometres of the epicentre. Of those who heard a sound, 42 per cent reported hearing it before the quake hit and 54 per cent heard something during the quake. The number of people who heard a sound increased with the earthquake's magnitude but decreased with the distance from the epicentre. So, the more powerful the quake and the closer you are to it, the more likely you are to hear sounds. But what exactly are these mysterious rumblings?

Seismic energy released as an earthquake travels in two different types of waves: P-waves (short for primary or pressure waves) and S-waves (secondary or shear waves). P-waves travel quickly through both liquids and solids, while S-waves travel more slowly through solids. When P-waves travel from the epicentre of a quake, spreading out from the source, they vibrate like a speaker. These vibrations can sometimes transfer into the atmosphere, creating sound waves that are in a range audible to most people. The P-waves travel faster than the S-waves, so arrive several seconds before them. The 'rumbling' sound that so many witnesses report hearing is the approaching P-wave vibrations and, in some instances, these are thought to be powerful enough to vibrate buildings. The slower S-wave arrives several seconds behind and this is usually when the shaking starts. So, in most cases, the P-wave is what you hear and the S-wave is what you feel. But there is one 'abrupt geophony' that can make sounds so loud they can be heard on the other side of the planet.

Scan to hear the sound of a powerful 9.0 magnitude earthquake in Japan recorded by undersea microphones in Alaska, March 2011.

On 27 August 1883 a sound emerged from the Earth that was louder than any sound ever recorded in human history, before or since. It was the colossal volcanic eruption of the island of Krakatau.

Back in 1883, Krakatau (perhaps better known as Krakatoa – a historical misspelling) was a small archipelago of islands in the Sunda Strait between Java and Sumatra. In those days, the strait was alive with shipping. The huge volcano had a history of 'activity', with several ancient large-scale eruptions, but in the years preceding 1883 things had been hotting up. Seismic activity had been building and in 1880 earthquakes were recorded as far away as Australia's Northern Territory. Hydroacoustic waves (sound waves from seismic activity – travelling through the ocean) had been recorded travelling from the island all the way to Singapore, where they reportedly caused noisy interference on telephone lines that was enough to drown out people's conversations. But these phenomena were just warning signs from the volcano as it built up to the main event. At around 1 pm on 26 August 1883 the eruption entered its 'climactic phase'.

Scan to hear the sound of an eruption from Italy's Stromboli volcano.

It's hard to comprehend the scale of the explosions that ripped Krakatau apart. For the rest of that day the volcano's eruption was almost continuous, with loud explosions coming every ten minutes or so. By 2 pm clouds of black ash that had been spewed from the island towered 27 kilometres up into the atmosphere. Shipping within 20 kilometres of the volcano was peppered with lumps of hot pumice, the size of small cannonballs, and ash fell like snow from the sky. The captain of an Irish merchant vessel – the *Charles Bal* – recorded the scene in all its terrifying detail.

> *Chains of fire appeared to ascend and descend between it (the volcano) and the sky, while on the S.W. end there seemed to be a continued roll of balls of white fire. The wind, though strong was hot and choking, sulphurous, with a smell as of burning cinders, some of the pieces falling on us like iron cinders.*

But these visions of hell were only just the start. A day later the volcano unleashed four enormous explosions. The first came at around 5:30 am, then 6:54 am, soon followed by 10:02 am and finally at

10:52 am. The first eruptions on Krakatau for 200 years had left voids in its underground magma chamber. This allowed for thicker magma to rise up into these spaces and mix with the thinner magma already near the surface. The mixing of these two magma types led to a huge build-up in gas and pressure and on 27 August it burst forth with deadly force. With each explosion, pyroclastic flows – fast-moving clouds of hot gas (around 1,000 degrees Celsius) and volcanic rocks tore down from the volcano at speeds of around 100 kilometres per hour. Some of these flows hurtled downhill with such force that they are thought to have travelled 40 kilometres across the Sunda Strait, destroying villages and forests all along the surrounding coastline. The immense submarine slides of tonnes of rocks collapsing into the ocean were powerful enough to trigger huge tsunamis. Giant waves, up to 40 metres high and travelling at 100 kilometres per hour, swept north across the Sunda Strait, taking just twenty minutes to travel 35 kilometres. One such wave impacted on Ketimbang village in South Sumatra, killing 8,038 people. The wave was funnelled into the narrow inlet of Lampong Bay, where it slowed but gathered height and wiped out South Sumatra's then biggest port, Teluk Betung, killing a further 2,263 people. The wave was powerful enough to wash large ships 3km inland. Away from the Sunda Strait, waves around four metres tall hit around the coast of southern Sumatra. One person was killed as far away as Sri Lanka and boats were rocked by a huge wave in South Africa. More than 36,000 people died.

The explosion at 10:02 am is widely regarded as the most volatile of the four and was so powerful it destroyed 70 per cent of the island in a few short moments. It obliterated 13 square kilometres of land, leaving a crater 5.6 kilometres across and 300 metres deep; 45 cubic kilometres of rock were blasted into the atmosphere (enough to cover the island of Manhattan to a depth of about 60 metres in ash). This material ejected from the volcano has been calculated to have been travelling at around 2,500 kilometres per hour with a similar force of about 200 megatons of TNT, roughly equivalent to four times as powerful as our most destructive thermonuclear weapons. The sound of the explosion was devastating. It's been estimated at around 31 decibels, so would have been lethal to anyone close to the volcano (130–140 decibels is considered dangerous to human hearing). The captain of RMS *Norham Castle*, just 65 kilometres from the blast, recorded in his log:

> *So violent are the explosions that the ear-drums of over half my crew have been shattered. My last thoughts are with my dear wife. I am convinced that the Day of Judgements has come.*

In Batavia (now called Jakarta), 160 kilometres away, the blast wave was strong enough to break windows and crack the plaster on walls. The 'booming of guns' was heard as far afield as Myanmar and Diego Garcia and it even rattled the windows in Mauritius. In Bangkok, Thailand, the sound was mistaken for the firing of guns as a distress call from a stricken ship. The sound of the 10:02 am explosion on Krakatau was heard over one-twelfth of the Earth's surface, including 3,100 kilometres away in Perth, Western Australia, and 5,000 kilometres miles away in Rodrigues in the Indian Ocean. But the audible explosion is only half the story. Krakatau's big moment also generated sound waves in the infrasonic spectrum (sounds below the 20 hertz limit of human hearing) that were picked up on barographs (instruments measuring air pressure) all over the world. Needles were sent scrawling on instruments as far afield as South Georgia in the South Atlantic, to San Francisco, Alaska and even England. These pressure waves are thought to have been strong enough to circle the globe nearly four times. The eruption of Krakatau in 1883 is to this day the loudest noise ever heard by modern humans and it remains a natural sound so powerful that it is almost beyond our comprehension.

Krakatau's big bang occurred when our abilities to record sound were only in their infancy and sadly there are no recordings of the blast for us to listen to. These days seismic and volcanic activity is monitored by countless microphones and recording devices all across the globe, and we can listen in to the dramatic sounds they capture.

The recordings from one particular eruption have given us our best example yet of what a blast like Krakatau's may have sounded like. In December 2021 a volcano in the South Pacific's Tongan Islands began to erupt. Hunga Tonga–Hunga Ha'apai was a submarine volcano, its peak just poking above the ocean. At first the eruption spewed a large ash plume that extended up into the atmosphere and was clearly visible from 70 kilometres away in Nuku'alofa, the capital city of the island of Tonga. The volcano's activity then decreased, so much so that the Tongan Geological Services classified the volcano as 'dormant' on 11 January. But Hunga Tonga had a terrible surprise in store. On 14 January, the mountain started erupting again and at 5 pm the next day the volcano exploded with an incredible force equivalent to 18 megatons of TNT. It was powerful enough to send an ash cloud 40 kilometres into the sky and it rained ash over Tonga. The blast also triggered tsunami waves up to 20 metres in height. The centre of the whole island had disappeared beneath the sea, leaving two smaller islands separated by a 2 kilometre gulf of empty ocean where the peak of Hunga Tonga had once stood.

Residents on Tonga, filming the ash cloud with their mobile phones, recorded the explosion that sounded like a loud cannon being fired; in one video posted online, the shock was enough to knock one person to the floor. The explosion was heard in Samoa 840 kilometres away and 2,000 kilometres away in Aotearoa New Zealand. In the small town of Whitehorse in northern Canada's Yukon territory, 9,700 kilometres away from the blast, one earwitness described the sound as just like 'a large truck passing by' and reported that the sound had gone on for about an hour. It's incredible to think that someone in the Yukon, dressed up against the sub-zero winter cold, shovelling the latest snowfall from their driveway, would hear a sound with its origin a world away in the tropical South Pacific!

The blast has been estimated at more than 100 decibels, making it the most intense sound on the planet for 139 years and the second loudest sound ever experienced in modern human history.

Atmospheric shockwaves were sent around the globe. Instruments in Japan and Utah recorded that, just like with Krakatau, the pressure wave circled the globe as many as four times. Eight hours after the blast, in Idaho, specialist microphones buried to record the characteristics of the local snow pack picked up the blast. The geophysicists behind the study were able to use software to speed up the infrasonic waves by 10,000 times, shifting it into a range we can hear with our own ears. Their recording of an explosion nearly 10,000 kilometres away shows us just how powerful our planet's natural forces can be and how the sounds of the Earth can create moments of global history.

Scan to hear the blast from Hunga Tonga–Hunga Ha'apai recorded on a mobile phone by witnesses.

Scan to hear the pressure wave from the explosion as it hit Idaho, 10,000 kilometres away and eight hours later.

Spirits' footsteps

I WALKED OUT INTO the night, leaving the old wooden hut for the last time. It had sheltered us from the Arctic winter, protected us from bears and earthquakes and had been our cosy, if cramped, home from home. For the last five days we had been stuck inside, watching the blizzard race past the small window, spending the time in detailed conversation about the exact type of pizza we would order when back in town. Our taste buds were growing more than a little bored of the packets of dehydrated food we had been living on. We had only braved the outside world to pee, before retreating back to the warmth, fingers and noses cold, beards frosted over and hoods filled with snow. But today the sky had cleared. All was still. The sun had set below a cloudless sky and we had spent the day furiously packing up our gear. It was time to escape home. Looking closely at the forecast we could see that this was a short lull in the weather and the next storm was due to roll in tomorrow. After much discussion we decided to make a run for it. Nobody wanted to get snowed in again.

We loaded up the snow machines and sledges, struggling in the cold with bare hands to tighten down our stacks of filming equipment under a spider's web of ratchet straps. It was hard not to get distracted by the world around us. Beyond the icy clouds of our own breath, caught in the beams of our head torches, we could see a wonderland. With the clouds gone, the dim light of the low moon shimmered over the sea ice. Across the bay, a coastline of pale ghostly mountains, cloaked in snow, rose above the blunted snouts of glaciers as they carved their way down to the ice-bound sea. Above us the sky was strewn with more stars than I had ever seen. The Arctic seemed impossibly huge and beautiful, and I was sad that we had to go.

Firing up the snow machines and climbing on board, we took one last look at the hut before driving down to the shoreline and out onto the frozen sea. We followed the coastline before turning west to head into the bay, forming a convoy of skidoos and sledges, the acute beams of our headlights bright comets in the deep blue darkness. The going was tough as the storm had blasted the snow into endless fields of frozen sastrugi (ridges of hard snow, shaped by the wind) that jolted and jerked our snow machines, threatening to tip us over if we didn't take things slowly. Following our guide out front we steered down onto the fast ice, trapped solid in the head of the bay and jetting beneath the shattered wall of the Strongbreen glacier as it towered above us. It looked like an impossible barrier barring our route south, but it had a weakness. Between the mighty river of ice and the mountain on its flank was a steep narrow pass up onto the top of the glacier. A series of snow-covered lateral moraines (the piles of rock debris carved out by the glacier) gave us a way through, although the route was horribly steep and deep with powdery snowdrifts. We had to pull full throttle and 'gun it' up to the top. I held my breath, leaning forward in my seat; with the engine already full tilt and screaming, still a long way from the top, I could feel my momentum slowing. Fearful of sinking in the snow or, worse, sliding backwards down the mountain, I gritted my teeth and finally shot over the lip of the pass and up onto the top of the glacier. I was sweating buckets and my exhalations had fogged up my goggles. The condensation soon froze solid in a lattice of ice crystals. I couldn't see a thing and I had to drive with my head awkwardly tilted to one side so I could peer out of a small clear corner at the bottom of my goggles.

We followed our guide up onto a high point on the ice and came to a stop, side by side. I could hear the excited gasps of the crew but could see nothing through my fogged-up goggles and I struggled to pull them aside. Finally, unblinkered, I could see the world once more. We were parked on the top of the glacier overlooking the distant wall of mountains. The landscape around us was of gentle rolling hills of pristine snow, unblemished and unbroken by tracks or footprints. We had been drilled not to step off our snow machines on the glacier, if we ever stopped like this. The blanket of snow hid hungry crevasses and this place had a history of swallowing those who wandered too far from their vehicles. (The snow machines, being broader, were less likely to sink into a crevasse than someone on foot.) Under the low moonlight, the frozen landscape was magical. But it was the sky that struck me silent.

Swirling ribbons of green unfurled across the heavens, like a breeze drifting across a veil. They danced in rows, rippling from unseen origin beyond the mountains, towards us and over our heads. Sharp-lined and bright along their edges closest to Earth, then ascending into diffuse clouds where the waves of phthalo green rose up into space. They arced and folded, flickering and fading, as they held us under their spell, it was impossible to look away. Bright bursts of energy pulsed along the ribbon, heading away to the horizon, leading our eyes across the heavens as if they were beckoning us to follow. It was the aurora borealis. At last, on the way home and far too late to film them, the northern lights had come to call.

Aurora borealis is a phrase with Greek origins, aurora meaning 'sunrise' and borealis from the 'north wind'. The solar wind is material ejected from the sun and sent out into space. When these winds reach our planet, they are guided by the Earth's magnetic field towards the polar regions (Antarctica has the aurora australis to mirror the aurora borealis in the Arctic). The solar winds are made up of charged particles from the sun, which collide with the gases in our atmosphere, exciting the gases to make the lights of the aurora.

The atmosphere is made up of different gases, so when the charged solar particles collide with nitrogen in the upper atmosphere they glow red, and when they collide with oxygen lower down they burn green. Looking up at the sky it felt as if the lights reached out to us. I could almost imagine stretching out a gloved hand and touching them directly. But in truth they were likely 100 kilometres above us and, at their furthest extent, reached up 300 kilometres into the atmosphere. Despite being more commonly known as the 'northern' lights, we were standing looking at them facing almost directly south. Because of the way the Earth's magnetic field draws the solar wind towards the Earth, they interact with our atmosphere in a ring called the auroral oval, that typically sits between 60 degrees and 75 degrees north, although on rare occasions this can extend as far south as 50 degrees north (where they can sometimes be spotted from Cornwall!). Up on the Strongbreen glacier, we were at around 77 degrees latitude north, so further north than the auroral oval – meaning we had to face southwards to see them.

The lights are born of a physical interaction of charged particles and gases, but watching them dance across the sky, it was hard not to think of them as something more spiritual. All across the northern hemisphere there are many beautiful beliefs and stories explaining their origin. The Makah people of Washington State tell that the lights are fires made by a tribe of dwarves who use them to cook whale blubber. While, conversely, the Mandan people in North Dakota believe them to be the cooking fires of a tribe of northern giants, who lit enormous fires to cook their enemies before they ate them. The Algonquin people of Canada believe the lights were from the hearth fire built by their creator god, Nanahbozho. His fire was a sign, reassuring the people that he was watching over them.

In northern Europe, too, the lights have their own colourful origin stories. The Vikings shared tales that the lights were the glow from the armour of fallen warriors, marching their way to the afterlife. One story says that the aurora is the glow of the 'Bifrost bridge' a magical archway leading to Valhalla. The Sami people of Lapland believe that the lights are the blow of a great whale, and one Swedish legend says the pulsing in the sky is the reflection from large shoals of herring, so seeing the lights is a sign of a good fishing to come. In Finland the lights are supposedly made by sparks flying from a fiery torch, tied to the tail of a celestial fox. As he runs across the sky, he leaves a trail of sparks for all to see. One old story from Iceland associates the lights with childbirth, warning that if a woman in labour looked directly at the aurora, her child would be born cross-eyed. Perhaps the saddest story is from Greenland, where some still believe the lights to be the dancing souls of stillborn babies.

There are many stories that see the lights as a tangible link between our own world and the realm of spirits. But in some cases, this link isn't just a visual one. There is also a long-held belief that the aurora makes a sound.

Lieutenant William Hooper was a Royal Navy officer who sailed north into the Arctic onboard HMS *Plover* in 1848. He was part of a mission to find the lost remains of the Sir John Franklin expedition that had set out in 1845. Hooper spent the winter of 1849–50 near Fort Franklin high on the edge of Bear Lake, now in Canada's Northwest Territories. He wrote in his journal:

> *I have heard the aurora, not once, but many times, not faintly and indistinctly, but loudly and unmistakably. At first it seemed to resemble the sound of field ice, then it was like the sound of a water mill, and, at last like the whirring of a cannon shot heard from à short distance.*

Hooper wasn't the only early Arctic explorer to encounter the sounds of the northern lights. Knud Rasmussen was born in 1879 in Ilulissat on the west coast of Greenland. He grew up in the heart of the Kalaallit community, speaking their language and learning how they lived off the land. In his 1927 book *Across Arctic America* he wrote:

> *My playmates were native Greenlanders; from the earliest boyhood I played and worked with the hunters, so even the hardships of the most strenuous sledge-trips became pleasant routine for me.*

Not only did this upbringing in an Inuit community make Rasmussen a useful man to share an Arctic adventure with (he became one of the most successful early European explorers of the frozen North), his writings also opened a window onto Inuit culture, albeit through a European lens. He interviewed many Inuit communities he encountered on his travels and, while he has been criticised in some quarters as 'romanticising' the Inuit people, he set out to preserve their oral traditions at a time when Indigenous voices were largely supressed by colonialism. In his wonderfully detailed *Intellectual Culture of the Iglulik Eskimos*, he recorded the belief that the northern lights were actually the spirits of the departed, playing football with the skull of a walrus:

It is this ball game of the departed souls that appears as the aurora borealis, and is heard as a whistling, rustling, crackling sound. The noise is made by the souls as they run across the frost-hardened snow of the heavens.

But it seems that Rasmussen discovered that the spirits in the northern lights didn't just make a sound. It was even possible to communicate with them:

If one happens to be out alone at night when the aurora borealis is visible, and hears the whistling sound, one only has to whistle in return and the lights will come nearer.

In his 1916 book about the cultural lives of the people of Labrador, American anthropologist Ernest W. Hawkes also recorded a belief that the lights made a sound:

The whistling crackling noise which sometimes accompanies the aurora is the voice of spirits trying to communicate with the people of the Earth. They should always be answered in a whispering voice.

In 1986 the Nunavut Arctic College, based in Igloolik on Canada's Baffin Island, fearful that the oral histories and traditions of the Igloolik Inuit were being lost, began a project to interview their community elders. The Igloolik Oral History Project spoke to over 600 elders and recorded their memories, culture and history. The project ran for thirty years and remains one of the most incredible archives of oral history anywhere in the world. The recordings contain some wonderful recollections and stories about the aurora.

Aqsarniit, meaning 'football players', is the Inuit word for the northern lights throughout the eastern Arctic. One elder, Mark Ijjangiaq, describes the lights:

I have heard that they used a walrus head for a football, and one can see the football players moving around. I have not heard what aqsarniit are made of but you can hear the swishing sound they make. If they get too close you can chase them away by twisting your tongue to the upright position. We used to do this when aqsarniit got too close and it always had an effect. When one was watching them, you could see them getting closer and closer until one could hear the swishing sound.

Elder Catherine Arnatsiaq recalls that the lights made her afraid:

I heard it said that the aqsarniit cut people's heads off. I tended to believe this because I was also aware of the saying that the aqsarniit used walrus heads for footballs, so I was scared of them! The other thing was when we whistled at them, they would make a swishing sound and would pick up speed. When the aqsarniit appeared, we would whistle at them and they would increase in speed and colour.

George Kappianaq was also fearful of the aurora appearing:

We were forbidden to make fun of the aqsarniit. We were told that we should never whistle at them to make them closer because it was possible

> *they might take us up to the skies, which they are capable of when they get too close to the ground. We would drive them off with sounds made by rubbing our fingernails together.*

But elder Niviattian Aqatsiaq recalls the aurora spirits being more playful:

> *When we would play outdoors, we would whistle at the northern lights to make them come closer. They would make a swishing sound. I don't know what they may be; perhaps they were once alive among the living.*

Despite the plethora of eyewitness accounts and traditional stories, Eurocentric science has always been sceptical about the 'sound' of the aurora. These opinions range from colonial prejudice to conventional physical theory. Scientific polymath Alexander Von Humboldt wrote in his 1845 five-volume exploration of nature, Earth and space, grandly titled *Cosmos*, that auroral noise is 'now rendered extremely doubtful, since the testimony of the Greenland sledgers, and the Siberian fox-hunters, is no longer taken unconditionally. The northern lights have become more silent since they have been examined more carefully with the eye and the ear.'

As early as the late 19th century, scientists were sceptical that the aurora could make any sound audible to human ears. They argued that due to the aurora's enormous altitude, any sound made could never be heard by someone on the ground. Reports of auroral 'crackling', 'whistling' and 'swishing' were written off as illusion or imagination. Carl Størmer, a Norwegian physicist who studied aurora by photographing them and calculating their heights, concluded in 1955 that 'it is impossible that real sounds from the aurora can reach the ear of man'. He went as far as to suggest that reports of sounds were 'subjective impressions'. The scientific consensus was that auroral sounds were either a case of mistaken identity or even psychological illusion. The suggestion was that the awe and visual stimulation of seeing the aurora might lead the witness to become hyper-aware of ambient sounds (ice cracking on a nearby frozen lake, branches creaking, the wind blowing through telegraph wires etc) and mistake these as originating from the lights themselves.

In the 1950s, scientist Robert A. Helliwell and his colleagues from Stanford University began to study atmospheric radio waves monitored from a series of remote polar locations. They picked up the first scientific recordings of an 'auroral chorus'. The strange sounds they heard occurred during strong geomagnetic storms. They were caused by electromagnetic waves in the ELF (extreme low frequency) and VLF (very low frequency) spectrum. These waves are generated when charged particles from the sun are funnelled along magnetic field lines, causing them to agitate plasma in the atmosphere. This activity can only be picked up by specialist VLF receivers and, even then, needs conversion into sound waves so that we can hear it. The result is a surreal and ghostly chorus of rising tones broken by an odd chirping sound, a bit like a bird.

In the early 1980's a Californian radio enthusiast named Stephen P. McGreevy became interested in the propagation of radio waves from the northern lights. He noticed that the Aurora can attenuate short wave radio, garbling the signals transmitted from countries where the signal crossed the auroral zone. This phenomenon set him on a life-long quest to record the sounds of radio waves generated by the aurora. McGreevy recalls one such special trip in September 1993, when he and a friend took the 8000 kilometre drive from his home in California to Saskatchewan in northern Canada. That autumn the aurora activity was high and the lights seemed to fill the heavens. McGreevy described the display above him as, 'Red, purple and green. Light like paint being poured down by an invisible hand in the sky.'

Using two large loop coil antennae to pick up VLF waves in the magnetosphere he was able to record the rising whistling and swishing tones. Over the years McGreevy has spent many nights chasing recordings of auroral choruses. You can listen to one of his incredible recordings below.

Scan to hear a compilation of sounds from an auroral chorus.

Since his obsession began, McGreevy has amassed hundreds of recordings of this 'music of the magnetosphere' and has shared them online, encouraging visitors to his website to listen in, believing that 'like stargazing, natural radio listening redirects the mind and heart towards the wonder and beauty of the natural world.'

During his adventures, McGreevy has himself wondered about the origin of the strange sounds that have been heard in relation to the northern lights. On one of his recording trips to Canada he encountered some members of a First Nations people called the Dene. When he played them his recordings they seemed to recognise the sounds and shared their traditional stories related to the lights.

While they are wonderfully beautiful, these choruses originate far up in the magnetosphere, so the scientific consensus has been that they cannot be heard by anyone witnessing the northern lights from the ground. But having heard for himself the stories of the Dene people, McGreevy now has his own ideas. 'I am very certain that long ago, during epochs when the ELF-VLF audio-frequency band "signals" were so strong they could "transduce" within the ear-brain systems in humans and possibly other creatures, enough to be heard on the ground and incorporated into their various songs and legends.'

Despite the historic doubts of mainstream science, people didn't stop reporting sounds coming from the northern lights. For many witnesses, the experience was often strange and magical and made all the more enigmatic by the scientific denial. It took the lifelong dedication of one extraordinary man to perhaps provide a final answer to the mystery.

Back in the early 1990s, a Finnish scientist called Unto K. Laine was returning late from a music festival in Finnish Lapland when he and his friends stopped to watch the northern lights. Laine remembers his surprise, as they could hear crackling sounds that seemed to be coming from the aurora above them.

> *This experience never left me. We had to concentrate – we did not move or talk at all. A few of us did not hear it, because at that time, the aurora wasn't very strong, and it was a very low-intensity sound. I could never forget this experience; it was so strange. It was very cold weather, about minus 35 degrees Celsius with clear skies, no clouds and no wind. So, it was absolutely the best conditions to hear the sounds.*

That night inspired Laine to begin a quest to record the sounds he and his friends had experienced and to understand what processes might be behind the strange noises. But even though he knew that the sounds were real, it was another challenge altogether to try and record them. I know from my own experiences trying to film aurora over thirty years that nature hardly ever cooperates. The aurora forecast might seem positive, with high levels of solar winds impacting the atmosphere, but you can set up your cameras and stand in the freezing cold all night and the whole sky be covered in dense cloud. If filming an aurora is tricky, then attempting to record its rare and phantasmagorical sounds is a much bigger challenge. Laine spent years and countless winter nights out alone placing microphone arrays around the snowy fields of his village, hoping to record any sounds. 'During all these years, I have checked the space weather two to three times a day, so not to miss any aurora events – and always, when the weather conditions are good, I go.'

Unfortunately for Laine, his research coincided with an eight-year-long 'solar minimum', meaning a decreased level of solar activity. This led to fewer cosmic 'solar winds' and a marked decline in aurora. But in 2011 solar activity increased again and Laine began using a VLF loop antenna to measure magnetic fields and a microphone array to help him source the origin of any sounds he picked up. On the nights of 17–18 March 2013, Laine finally succeeded in making clear recordings of the sounds of the aurora. He captured a series of faint crackling sounds, popping noises and muffled clapping sounds. The sounds were often short and low amplitude but they did seem to match many of the noises that so many witnesses had reported, going back for centuries. Listening to the recordings, Laine was surprised at what he heard. 'The sounds are diverse and can vary quite a lot, and it is very possible that there are many different mechanisms creating the sounds.'

By lining up the results of the magnetic field measurements alongside the sound recordings, Laine was able to see a link between the two, with pulses of magnetic energy observed just before the auroral sounds were recorded. Laine was able to rule out the sounds of trees and frozen lakes as he had set out his equipment in the middle of open fields, far away from any forests. By triangulating the array of microphones, he was able to locate the source of the sounds and discovered that they were coming from a height around only 75 metres above the ground, challenging the long-held view that auroras were too high for us to hear them. The biggest remaining part of the mystery now was, exactly how were the aurora making the sounds?

Laine compared his data from March 2013 with temperature records made by the Finnish Meteorological Institute for the same night. He discovered that they had measured a thermal temperature inversion in the atmosphere. This phenomenon takes place when a blanket of warm air traps cold air next to the ground and it occurs at almost exactly the same height that the noises originated from. Laine proposed that the sounds are caused by the build-up of electrical charges in the warm inversion layer, and an opposite build-up of charges in the cold air trapped below. When an aurora appears in the skies above the inversion, it disturbs the Earth's geomagnetic field and causes the stored electricity in the inversion to discharge and spark. These sparks of electrical charge create measurable magnetic pulses and sounds that are audible to our own ears. Laine also discovered that the volume of the sounds he recorded appeared to change with the intensity of the light's display.

Our scientific discoveries about the northern lights, from their patterns, colours and sounds, are wonderful and fascinating, but high on the glacier looking up at the painted night sky, I was equally reminded of the original stories. Seeing the aurora was for me something of a spiritual experience and it was hard not to think of them as being alive in some way. The lights appeared to fade and then grow again, burning brighter and coming closer so that they seemed to fill every corner of the sky. I wasn't aware of any crackling or popping sounds, but I did have my ears buried in layers of fleecy balaclava and a deep hood. Looking up, I pulled down the warm covering from my lips and attempted to whistle. In the cold, my lips were instantly numbed and useless, leaving me with no chance of calling out to the spirits. I had to make do with watching them ripple from a distance instead. As if the lights had the power to bend time and memory, I don't recall exactly how long we sat there gazing up at the sky. It was hard to drag ourselves away but, with fingers throbbing and faces frozen, the cold was growing and it was time to leave for the long drive home and the opulent promise of fresh pizza. I recalled all those nights of storm without so much as a glimpse of the night sky. Despite missing out on filming the aurora,

I couldn't believe what we had just witnessed with our own eyes. We fired up the snow machines and headed back to town over the glacier, as the aurora continued its dance above us. Phantom light breathing across the darkness.

Scan to hear Unto K. Laine's recordings of an Aurora Borealis.

Warnings from the ice

MY LUNGS WERE bursting. It was only a short 100-metre climb from our lodge to the top of the moraine cliffs but, at an altitude of 4,790 metres, our daily 'commute' to the glacier never seemed to get any easier. On this particular morning we were followed up the snaking pathway by an oddly curious yak. I've never had much of a love for Nepal's yaks, as on a previous visit I had been woken in the middle of the night by one as it was grazing and trying to push my tent aside to get at the grass beneath. In the delirious half-asleep, half-awake state that comes with high altitude, I was convinced that some kind of wild mountain Yeti was trying to break into my tent and steal me away. On a previous visit here, I had dozed off reading in the sunshine outside a trekking lodge, only to wake and find a large yak munching on my book. By the time I had rescued it from the beast's slobbering jaws, the yak had eaten all the pages of the second half, leaving me robbed of an ending. The yak now following us up the hill did at least keep us moving. There was no way I wanted to be anywhere near those horns and we reached the end of our climb much faster than usual.

The view at the top demanded you stop and take it all in. Our eyes followed the glacier, a huge river of rock and ice, as it crawled down from the mountains of its birth. In the far distance the rising sun had already set fire to the tips of the mountains, making them glow like waking embers in an ash-cold hearth. The peak that most demanded our attention was the mighty Cho Oyu; at 8,188 metres it's the sixth highest mountain in the world. Its name means 'Turquoise Goddess' in Tibetan, but this morning its shadowy blue ramparts of snow were rapidly turning pink, then orange, with the touch of the sun. This was my third visit here and this view had become my favourite of any in the world. Seeing Cho Oyu again, shining at the head of the valley, was like being reunited with an old friend.

Our team had come to Nepal's Khumbu region to try and record the sounds of glaciers for a documentary. With four of the world's top six highest mountains, including the tallest, Mount Everest, the region is known for its stunning peaks and some enormous glaciers. We had trekked for five days to reach Gokyo, home to the mighty Ngozumpa glacier. At 36 kilometres from source to snout, it's the longest found anywhere in the Himalaya. This morning, the Ngozumpa was shrouded by a bone-chilling mist and we stood on the edge of a swirling river of cloud that cut through the mountains. With the rising sun the mist slowly vanished and we could look down along the length of the huge river of ice. The Ngozumpa is not a pretty glacier. There is no blue crystalline ice to be seen. Instead, it wears a deep layer of broken grey rock debris, carved out by the glacier as it makes its way down the valley. We stood on the glacier's 'lateral moraine', the large deposits of eroded rock and earth piled up each side of the river of ice, 50–100 metres above the glacier's surface. Looking down, we could see that the ice was covered by so much rock debris, it had become piled up into its own miniature Himalaya, with an endless maze of peaks and troughs.

Armed with an array of microphones, our first job was to get down onto the glacier itself. Looking at the plummeting drop before us, I wasn't really sure how we might find a way down. The cliffs of the lateral moraine were seriously unstable. Constantly undercut, there were signs of landslides along their length and there was a real danger they might collapse beneath us. We made sure to wear helmets and also brought along a rope and harnesses in case we might need them. Our sherpa Sirdar led the way cautiously down the cliff, following a narrow path that hovered over the void. The steepness made it slippery and the rock dust slid away with every footstep. It was all too easy to dislodge a rock embedded in the cliff wall, and several times we shouted 'BELOW!' to warn those at the front of the column to watch out for tumbling rocks from above. The last part of the slope was so steep you had to run down, and my momentum carried me onto the glacier itself.

It was a huge relief to get the cliffs behind us. We found ourselves in a monochrome world of broken and splintered rock, piled into great hills and shadowy valleys beyond the touch of the sun. Across this most alien of landscapes, I could see an indistinct path made from repeated footsteps compacting the rock dust as it snaked across the glacier in a narrow line until it disappeared in the labyrinth of hills. We followed the path as it wound up and down and along ridges of rock debris. We passed strange-looking lakes, dotted all across the glacier's surface. In a couple of places our route traced the apex of ridge line atop a tower of ice. Here the powdered rock underfoot tumbled away like a sand dune with every footstep, leaving us on the edge of a deadly thirty metre slide into the icy meltwater below.

Taking it very slowly, finally we worked our way down to the shore of one of these glacial lakes. The crew set about placing our microphones, burying a low-frequency infrasonic microphone in a hole where the ice was exposed on the surface. Our hope was this might record the sounds of the ice itself. We set up an atmospheric mic on a tripod – hoping to record the overall soundscape of the glacier – and ended our work by plunging two hydrophones into the milky water of the lake. Taking a moment to listen to this broken and threatening landscape, I was aware that it was a place in flux. The quiet was punctuated by the rattle of sliding rock debris and occasionally a loud 'splosh' as the rocks tumbled into the water. More ominous, though, was the deep booming crack and thunderous rolling that came from large boulders falling from high on the moraine cliffs, liberated by the glacier undercutting the valley side.

Scan to listen to the sounds of the Ngozumpa glacier.

For several years now, geologists have known that the Ngozumpa is changing. The Himalaya have been warming significantly due to climate change. Local people have noticed dramatic changes in their surroundings over the last couple of decades. Hillsides once covered in snow are now bare and dry. Snow is melting earlier and there is more rainfall. Glaciers, ice and snow cover are receding more rapidly than the world average and researchers from Nepal have calculated that the 5,500 glaciers in the Himalaya (including in the Everest region) could reduce in volume by 70–99 per cent by the end of the century. And one study in 2013 found that some glaciers on or around Everest had shrunk by 13 per cent in the last fifty years, with the snowline 180 metres higher than it was fifty years ago. These rivers of ice are disappearing faster every year and some of the region's smaller glaciers are now only half the size they were in the 1960s.

With warmer air temperatures, the ice of the glaciers of Nepal are melting away to nothing. On the Ngozumpa and other glaciers, the disappearing ice is transformed into meltwater, which pools in lakes on the glacier's surface. An analysis of satellite images of the glacier, published in 2020, discovered that the Ngozumpa now supports over a thousand of these lakes. This new water world on the glacier is constantly changing and updating. With the accumulation of meltwater, the lakes can grow quickly but, surprisingly, they can disappear overnight too. A 2017 study by glaciologists from Scotland outlined the remarkable process of the changing lakes. One lake – named Lake 7092 – began to expand rapidly, growing in depth by nearly 9 metres between October 1998 and October 1999. In just a year, water from the melting glacier had swelled the lake from an area of 17,890 square metres to 52,550 square metres.. But remarkably, just a year later, the lake had almost completely disappeared. Satellite analysis worked out that the exposed ice cliffs along the eastern and southern edge of the lake had been in constant retreat, calving and collapsing into the water as they melted. Altogether the area along the edge of the lake had lost 340,000 cubic metres of rock and ice. With the barrier holding the lake in place melted, the water of Lake 7092 drained away.

Researchers from the University of Colorado have used cameras set up on the glacier to study this filling and emptying process. They have revealed that the volumes involved can be prodigious, with one camera recording an emptying lake losing over 100,000 cubic metres of water in just two days. Debris-covered glaciers like the Ngozumpa don't melt in the same way as clean-ice glaciers. All the rock on top insulates the glacier from the heat of the sun, but once you remove this protective layer, exposing the ice, as happens when the glacial lakes expand and contract, then the rate of melting increases. The bare ice walls of a draining glacial lake melt more quickly in the sun. For ice below a layer of rock debris, the melt rate is about 2 centimetres a day, but on exposed ice walls, it can be as much as 4 centimetres a day. The cameras revealed that when one lake empties another one fills, so it looked as if the lakes might be connected in some way beneath the ice.

A team from the University of Svalbard donned their helmets, harnesses and head torches and set out to follow the path of the water. Their explorations took place outside of the summer melt season, when entering the glacier would be just too dangerous. They discovered a series of 'ice pipes' – tunnels beneath the ice, some of which opened out into spectacular caverns. It seemed that not only was the glacier melting on its surface, it was being eaten away from the inside as well. One of the Norwegian scientists even compared the Ngozumpa to a 'Swiss cheese'. The ice tunnels act as lines of weakness in the glacier. When the ice melts, the roof falls in and exposes more clean ice to the heat of the sun, increasing the rate of melting yet further. All the water escaping from lake to lake through the ice tunnels has to drain somewhere and in the case of the Ngozumpa it is running downhill and forming a huge lake right at the snout of the glacier. Here the water hits a dead end with a massive wall of debris called the 'terminal moraine', which acts just like a dam. This lake – called the 'Spillway Lake' – is expanding rapidly. First reported in 1984, the lake started to grow slowly, but since 2001 it's been growing at around 10 per cent a year. In 2009 the lake measured 300,000 square metres with a volume of at least 2.2 million cubic metres. Research published in 2017 used sonar scans to show that the lake was also getting deeper.

These lakes are appearing all across the Himalaya and are a growing threat to the lives of mountain people. Heavy rainfall, snowfall, avalanche and glacial collapse can lead to the moraine dam failing, causing a sudden and violent release of water from within the glacier. Known as Glacial Lake Outburst Floods or GLOFs, there are thought to be around fifty lakes in Nepal alone that are at risk of bursting through. The Ngozumpa's Spillway Lake is one of many lakes in the Khumbu region that are causing concern for local communities. The Dig Tsho lake in the Langmoche Valley burst its banks in 1985 and is growing once again. Beneath the gravity-defying peak of Cholatse, the newly formed Chola Lake has appeared as the mountain's glacier melts. On the Imja glacier, beneath the wall of Lhotse (the world's fourth highest peak), sits the Imja Tsho lake. Within the lifetime of the local herders, the lake has grown from nothing to a body of water measuring one square kilometre in area and 45 metres deep. The threat to the sherpa villages is very real. For an example of the destructive force of a GLOF, you just need to head over to one of Gokyo's neighbouring valleys.

Beneath the snow-crowned wall of Parchamo (6,273 metres) and Teng Ragi Tau (6,943 metres), the Thyangbo glacier sweeps down to feed the Thame Khola River. Just over 6 kilometres downstream from the glacier's snout sits the sherpa village of Thame. It's located on an ancient pathway where traders from Tibet, crossing the challenging Nangpa La pass, would bring salt to sell to the sherpas in exchange for rice and barley. I was lucky enough to visit Thame on a previous journey in 2000 and I remember the place had a real sense of peace. Sitting in a valley away from the main trekkers' route to Everest, it wasn't swamped by overseas visitors and it felt as if this was a good place to see the real Nepal. I remember the village was surrounded by terraced fields growing potatoes, and this crop – alongside a few trekking lodges – has long been the people's main income. The village was most famous for being the childhood home of the great Tenzing Norgay, who alongside Edmund Hillary first climbed Everest in 1953. By all accounts Thame kept its laidback feel long after my visit, but at 1:30 pm on 16 August 2024 that peace was shattered.

It started with a sound. One villager recalled in an online video, 'It came with a huge roar, the water and boulders just rushed down.' A destructive wall of churning grey water, thickened with tons of silt and huge rocks, swept down from the glacier, following the Thame Khola, and wiped out the centre of the village. According to eyewitness Mingma Rita sherpa, the flood came in three waves:

> *At first, we saw that this flood is not that strong … we thought we're safe now … but again, such an unfortunate thing happened – a second flood came, and this flood was much stronger … the third time was the strongest, from the top it slowly swept away the village. We could not think, it was just like a dream.*

The torrent obliterated several homes, the village health post and the local school. It must have been terrifying. People had to run for their lives, trying to reach higher ground. One villager reported that everything was 'destroyed within a few minutes, and we were not even able to save our shoes – we just ran away … everyone was crying, not able to think about what had just happened.'

Luckily, being the middle of the day, many people were out in the fields. It was market day in the sherpa capital of Namche Bazaar and people had travelled away from Thame for a day or two. And, most fortunately, the local school had closed earlier that morning, sending the children home. Surprisingly, nobody was killed by the flood, but it did displace 135 people including 40 children, leaving them homeless. The power of the flood was such that its destruction didn't end at Thame. It continued to charge downstream and into the Bhote Koshi river and then on into the mighty Dudh Koshi, the river rising from the Gokyo Valley. Here, on a bend in the river, the flood scoured away the steep river bank, undercutting the pretty hamlet of Toktok, which perches above the gorge. It was enough to cause a landslide that left a row of houses precariously balanced on the edge of the void. The flood washed down the Dudh Koshi and damaged an important steel bridge at the village of Adheri, 47 kilometres downstream.

Analysis of the disaster by a Nepali government investigation was able to piece together the events building up to the flood. The area had seen unusually high temperatures for that time of year. On 9 August things became warmer, with temperatures sitting almost two degrees above the normal average. On the day of the disaster the temperature was recorded as 15 degrees Celsius, a full 5.3 degrees above the average. This heatwave and a continuous rainfall caused a chain reaction among a system of small glacial lakes that sit beneath the peaks of Parchamo and Teng Ragi Tau. The rainfall, perhaps boosted by an increase in avalanche activity, caused the highest lake, the Upper Tsomutse, to overflow into the smaller Lower Tsomustse (only about the size of an Olympic swimming pool) with enough power that the glacial moraine, holding back the lower lake, burst asunder, allowing 0.34 million cubic metres of water to charge down the valley. In some ways the people of Thame had been fortunate. If the GLOF had struck in the middle of the night rather than in the quiet part of the day, many of them would have been swept away in their beds.

In a rapidly warming world, scientists utilise a number of techniques to measure the changes to frozen landscapes. Comparing satellite data over time, setting up cameras to record physical change and collecting eyewitness testimonies are all widely used approaches to keep track of diminishing ice. But a relatively new method in their data-gathering tool kit is to remotely record the sounds of ice. By passive listening to the sounds made by glaciers and ice caps, scientists can record the sounds of calving, iceberg collisions and tidal flows, and link these to changing rates of ice flow. By placing hydrophones in glacial lakes, scientists can tell what is going on beneath the surface of the ice. They will regularly hear a soundtrack of near constant 'popping' noises, like a line of firecrackers going off. These are in fact bubbles released from the melting ice, bursting in the water. By sampling the ice it's possible to learn how many bubbles it contains and by counting the sounds of the bubbles released in the water and tracking them over time, scientists can determine the rate of melting.

Researchers at the Scripps Institution of Oceanography have been listening in on an Arctic glacier in Svalbard. The study set out to analyse the underwater recordings from a set of hydrophones positioned near the snout of the Hansbreen glacier as it calves into the ocean at Hornsund fjord. The hydrophones were placed by scuba divers on the ocean floor 900 metres from the glacier's snout. Any closer would be highly dangerous, as huge blocks of ice calve into the water at regular intervals. The hydrophones were able to capture the cracking of the ice and the bass rumbling as icebergs broke from the ice cliff. They also recorded the hissing static sounds of air bubbles bursting from the glacier as its ice melted. Three timelapse cameras positioned to film the glacier snout as it calved into the water allowed the researchers to work out the volume of each calving iceberg and their drop heights. In total they captured 169 calving events and by comparing the photos with the acoustic recordings the team were able to match the sounds and pictures. The result is that the researchers were able to derive a formula to calculate the mass of the calving ice just from the noise it made. Deploying hydrophones allows for a cost-effective, long-term method of remotely recording ice loss at glaciers that are often hard to reach and expensive to study.

Across the Himalaya, local authorities and research teams have started to use sound to monitor glacial lakes and are working towards a network of early warning systems for mountain communities. India's National Disaster Management Authority is leading a mission to instal ultrasonic sensors at 190 high-risk glacial lakes. These sensors emit high-frequency sound waves to measure the distance from the sensor to the lake's surface and detect any sudden drop in water levels that might signal an impending GLOF. In Uttarakhand, geophysicists are using seismometers to detect the acoustic vibrations in the earth that are caused by collapsing ice and failures of moraine dams. They are aiming to instal a network of one hundred monitoring stations across the mountains. When applied to one major GLOF disaster in Chamoli in 2021, which killed around 300 people, case studies have shown that seismic sensors could have provided up to thirty minutes of advanced warning, which would have been enough to save many lives.

While it has yet to be used for monitoring glaciers, there is a new technology called Distributed Acoustic Sensing (DAS) that uses thousands of discrete fibre-optic cables as vibration sensors to give an accurate early warning of volcanic or seismic activity. Perhaps this new system will be equally useful in helping give notice of glacier collapse. In a warming world, the threat of catastrophic mountain floods is likely to grow. But listening in on the sounds of glaciers might just give us clues that could be used to avert future catastrophes.

With our microphones now deployed on the Ngozumpa, it was time to get off the glacier. Our way back up the cliff took us dangerously close to a huge gravity-defying boulder, hanging precariously over the pathway. A ticking timebomb ready to discharge. We crossed beneath it one at a time, mindful to keep moving quickly, despite our calf muscles and lungs burning in the thin air.

Once safely at the top of the moraine cliff and looking back down, it took me a while to spot our tiny microphone and tripod. I could see the many lakes dotted over the glacier's fractured surface. Some were a milky grey, others pale green and some were coloured a stunning blue like scattered gemstones. The sound of far-distant voices rose up from the glacier and I could just about pinpoint a line of heavily laden porters, tiny ants wandering lost over an endless gravel road. They were crossing on their way to the hamlet of Dragnag and the Cho La Pass, which would lead them down on towards Everest. At the head of the valley, a rising wind tore a flag of powdery spindrift from the summit of Cho Oyu. The mountain had transformed from a turquoise goddess to one of sheer brilliant white, so bright that it was painful to look at. A tumultuous boom shook the cold air, followed by an echoing growl. The sound sent tremors through my core, making my heart flutter. A huge boulder, bigger than a minibus, had fallen from the moraine cliff on the far side of the glacier, sending up a smoke of dust, its crash of rolling thunder a portent of collapse and flood. Its echoes bounced back and forth across the valley, a warning from a rapidly disappearing world.

Scan to hear the calving of icebergs into the ocean, from a glacier in Greenland.

5. Voices of the Deep

MYSTERIOUS SOUNDS FROM THE OCEAN

Making friends with a whale

THEY SAY YOU never forget your first encounter with a whale. Climbing down the boat ladder into the azure-blue ocean I felt a familiar uncertainty. Since I was a boy, the sea and everything in it had held a huge fascination. But this excitement was always tempered by a nervousness. When I was a kid, my sister and I had been swept out to sea during a family holiday to Cornwall. I still remember peering over the edge of our vinyl plastic dinghy and shivering as I looked into the water below. What amazing creatures lived down there? What would they make of us, should our flimsy inflatable, a rather inadequate barrier between two worlds, deflate and sink?

Now, on a boat 200 kilometres off the Australian coast, I was reunited with both my worries and wonders. The ocean had never been my element. Always happier with my feet on dry land, it had taken several days to get my sea legs. I had spent long hours lying flat on the bed in my cabin, trying to adjust to the swaying and shifting of our vessel. The night before I had sat around the table sharing stories with the team. Our dive camera operator had adventurous tales from a lifetime of filming Australia's marine wonders, telling of a terrifying encounter with three tiger sharks. The boat's skipper, a deep-sea fisherman and sport diver, shared epic yarns about battling a giant marlin, and our expedition leader, who had spent close to sixty years exploring underwater, told tales of the ocean so filled with whale sharks you could 'walk across their backs'. As each took turns to regale us with their stories, it started to feel a bit like that scene in *Jaws* where the crew show off their scars. I was definitely Chief Brody. I considered for a moment hitting them with my best ocean story. A scarily close encounter with the pincers of an edible crab 'the size of a Cornish pasty' while fishing off the pier in Weymouth. But I think they sensed my nervousness and thankfully the conversation turned towards the subject of our current voyage.

We had come to the Great Barrier Reef off the coast of Queensland in Australia to film a very important meeting: a unique gathering of humans and whales that's been described as the greatest wildlife encounter on the planet.

In 1981, a snorkeller 53 kilometres north-east of Port Douglas was approached by a seven-and-a-half-metre long creature, its skin a liquid patchwork of dark blue, black and white. The animal was so curious and came so close he described the encounter as 'spiritual'. And so a new type of whale announced its presence to us: the dwarf minke whale. Related to the more standard northern minke but smaller and with a complex and beautiful swirling colouration, it's different enough that it may even be a distinct species.

The smallest of the baleen whales (related to the blue, humpback and fin), dwarf minkes gather inside the outer 'ribbon' reefs of the Great Barrier Reef every May to October. They come from the open ocean of the Pacific to spend time hanging out together in the warm, shallow, protected reef waters, before heading south and leaving for Antarctica, where they likely feed. During their time on the reef, they aggregate in large gatherings and are often drawn to boats and any humans in the water. This event now has its own dedicated tourist industry, with humans equally curious to swim with the whales.

As I stepped off the last rung of the ladder, looking down into the blue depths felt a little like vertigo. I pulled myself along a rope trailing off the back of the boat and passed my fellow snorkellers, each hanging off short loops in the rope so that we appeared like human bait hooked on a line. Taking up a space on the rope, I clutched hard at the loop, my only connection to the world of solids. For a while we waited. The sea was a bit choppy and the rise and fall of the swell pulled the rope and its passengers in long snaking arcs. I struggled to put on my fins and my mask fogged up before I swallowed a face full of wave as I took it off to wipe it clear. Below us the surface contortions split the sun, sending shimmering searchlights dancing down into the deep.

And then, seemingly out of nowhere, the whales appeared, their sleek torpedo forms gliding effortlessly through the water as if propelled by an unseen force. One large whale passed along the line of the rope, getting closer. My first thought was, 'Who the hell chose to call these things dwarf?' To me they seemed huge. Suddenly they were coming at us from all directions. I could hear the excited squealing of my fellow snorkellers, muted behind their facemasks. This was what the skipper of the boat had described to us as 'whale soup'.

I counted about ten whales in the water, maybe thirteen. To human eyes, ocean life can look pretty similar. Individual sharks, dolphins and fish are hard to distinguish from others of their kind, but looking more closely you could see the variations in the whales' beautiful markings. And beyond that, there were clear differences in their behaviour. Some whales hung back, seemingly a little nervous. One huge whale was more confident and would pick a target human on the line and head straight at them, forcing the snorkeller to float flat on the surface to allow the whale just enough space to pass beneath.

But there was one particular whale that seemed to choose me. As it approached, it felt like a scene from a sci-fi movie where I was the representative of humanity about to meet a strange and wondrous alien. And it made me a little nervous. As the whale came at me, I could see it was about four and a half metres long; its patterning was interrupted on its left side by a semi-circular gouge, a scar from the bite of a cookiecutter shark. It came so close beneath me that I had to fold myself into a ball to stop my fins touching it. As it passed, it rolled onto its side so it could look at me. Its eye swivelled, focused and took me in. It had a profound curiosity and an intelligence that made me feel small, as if I was in the presence of a character much cleverer than me.

I was eye to eye with a minke whale. My nervousness was replaced by an overwhelming joy. I wanted to reach out and touch it as it passed to make our connection even stronger, but the strict code of conduct wouldn't allow it. How do you communicate with a being from another world and let it know this moment is special for you too? All I could think to do was wave madly, with all the childish enthusiasm of a kid shaking a flag at their favourite sports player. It's impossible not to add my human interpretation to the whale's behaviour, but it seemed to me that this action made it somehow even more curious. I had made friends with a whale. Our encounter lasted for five hours straight and nothing could get me off that line (even when I mistook the rope loop for a passing venomous olive sea snake and, reaching out to grab hold, gave myself a bit of a fright!). My minke passed by again and again before, seemingly tiring of this particular flapping human fool floating in the water, it moved on to another. By the end of the day, it was hard to know whether the humans or the whales were the true tourists.

That night on the boat, everyone onboard seemed to float in a euphoric bubble as our skipper played recordings of the minkes' voices, captured with a hydrophone. Minke whales are known to vocalise and create sounds that include clicks, grunts, 'pulse trains', 'ratchets', thumps and recently discovered 'boings'. But their most interesting call seems to mimic the central coda of Beethoven's fifth symphony: *'Da, da, da, daaaaa. Da, da, da, daaaaa.'*

Scan to hear the strange call of a minke whale.

I didn't hear the minkes myself, but others on the line reported hearing their voices and even feeling the vibrations in their chests. It's been hypothesised that these strange sounds may be made by males looking for a mate, but really there is so much we just don't know. It felt otherworldly to look into the eyes of an ocean alien, but when you consider the mysteries of their vocalisations, the minkes and all other whales really do exist on another planet to us. To understand why this is, you need to know the differences between water and air.

On the surface, vision is the primary sense. Light travels huge distances. Our eyes can perceive the light from the Andromeda galaxy, 2.5 million light years away. But underwater, vision is less dependable. Divers get excited about visibility of just 50–100 metres. And then you realise that the majority of the ocean doesn't even receive any light. The aphotic zone is deep beyond the reach of the sun and makes up about 90 per cent of the ocean.

Underwater it is sound rather than vision that is the dominant sense. Sound travels both further and faster underwater than it does through air. In the air, the speed of sound (defined as the distance travelled per unit of time by a sound wave as it propagates through a medium) is approximately 343 metres per second. At similar conditions of temperature, but in the water, the speed of sound is a staggering 1,480 metres per second.

Think of sound as a wave of compression travelling through a material. That material is made up of a matrix of atoms (imagine these as basketballs) joined together and held in place by connectors (or bedsprings). When a sound impacts on the material, it pushes the basketballs closer together as it moves, by compressing the bedsprings. As it passes, they bounce back, separating the basketballs to their former position. And so, a wave of sound travels through a material. Stiffer materials propagate sound at higher speeds. The stiffer bedsprings snap back more quickly into place, leading to faster transfer of the compression wave. Compared to air, the matrix of water molecules is much stiffer, making it better suited to the rapid transfer of sound waves.

These properties of water make the ocean just about the best place on the planet to use sound, both as a communication tool or as a means to navigate or find food. And of all the ocean's wonderful creatures, it's the whales and dolphins that have evolved to use sound in ways that are simply extraordinary.

The big one

THE BLUE WHALE could easily claim to be the most spectacular animal that ever lived. Supported by seawater that negates the size-limiting effects of gravity, the blue whale has grown to a gigantic scale, far bigger than any dinosaur, to become the largest living creature that has ever existed on the planet. The figures are mind-blowing. The longest blue whale on record was a female, measured at the South Georgia whaling station in 1909, that was a staggering 33.58 metres long. That's as long as three double-decker buses. The heaviest blue whale on record was also a female, hunted in South Georgia in 1947, which weighed 190 tonnes, the same as thirty African elephants. Even the average blue whale measures 22 metres and weighs 145 tonnes (that's still twenty-four African elephants!).

When a blue whale comes to the surface to breathe, its exhalation explodes from its lungs in a hot, moist cloud that can reach 9 metres into the air. A new-born baby blue whale measures 7 metres long and weighs almost 2.5 tonnes. It gains weight at a staggering 4.5 kilograms an hour. For krill, a blue whale is less of a gentle giant, more of a terrifying monster. A hunting blue whale will eat enormous quantities of these tiny shrimp-like crustaceans. It can eat three to four tonnes of krill in a day. To put this into perspective, if a typical Western human adult consumes 2,000 calories a day, a blue whale can gulp down 457,000 calories in a single mouthful. That's over seven months of food for us in just one bite. And the whale won't stop there.

Once a blue whale has spotted a cloud of krill, it will ramp up its speed, opening its huge throat sacs, that extend almost half the length of its body, and take an enormous gulp of krill-packed seawater. The whale takes in so much water that it weighs more than its own huge body. Once the krill are inside, the whale closes its mouth and heaves the water out with movements of its elephant-sized tongue. The krill are left strained up against the giant three-and-a-half-metre-long baleen plates and swallowed. This titanic feeding manoeuvre is thought to take up so much energy for these whales that they will only lunge after the biggest, densest clouds of krill. The small ones just aren't worth the energy they'll expend from opening their enormous mouths.

The average lifespan of a blue whale is between eighty and ninety years and some scientists have speculated there may be individuals out there that are over a hundred years old. Scientists know this because they have sampled and analysed the whales' earwax. Even a blue whale's earwax is impressive. The 25 centimetre-long earplugs look like some kind of dark, creepy candle from Dracula's castle. A closer look reveals the wax has layers called 'lamina'. Blue whales live a life of feast and famine, following their favourite food of krill, which is seasonal. This means they have months of feeding followed by months of fasting, and this alters the composition and darkness of the lamina laid down in the earplug. Like the rings of a tree, scientists can count these layers and work out the age of the whale.

The *Guinness Book of Records* gleefully tells us that the blue whale has the biggest heart on the planet – approximately the size of a bumper car. In what is perhaps the best animal fact ever, David Attenborough, in *Blue Planet*, famously claimed that the blood vessels of a blue whale are so wide you could swim down one. In truth, it would be a very tight squeeze for an adult human, so actual swimming might be out of the question! Some biologists wish they had lived in the time of T. rex and the dinosaurs, but personally, I feel deeply privileged to have shared my time on this planet with the blue whale.

As you would expect, a creature of such superlatives doesn't disappoint when it comes to vocalisations. The biggest beasts make the biggest sounds and, while the blue whale isn't the loudest creature on the planet (more on that later), it's probably in the top three. Marine biologists have measured a blue whale's call at 189 decibels. To give that context, the ear-scraping din of a jet engine taking off is only 140 decibels. So, if the sea is full of these booming behemoths, why don't we hear their calls anytime we swim in the same ocean as them? It's all to do with the pitch. Human hearing is normally limited to picking up sounds as low as 20 hertz, about the same as the lowest pedal on a church organ, whereas the pulses, groans and grunts of blue whale speak come between 10 and 40 hertz. So, the majority of the sounds they make are below the range of our own hearing, and we have to speed up the recording some of of their calls by ten times to be able to tune in. Listening on my computer to calls that a scientist emailed me, the bass notes make the speakers wobble dramatically and I can feel the vibrations in the desk rumbling up into my chest. Just like humans, the bigger baleen whales make sounds from their larynx, although they don't have vocal cords like us and they don't have to breathe out to make a sound. This means they can call underwater without having to surface to take a breath, doing so by recycling the air already in their lungs.

The latest researchers studying whale communication are listening in on a truly remarkable sonic world and giving us an insight into lives lived in and shaped by a soundscape far beyond our imagination. A team from the Scripps Institution of Oceanography gathered 4,500 recordings of blue whale vocalisations in the seas off Southern California, over the course of fourteen years. They noticed that the calls came in three different types, which they named A, B and D calls. Overall male blue whales were noisier and, while both sexes made a variety of different single-note calls, only males would phrase these calls together to make 'songs'. The researchers cleverly synced these calls to the known movements of 121 blue whales in the area that had been fitted with suction-cup tags to record depth and GPS location. This allowed them to work out what blue whales were doing when they made certain calls and where they made them. The Team's analysis uncovered patterns that have allowed us to better understand blue whale communication.

Most of the whale's sounds were made in shallow water, less than 30 metres in depth, and most calls were made around dusk and on into the night when the krill had dispersed and they were not feeding. The 'D' calls consist of short short tones and were made by both males and females. These calls may be a way the whales maintain a social pair bond during feeding. The whale equivalent of polite dinner conversation.

The 'A' and 'B' calls were made only by male whales. The 'A' calls were 'pulsed' in nature but the 'B' calls were more tonal. These calls would last for about fifteen to twenty seconds and the males would sometimes join them together to make phrases. Because only the males performed these types of calls, it's likely that they are primarily used as mating signals.

To me, the single most incredible thing about blue whales is the potential that they may be communicating over long distances. The researchers found that males making 'A/B' type calls made repeated U-shaped dives to around 330 metres. These dives allow the singer to access an invisible sound channel, one that offers acoustic properties to concentrate the call. As you swim deeper into the ocean, the temperature of the water and the pressure it exerts change. Within this blue whale 'sound channel' the water is warmer at the top. Sound travels faster in warmer water and is forced in a downwards direction as it moves. Reaching the bottom of the channel, the water is near freezing but the pressure is higher. Sound travels faster at higher pressures, so at this point, the song is forced back upwards, back into the channel. This pattern of ups and downs is repeated again and again as the sound travels across the ocean. The changes in the speed of travel act to concentrate the acoustic waves, focusing them so that little is lost to the surrounding ocean.

This sound channel is better known by scientists as the SOFAR (Sound Fix and Range). It's typically found at depths between 800 and 1,000 metres and can carry sounds between 10–30 hertz for over 1,000 kilometres with minimal decrease in intensity. With the blue whale's 'B' call being 10–20 hertz and incredibly loud, it is perfect for long-distance propagation in the SOFAR. The deep dives of the 'B' call male blues in the study off the shallower southern Californian coastline wouldn't be deep enough to take them down to the SOFAR but they may still benefit from a less-developed acoustic channel, and their dives would still reduce any interference from surface noises and maximise transmission. The research team feel these dives may give the whales the opportunity to send their 'B' songs across the ocean for hundreds of kilometres to broadcast their presence and attract a mate. But what of those blue whale males who may get to sing at SOFAR depths? Could they be sending their songs even further?

With the end of the Cold War in 1991, the US Navy loosened its restrictions on a top-secret project to listen to the world's oceans. SOSUS (Sound Surveillance System) was an array of deep-sea listening stations along America's Atlantic coastline that allowed the US Navy to listen out for Soviet submarines and track their movements. From their base in Virginia, the navy could tune in to the whole of the North Atlantic Ocean and eavesdrop on enemy movements. But it wasn't just submarines they picked up on their headphones. They heard whale songs, lots of them. By 1992, the year that the Soviet Union fell, biologists were invited to the SOSUS headquarters to listen to whales. They were amazed to discover the navy had been sitting on the ability to record individual whales singing from all over the ocean and that they could see one hydrophone array picking up a blue whale's call and then see the same call appear on the sonogram print-outs at another far-away listening station many minutes later. This introduced the idea to biologists that the song of a whale has the acoustic properties to travel thousands of kilometres. The hard part for researchers is proving that other whales are hearing these songs, but although the evidence is thin, nature doesn't often furnish an animal with such incredible abilities if it doesn't then use them.

The idea of long-distance whale song, even as yet unproven, is astounding. As a blue whale sings, his song spreads out horizontally in a circular wave heading in all directions. It's just like the ripple you see coming from a raindrop landing in a puddle. The song of a male blue, calling off the Grand Banks of Canadian Newfoundland, will reach Nova Scotia just a few short minutes after it began. The song will ripple out across the North Atlantic, reaching the ears of blue whale females at Cape Hatteras in North Carolina, up to 2,000 kilometres away, just twenty minutes later. From a human perspective it's hard to fathom such a distance. Telephones and computers have made our world a much smaller place and allowed us to 'cheat' at long-distance communication. But just to give you an idea, a blue whale's call could be the equivalent of you standing in New York's Times Square and having a chat with someone paddling their toes at Miami Beach in Florida. Sceptics of long-distance whale communication ask what would be the purpose of such interactions between individuals who are so far apart? After all, if a female blue whale likes a male's song, it may take her weeks to reach him.

Scan to hear the long-distance call of a blue whale.

We have always imagined blue whales to be romantic loners, solitary giants that cruise their way through the ocean. The decline in their numbers after commercial whaling only adds to this sense of loneliness. Blues are most commonly observed by themselves. Only a lucky few people ever get to see a mother with a calf and only occasionally do the whales come together around feeding opportunities. Even then, they may be several kilometres distance from the next whale. The latest research listening in to their calls suggests that perhaps these mighty animals aren't so alone. They may be physically distant, but that doesn't stop them communicating. Are they truly alone or do they just exist in a startlingly different sonic world to own: an expanded social universe beyond our limited comprehension.

The loudest of all

Blue whales' calls may likely travel over the longest distance, but their voices aren't the loudest in the ocean. That title belongs to a very different animal, the sperm whale: the beast given global fame in Herman Melville's *Moby Dick*. Sperm whales are very different to their big blue cousins. Firstly, they have teeth: 20 centimetres long and each weighing a kilogram, some of the biggest teeth on the planet. They also have the largest brains of any animal. They have a peculiar body shape, more double-decker bus than streamlined ocean torpedo. Their huge heads make up almost a third of their body weight. If you were to design an ocean-going animal, giving it an enormous rectangular front end would seem a bit odd; it must take a lot of effort to maintain balance making it hard work to propel itself through the water. What possible function could there be for such a generous head?

It was the whale's head (or what was inside it) that almost led to their extinction. They were slaughtered en masse by whalers in the 1800s for the oil that can be found inside their huge heads. This oil, called spermaceti (literally 'seed of the whale' – for its likeness to seminal fluid), fuelled the lamps and lubricated the machines of the Industrial Revolution. It became so precious that at the height of whaling in the 19th century, as many as 5,000 sperm whales were killed every year. The whalers would call them 'carpenter fish' after the strange loud knocking or hammering they heard on the ship's hull when the sperm whales were about. These strange and threatening sounds weren't any kind of oceanic woodwork, but were in fact the 'clicks' that sperm whales use to communicate.

The whole enormous head of a sperm whale acts like a huge and powerful morse code machine. The spermaceti organ at the front of the head also contains a mass of oily fatty tissue called the 'junk'. The whale has two long nasal passages that wrap around the spermaceti and the junk. The left-hand passage runs up to the whale's blowhole on the top of its head. The right-hand nasal passage is twisted and folded to form a string of air-filled sacs. Near the front of the head sits a pair of dense collagen clappers called 'monkey lips', a little like a giant version of our own vocal cords. To make a 'click' the whale forces air through its right nasal passage and over the monkey lips, which snap shut. The resulting 'click' reverberates through the air-filled sacs. It travels through the spermaceti and to yet another reverberation chamber in an organ against the skull, before being bounced forward, back through the junk and the spermaceti and amplified out into the ocean. It seems the whale may be able to change the shape of the spermaceti organ and the junk and so manipulate the power and direction of the clicks.

Scientists have recorded four different types of sperm whale 'click'. There are 'slow clicks' made by males, which are probably something to do with mating; 'long-range sensor clicks'; 'creaks' sounding a little like a squeaky door (these are probably to do with catching prey); and finally 'codas', a series of clicks related to social behaviour.

Sperm whale codas are fascinating. The whales live in different sonic 'clans' that can be separated by their use of distinct codas – patterns of clicks. A sonic clan can consist of thousands of non-related individuals, spread across huge areas of ocean. Scientists are calling these unique clan codas 'dialects'. Even more exciting is that the dialect clicks differ ever so slightly between individual whales and may act as unique identifiers to that individual. Sperm whales may use something akin to human names, which help tell one whale from another.

We are just beginning to decipher the morse code of sperm whales and it seems that their clicks give an insight into their social complexity. But their sound-making abilities aren't just limited to whale talk – they may have sonic superpowers. The whale's extraordinary skillset is due entirely to its incredible ecology. Sperm whales spend only about 20 per cent of their time on the surface. Their true habitat is the deep; diving down into the inky blackness to depths of 1,800 metres, they can stay below for over an hour on a single breath. For a deep-diving whale, its clicks act as like a torch-beam of sound. The clicks spread out across the ocean and bounce back off objects they hit, reflecting off canyons, walls and trenches to give the whale a sonic picture of the deep ocean. The whales also use their clicks to find and actively hunt for prey. Jumbo squid – 1.8 metres long and weighing up to 36 kilograms – are the whales' favourites. A single sperm whale can eat more than a tonne of squid in a day. The hard chitinous beaks and suckers of the squid make for perfect sonic targets, bouncing the squid's presence back to the whale with extraordinary accuracy. A sperm whale's 'searchlight' is so accurate, it can detect a 30 centimetre-long squid from more than one and a half kilometres away.

The sperm whale makes the loudest sound of any animal on Earth. At 230 decibels, nothing else really comes close. Human eardrums will burst at 150 decibels, so diving with sperm whales can be risky. There are reports of divers being 'buzzed' by clicking sperm whales becoming temporarily paralysed with one even losing the use of their limbs for a few hours. It may be that the whales, using the sound-amplifying organs in their outlandish giant heads, are able to focus and aim their powerful clicks to incapacitate their prey. The whales' mysterious life in the deep sea makes it hard to study the full repertoire of their sonic skills. So, for now, we can only guess at the true extent of their abilities. Not only is their morse code a complex social dialect, it's a deep-sea navigation device, a sonic torch for finding prey in the darkness and perhaps even a weapon, stunning their prey with blasts of sound.

Scan to hear the loudest sound of any animal.

While the sperm whale uses clicks as a clever functional tool, one whale has lifted its vocalisations into the realms of performance art.

Song of the seas

IMAGINE YOU ARE on the deck of a boat, far out at sea off the coast of Hawai'i. The ocean surface is still, without a breath of wind; a mirror to the blue sky. Suddenly there comes a 'pruuuf' of exhaled air, rising as a warm cloud above the water. You lean over the side of the boat, dropping your hydrophone in with a splash before pulling on your headphones to listen to the world below. The voices you can hear are extraordinary: a near endless array of mechanical clicks, deep rumbles, staccato grunts, squeaks, whistles and trills. Some of the deeper bass tones seem to vibrate through the hull of the boat itself, leaving your internal organs quivering. You are listening to the most incredible and complex sound in the ocean: the song of a humpback whale.

Scan to hear the song of a humpback whale.

Being made up of different phrases and refrains, the calls of male humpback whales are referred to as 'songs'. Scientists studying humpback vocalisations have discovered that each song is an ordered structure of stereotyped sounds. Individual sounds called 'units' are sung in a set order called a 'phrase'. Phrases are repeated multiple times in what is called a 'theme'. Different themes are sung in a set order, each with a distinct configuration, to complete the song.

During the winter months, male humpbacks gather in areas that whale scientists call arenas. Incredibly, all the males in the arena will sing exactly the same song. It's hard for scientists to know for sure just what is going on here as they can't easily follow the behaviour of individual whales underwater. For now, the exact purpose of the males' songs still remains a delightful mystery.

They perform only during the mating season, so most scientists think it's likely that their songs play some kind of a role in attracting females. It has been discovered that sexually immature males join in with the chorus, perhaps giving them an opportunity to learn the ropes. This has led to the theory that these singing arenas are all about the group performance, with the overall choir doing a job to attract females into the arena, to the benefit of all the males. But surprisingly there is little evidence to suggest that females respond directly to any individual male's song, so it's equally likely that the males are calling as a territorial warning to their rivals and that the arena is just one big singing competition to sort out a hierarchy among the bulls.

Some whale scientists have come up with alternative functions for the whales' songs, from a helpful sonic navigation aid, to an elaborate 'signature' whistle for individual identification, or even a bizarre competition between males to see who can hold their breath the longest. There are also very eminent whale biologists who rail against our need to add a biological 'purpose' to the whales' singing, suggesting that it points to a deeper cultural element of whale behaviour. Could it be that the whales are singing for their own pleasure? Whatever is behind these songs, one thing for sure is that they are unique among the whole animal kingdom.

The longest humpback song ever recorded went on for a marathon twenty-two hours. In the time it takes to listen to just one whale song, you could play half of the Rolling Stones' entire back catalogue! So, whatever their purpose, these ocean performers are certainly persistent. To sing, the males (measuring about fourteen metres long and weighing up to forty tonnes) hang motionless in the water, noses pointed down and with their long pectoral flippers outstretched. In some places it's thought that they use features of the sea floor, such as coral valleys or ocean canyons, to resonate their songs, making them louder.

Remarkably, each population of humpbacks has a uniquely different song. Scientists have recorded the whales introducing novel sounds and phrases that they have picked up from other males. Just like a pop song with a new riff or a catchy lyric, this new element is quickly learnt and spread throughout neighbouring whale populations. Chance encounters between individual whales from these different populations means phrases are passed on, adapted and incorporated into their old songs, in a combination of their two styles. In humans the musical equivalent of these cultural exchanges would be the Beatles travelling to India or Run DMC crossing paths with Aerosmith.

Scientists can now track these novel phrases as they pass across the ocean, spreading out to dominate the airwaves, just like an annoyingly catchy pop song. Phrases from songs of whales on the west coast of Australia have been recorded appearing in those of whales on the east coast. And from there, scientists have tracked them as they are passed across the ocean to other groups. Phrases that started near Perth have spread all the way to the islands of French Polynesia, 8,000 kilometres away.

This constant exchange and learning of complex new phrases isn't really seen in any other animal apart from humans. So, humpback whales have developed among the most complex and sophisticated of all animals' voices. And brand-new research has recently recorded a very different vocalisation that some scientists think might be unique to females. Compared to the elaborate songs of the males, these new calls are simpler, sounding like a deep buzzing. Called 'pulse trains', they are far lower in frequency than any other humpback call. It's been theorised that these deep beats have the right acoustic properties to cut across the more elaborate male songs. Perhaps they are the only way the females can be heard above the din of all the males showing off!

Humpback whales may vocalise for love, but they are also known to sing for their supper. They do so by manipulating sound in the most extraordinary of ways. Across June and July, in the seas of the Pacific Northwest, millions of herring gather in huge shoals. They are attracted by plankton blooms that are thick enough to turn the water green and the fish in turn are a draw for humpback whales. Having arrived at the end of their long migration from the Tropics and not eaten for five months, the whales are hungry. They search for the herring and as groups they will dive in synchrony to start the hunt. Scientists from the

Alaska Whale Foundation and the University of Alaska have fitted some of these whales with small onboard cameras and microphones, attached temporarily to the whales' backs with a suction cup. The footage from these onboard cameras has given them a revealing view of the hunting whales, almost as if they were riding the whales themselves. The humpbacks use furtive low 'grunts' to keep in touch and coordinate their fishing. They first position themselves below a shoal of herring, then the lead whale rises and begins to blow a stream of bubbles from his blowhole, exhaling in a single breath that can last for a minute. As the whale swims through the bubbles, beats from its powerful tail break up the bubbles making them smaller, so they hang in the water like a curtain surrounding the fish in a 'bubble net'. From above we can see that the bubbles form a beautiful spiral pattern. But new science suggests that only by listening underwater can we learn just how the wall of bubbles works.

The onboard microphones revealed that the lead whale as it rises then gives a unique high-pitched haunting wail, which bounces off the bubble curtain. One researcher has theorised that this hunting call is perfectly tuned to be caught in the spiral of rising bubbles and that it may also be powerful enough and at the right pitch to vibrate the air spaces within the herring, causing them a great deal of discomfort.

The bubble net could be an acoustic as well as a visual barrier, forming the perfect trap to corral the fish, herding them towards the surface. With a final rallying call from the leader, the whales close the trap, driving up to the surface to burst out among the cornered herring, their huge mouths agape so that each of them can swallow a tonne of fish a day. Living underwater, it's not unexpected that whales would use sound as a means to communicate, but it's more surprising that they might use that sound as a tool.

Popping shrimp and squeaking fish

I COULD SEE ALL the colours before I even got into the water. Our team were taking a pause on our quest to film minke whales, to dive at one of the most famous spots of the whole Great Barrier Reef. Pixie Pinnacle is a 30 metre-tall, 15 metre-wide tower (or bommie) of coral that rears up from the ocean floor among the chain of remote outer reefs known as the Ribbon Reefs.

The others in my team were diving but, being an underwater rookie, I had to make do with just a mask, snorkel and fins. Slipping off the back of the boat into the warm water was always a bit awkward, especially getting used to wearing fins, and I achieved the transition with all the grace of a circus clown on a ladder. Once in the water it was like I had descended into a dream. The pinnacle appeared out of the depths, sweeping upwards out of the blue before stopping just a metre or two from the surface. I couldn't see the bottom of the tower as it vanished, dematerialising into fathomless cobalt, giving the sensation that the whole structure was just tonnes of rock floating in space. The waters were calm and clear, protected by the nearby Ribbon Reef No. 10, so the visibility was amazing. As I kicked my way over to the top of the bommie I could see it was covered with soft corals, sponges, gorgonians and delicate tube worms of pink, mauve and brown. This was a fantasy coral garden and home to an endless variety of fish. I spotted clown fish bustling about in their anemones, pulsing clouds of gaudy purple fairy and orange basslets darted back and forth, anxious not to drift too far from the coral. There were parrot fish biting lumps from the reef with their horny lips and, drawn in from the ocean, circling a short swim out into the blue, huge shoals of scissortail fusiliers dazzled electric blue in the sunlight. It was a sight so beautiful it literally took my breath away and I sucked a lungful of seawater into the snorkel. Snot streaming and choking, I panicked my way back to the surface to thrash around and get my act together.

A little embarrassed, I finally returned underwater and swam in a gentle circle around the bommie. The way the shoals of yellow snapper parted to let me pass allowed me to imagine I was some sleek oceanic shark, rather than a clumsy sunburnt landlubber. While snorkelling at Pixie Pinnacle revealed colour, abundance and wonder on a scale I could never forget, all my memories were visual ones. All that time underwater and I heard nothing beyond the gurgling of the sea.

Of course, our ears aren't designed to work well in the ocean. As sound travels differently through a liquid medium, it can be harder for our ears to pinpoint the direction of any sound and things end up being muffled. Underwater sound travels faster, so the time lag between our left and right ears picking up the noise is reduced and this means we struggle to work out where the sound is coming from. Back on land, sound travels through the air and into our ears, where tiny hairs pick up the vibrations and convert them to electrical signals. Plunge this system underwater and it simply can't process the sounds so effectively. But tune in to the underwater world with specialist microphones and the brightly coloured reef suddenly buzzes with secret sound.

Tropical reefs across the world are pulsating with clicks, pops, honks and groans from fish, with sounds as varied as the fish are coloured. These sounds play an important role in reproduction, defending a territory and feeding. On the reef, there are dusk and dawn choruses just like you hear with birds on the land, and when darkness falls over the reef, gangs of predatory groupers use 'foghorn' calls to stay together as they hunt.

New hydrophone arrays, combined with underwater filming, allow recorded sound to be referenced against footage, so biologists can now work out the direction a sound came from and attribute it to an individual fish or species. This is allowing us to better interpret fish behaviour and is leading to a more detailed understanding of life beneath the waves.

The ambon damsel is a pretty little yellow fish, about nine centimetres long, found across the Western Pacific including on the Barrier Reef. They are known to have an equally colourful sex life. A male will guard over a nest site on a patch of sand and try to attract several females to join him. Juvenile ambon damsels have a prominent eyespot on their dorsal fin, which usually disappears when they reach sexual maturity. But some mature males play cheat and retain their eyespot, allowing them to sneak into another male's territory and mate with the females. These fish are also known to change sex entirely, starting out as females then sometimes changing into males to gain a reproductive advantage.

Several species of damsel fish are known to make sound. They produce pulsing 'pops' when males snap their jaws shut and longer 'chirps' where these pulses are joined together. But researchers from the University of Liège recording at a reef in Taiwan captured a new sound. These Taiwanese ambon males were making a strange delicate warble, a bit like a cuckoo but with a 'rubberier' quality. They compared it to a squeaking windshield wiper on a dry windscreen. The male ambons made the call during courtship with females or territorial chases with other males. Having never recorded the call before it seemed it was new and the researchers speculated that on a noisy reef, where lots of fish are making all kinds of racket, a new – more distinct – call might help the damsels stand out from the crowd and make it easier to identify their own species.

Many fish make sounds using specialist muscles, called 'sonic' muscles, that are attached to the fish's swim bladder (an air-filled sac that helps the fish stay buoyant). These muscles are the fastest-contracting muscles in the vertebrate world, squeezing and relaxing at frequencies above 100 hertz and up to 400 hertz without the muscles succumbing to a state of permanent contraction. The muscles pull on the swim bladder, beating it like a drum, and the air-filled chamber resonates, amplifying the sound. But the frequency of the ambon damsel's squeaky windscreen wiper is a staggering 645 hertz, so way beyond what a muscle contraction could achieve, meaning the small fish are generating the sound in a way that has yet to be discovered.

The ambon damsel's new call seems to be spreading and is now heard on the Great Barrier Reef. A little like the songs of a humpback, perhaps fish can learn to make new sounds that may spread socially through the population and then across oceans.

Scan to hear the call of ambon damsel fish.

Fish sounds have been recorded all across the ocean and not just on tropical reefs. On the coarse sand flats of the North Atlantic's Dogger Bank in spring, a strange rumbling and grunting sound can be heard running through the cold water.

This is the 'drumming' of the North Atlantic cod. Males have gathered together to compete for females. They make their drumming sound by vibrating their muscles against their swim bladders and the sound acts as both a challenge to rival males and to attract female cod. Should a female appear, a male cod will escort her as she swims through his patch. She will settle on the sea floor and the male will dance around her, flicking his fins to impress her. Then if all goes well, the male cod will begin his drum solo. It's been discovered that males with larger drumming muscles have more offspring, which would suggest that his drumming is an important factor for females looking to choose a mate. To seal the deal, the female will swim up off the sea floor and the male will chase her and turn his belly to hers, their anal fins locked together. They will 'hum' at each other, which may help synchronise the release of her eggs and his sperm. The lucky male will get to fertilise about 90 per cent of the female's eggs, but the other 10 per cent escapes into the water and these eggs are up for grabs for any other male in the area. Tails beating frantically, they will rush in and release their sperm for the chance to fertilise the last few remaining eggs. In places, spawning fish make such a hullabaloo that the sound can be heard inland by people in coastal towns. In 2021 the residents of a neighbourhood in Tampa, Florida, were so bothered by a loud humming, that they started a GoFundMe campaign to investigate the source. The mysterious sound was reported by households living up to a kilometre inland. Some believed the sound to be from a secret military base under the sea; others thought it was likely the noise from 'rave' parties on yachts anchored off the coast. But it was a local marine biologist armed with a hydrophone that discovered the hum came from mating shoals of black drum fish, the males making a low frequency hum to attract female fish to their spawning sites.

The sounds made by fish can be heard right throughout the ocean, but there is one small marine animal that generates a sound that is so ubiquitous, it has been called the signature sound of life on planet Earth itself. Lower a hydrophone into shallow tropical seas almost anywhere in the world and you are likely to hear a background undercurrent of sizzling bacon. The source of this crackling is countless tiny 'pistol' or snapping shrimp. Growing around three to five centimetres long, there are over a thousand species of these crustaceans inhabiting the reefs, sand flats and sea-grass meadows of our tropical seas. The continuous popping sound they make is so dominant that it has been known to interfere with our sonar and fish finders.

Research has shown that whales and dolphins might even rely on the shrimp's constant symphony as a navigational tool to orientate themselves with the coastline. Each individual shrimp has one giant claw that can be more than half the length of its body so it looks like it's wearing an oversized boxing glove. The pincers on this claw have become modified so that one half – the hammer – can be cocked back to a right angle that when released snaps shut with huge energy. The pincer's other claw contains a small cavity and when the pincers snap shut, the seawater within it is violently forced outwards at speeds of around 145 kilometres per hour. This high-speed jet is enough to tear apart the water, leaving a sort of vacuum and creating a bubble of air. The air bubble is immediately under huge pressure from the surrounding ocean and collapses in a millisecond. This happens with enough energy to create light and heat equivalent to 4,700 degrees Celsius. That's four times hotter than lava and almost as hot as the surface of the sun (5,500 degrees Celsius). The 'popping' sound is made by the collapsing bubble and not when the two pincers snap together. It's probably the second loudest sound in the ocean, with the snap of a tiger pistol shrimp reaching 210 decibels.

The shock waves from this bullet of sound are enough to stun small fish or other shrimp, damaging their brains, eyes and gills and leaving them prone as easy prey. Recent research has discovered that the pistol shrimp themselves have developed specialist protective headgear to survive their own high-pressure attacks. The shrimp has armour on its head, called an orbital hood, which reduces the pressure released by the snap on its own brain by nearly half. When the shrimp snaps, water is redirected out of the head through small holes just below the eyes and this repels the shock wave coming from the snap, helping to protect the shrimp's brain. The shrimp's sonic snap is so potent that not even Kevlar will stop it, so physicists are excited to explore the potential anti-ballistic properties of this natural safety helmet.

For the shrimp, their powerful snap isn't just a weapon. It's thought that it's also used as a warning to deter other shrimp entering their burrows and defend their territories. But recently scientists listening in have discovered that, hidden in the shrimp's constant snapping, there might also be a warning for humans. Researchers from Woods Hole Oceanographic Institution have discovered that shrimp off the coast of North Carolina increase both the volume and the frequency of their snapping when the water gets warmer. They found that for every degree Celsius rise in seawater temperature, the shrimp's snapping would increase by one to two decibels and snapping frequency would increase by fifteen to sixty per cent. Could even louder snapping affect the shrimp's own behaviour, or even have a negative influence on other animals sharing the reef? It's too soon to say, but listening in to the pistol shrimp could give us clues about the location and level of rising sea temperatures. The presence of the 'crackling bacon' sound of shrimp on a tropical reef has long been a sign that the reef is healthy and full of life, but these days it might also be an alarm bell for our warming oceans.

Scan to hear the 'sizzling bacon' sound of snapping shrimp.

Having completed our filming with the minke whales, we were on our way back to Port Douglas, when we stopped at the world-famous Opal Reef. I was keen for the crew to get some shots of the amazing coral gardens there. They had featured in the BBC TV documentary series *Blue Planet II*, with gorgeous drifting shots of near endless colour and vivid fish. I wanted some of that magic for my own film, so our skipper anchored the boat and the crew suited up and fitted the camera in its special pressurised waterproof housing, ready for some filming. As I passed the heavy camera off the back of the boat to the team in the water and they disappeared below, I was kicking myself that I hadn't yet got around to learning to dive. Our skipper made me a bacon sandwich and I sat watching the water and waiting. Perhaps growing bored of my sulking, he encouraged me to go for a snorkel, telling me cryptically with a broad grin that I would get to meet 'Angus'.

As I slipped (quite literally) off the end of the diving deck and into the water with a splash, I was suddenly face to face with an enormous fish. About two metres long and probably weighing close to 200 kilograms, this was Angus, a humphead Māori wrasse. His skin was a remarkable patchwork of blues and greens and his beady eyes swivelled to look at me. He lived up to his name, sporting a huge lump on his forehead that was speckled with bright green spots, and his thick rubbery lips gave him a rather doleful expression. Angus seemed very curious and was known to be friendly to snorkellers; perhaps hoping for a handout of galley morsels, he came right up close. The whole experience was wonderfully unnerving. You don't really expect fish to be so big and so friendly, and at times I felt as if I was meeting a pet Labrador rather than a wild animal. But I didn't have him to myself for long and as another boat pulled up, he swam over to see if there were any new humans to meet.

With Angus gone, I decided to kick over the coral and explore a little, hoping for a repeat of the amazing experience I had swimming at Pixie's Pinnacle. But it soon became clear that the reef here was very different. The coral seemed grey-brown and there were fewer fish to be seen. It was like someone had switched the TV from colour to black-and-white, so startling was the lack of hue. As

I swam on, I could see here and there splashes of colour from living corals that stood out from the rest of the reef, but most of the coral seemed almost dead and many were crumbling away. Heading back to the boat, Angus approached once more and I felt sorry for what had happened to his home.

When the crew joined me onboard, their faces said it all. The magical coral gardens we had come to film were ruined and I could see the sadness in the eyes of our marine biologist, who had grown up on the reef. We sat in stunned silence as the skipper pulled up the anchor and we turned about, leaving Angus and his dying reef as we headed back to port.

The famous coral gardens at Opal Reef were first badly hit by coral bleaching the year before my visit in 2017 and have since been bleached again in five separate years. Bleaching occurs when water temperatures rise a few degrees above the 'just right' figure of 26–27 degrees Celsius. Corals get their amazing colours from zooxanthellae or 'zooks', tiny organisms that live in the tissues of the coral polyps – the colonial animals that make up the structure of the reef. The onboard zooks convert energy from the sun to make food, but their relationship with the coral polyps is a sensitive one. With even small increases in temperature, the zooks begin to make toxic chemicals that the corals cannot handle and they begin to expel them. I once watched this aghast in a research laboratory at the University of Brisbane as corals in tanks exposed to warm water jettisoned their tiny zooks in clouds of inky colour released into the water. Without the zooks, the corals can survive for a few weeks, but if the warming of the water is prolonged, they eventually will die.

The latest bleaching event on the the Great Barrier Reef occurred early in 2024 and was so bad that marine biologists have called it 'catastrophic'. A study by the Australian Institute of Marine Science observed that one section of the reef near Lizard Island experienced the largest annual decline in hard coral cover in thirty-nine years, with more than a third of hard corals lost. The University of Sydney's

Great Barrier Reef research station at One Tree Island discovered that in February 2024 66 per cent of their monitored corals were bleached. By April this had escalated to 80 per cent, and by July 44 per cent of those corals had died. One species of the beautiful Acropora coral had experienced an astonishing 95 per cent mortality in just a few short months.

The effects of coral bleaching and coral loss on the animals that depend on the reef, from the snapping shrimp to the minke whales, is worrying. We know that climate change (alongside other factors such as cyclones and water pollution) is changing the levels of biodiversity all along the reef. Even the fish are adversely affected. One study from James Cook University found that bleaching was a major factor affecting the survival rates of young wrasse. Perhaps we will be less likely to see fish like Angus in the future.

Carefully listening in on coral reefs can help give scientists a gauge on how warmer seas might be affecting biodiversity. They can record which species are present and if any suddenly disappear from the soundscape. Some fish are thought of as keystone species and their presence is important to keep the reef functioning. Parrot fish, for example, act as gardeners, grazing on algae that might overwhelm the corals, while triggerfish are important predators that keep populations of sea urchins in check. By listening to the reef, conservationists can keep tabs on its health and vitality and record any species declines. But sound might even play a part in helping reefs recover. Scientists working in the seas off the US Virgin Islands in the Caribbean discovered that coral larvae – the free-floating miniature 'baby' coral – were up to seven times more likely to settle at a degraded reef where the scientists were broadcasting recordings of sounds from a healthy reef. While such research gives hope that we might one day rebuild the world's coral reefs, any concrete expectation of their recovery depends on our ability to reverse the rise in ocean temperatures.

Fuelled by climate change, 2024 saw ocean temperatures rise to record highs. Analysis of the EU's Copernicus climate service observed that the world's oceans broke temperature records every single day. The first five months of 2024 alone shattered the existing records for that time of year by the largest margin seen since satellite analysis began. Time is running out. It is essential we reverse this rise in water temperatures, if future generations are to hear the amazing pops, clicks and whistles of a coral reef to swim with giant fish or even make friends with a whale.

New frontiers

SOMETIMES THE WORLD can feel like it's getting smaller. Our technology closes the gaps between continents, compresses time zones and can reduce our exposure to wild places to short video clips on social media and in nature documentaries. But if there is one great mystery, one last wild frontier here on Earth, it has to be the deep sea. More people have left our planet and journeyed into space than have explored the depths of the ocean. The deep sea is the largest habitat on Earth. It makes up about 90 per cent of our planet's available space for life. Our knowledge of this great wilderness is growing, but we have only just begun to shed light on the ocean depths, with just one per cent of the deep sea having been properly explored.

As sound travels further and faster underwater, recordings of the deep ocean are one of the best ways to 'explore' the remaining ninety-nine per cent. Acoustic exploration began as early as 1917 when scientists used a contraption called a Fessenden oscillator to reflect sound signals off icebergs and the bottom of the ocean. Since then, the number of remote deep-sea microphones, positioned by both governments and independent scientists, has multiplied and what they have recorded has dramatically changed our understanding of life in the depths. The common perception of the deep sea is that it is a barren void of endless darkness and silence. But the recordings from these remote acoustic monitoring stations have been revelatory. The deep ocean is alive with constant noise and is a surprisingly rich soundscape. From the snapping of benthic worms to the deep thud of a dead whale coming to rest on the ocean floor, these sounds of the deep sea are some of the weirdest to ever be heard.

The sources for many of these strange sounds remain unidentified to this day, which of course has led to plenty of speculation both by scientists and conspiracy theorists online. The most famous of these mystery recordings was captured in 1997 by US National Oceanic and Atmospheric Administration (NOAA) and originated from a location in the southern Pacific Ocean. The sound was picked up by NOAA's remote hydrophone network using US Navy technology originally designed to detect Soviet submarines. The mysterious sound became known as the 'Bloop'. There have been many colourful theories about what's behind this strange sound, from mermaids to alien spacecraft and everything in between. One thing we do know is that it is very loud, having been picked up by hydrophones across a range of over 5,000 kilometres. NOAA now thinks the sound could be what they call 'cryoseisms' or icequakes. These are the large-scale movements of ice that occur when huge frozen chunks calve off glaciers, becoming icebergs which, driven by currents, then go on to gouge at the sea floor.

Scan to hear the mysterious 'Bloop'.

Another mysterious deep-sea sound recording, which first generated headlines in 1989, is that of the 52-hertz whale, also called the 'loneliest whale' in the ocean. Recorded by scientists from the Woods Hole Oceanographic Institution, the sound resembles the call of other whale species, but differs in its frequency. Blue whales commonly call in a frequency range of 10–40 hertz and fin whales at around 20 hertz. The voice of the 52-hertz whale is higher in pitch than these other whales and is just a little higher than the lowest note on a double bass.

As far as we know, no one has ever seen this whale and we only know of its existence through these mysterious sound recordings. It's possible therefore that it is an entirely new species, either one individual of many that are yet to be discovered, or even the last and only representative of its kind. By tracking the recordings, scientists have been able to plot a migration route for the whale. It is detected in the Pacific Ocean every year between August and December but moves out of range of hydrophones in January and February. It's been traced as far north as the Aleutian Islands in the North Pacific and as far south as the California coast and can cover up to 70 kilometres a day. Its migration route is somewhat similar to blue whales but the seasonal timing of a fin whale's journey, has lead to speculation it could be a hybrid species. Over the years, the whale's call has slightly deepened to 50 hertz, suggesting the whale has grown and matured.

Not everyone agrees with the idea that the whale is isolated in its ability to communicate, as blue whales would still likely have the ability to hear 52's signals. And in 2010, sensors off the coast of California picked up calls that matched the mystery voice but occurred across a wide area, leaving scientists to speculate that there may be multiple animals calling. Maybe the 52-hertz whale isn't so lonely after all.

Scan to hear the 52-hertz whale.

The final, and perhaps most sinister, mystery sound of the deep sea is known as the 'Upsweep'. It's worth saying that if you are reading this in bed, now is probably not the best time to listen to this sound, especially if you want to avoid nightmares. It's been described as the 'choral choir from hell' and has a deeply disturbing quality that puts your senses on edge. This is probably why some online speculators and comic horror fans have suggested it's the voice of Cthulhu, the giant squid-headed being that haunts the ocean in H. P. Lovecraft's sci-fi stories. Thankfully the scientists at NOAA offer us some comforting reassurance. Having analysed the recordings, they tracked the source to the Pacific Ocean somewhere between Aotearoa New Zealand and South America and have theorised that it comes from underwater volcanic activity. Whether they cause intrigue or horror, it's exciting to think that these deep-sea recordings are some of the last natural sounds on the planet ever to have reached our human ears.

Scan to hear the startling 'Upsweep'.

Drowning in noise

LOOKING OUT OF the helicopter window, I could barely believe that the landscape was real. The coastline to our left stretched northwards to the horizon, a jawline of jagged icy teeth rising out of the sea. Drifting on a dark ocean speckled with rafts of shining white, a pristine iceberg passed by just centimetres below us, its immense fluted turrets indifferent to our tiny presence. It was a landscape wholly suitable for the quest to find a mythical creature. We had travelled to Canada's Baffin Island to film the unicorn of the Arctic – the narwhal.

Every summer, the frozen seas of Baffin Bay – the 689,000 square kilometres of ocean between Baffin Island and Greenland – slowly begin to melt. Driven by wind and currents, the frozen surface starts to split. Giant cracks called 'leads' appear in the ice and these provide a pathway north for Arctic whales. Belugas, bowheads and narwhals all migrate north hoping to feed in the rich waters opened up by the retreating ice. We would be trying to film this migration from the air, something nobody had successfully attempted before.

Our expedition was truly epic in scope. To reach the far north of Baffin Island and film the narwhals' journey, we had chartered the nearest available helicopter. This just happened to be based out of the small isolated tundra village of Kuujjuaq in northern Quebec, 1,500 kilometres south of our destination. Our flight north would take several days and follow the dramatic spine of fjords and mountains along Baffin's eastern coastline.

In the days before the proliferation of drones, if you wanted to film wildlife from the air, your best bet was to use a helicopter. Mounted on the front of our sleek black chopper was a gimbal camera, a digital camera with a powerful zoom lens, suspended in a gyro-stabilised cradle, which allowed you to zoom in but keep the camera perfectly steady. The addition of gimbal cameras had revolutionised wildlife filmmaking, allowing you to shoot close-ups of the animals while being far enough away to not disturb them. Our crew numbered four. Me, sitting next to the pilot in the front; our camera gimbal operator and a helicopter engineer sitting in the back. With our survival jumpsuits, aviator shades and headsets, this was as *Top Gun* as a zoology nerd was ever likely to get. But despite looking the part, it had taken my stomach a few days to get used to the helicopter's dips and bounces.

Our aerial journey along the coastline of Baffin Island had been an adventurous one. On our first attempted crossing over Cumberland Sound, we had run into a thick fog bank that swallowed us up. With the sea below us partly frozen, it created an alarming white-out and our pilot had to make an abrupt and stomach-churning turn to find a way back out. Towering icebergs would emerge suddenly out of the fog, making us nervous. We had been stranded for several days in Baffin Island's capital of Iqaluit and forced to wait out low cloud and high winds that had grounded all the flights.

Finally airborne, we had seen lonely polar bears wandering far out on the sea ice and giant bowhead whales ploughing northwards, their huge heads shattering the thinning ice with every stolen breath. Ponds of open water gave shelter to flocks of eider ducks that left glinting V-shaped wakes as they kicked their webbed feet and skittered across the surface.

We had to stop to refuel at occasional outposts along the way. I was always surprised when these small Inuit communities suddenly emerged out of the wilderness, their colourful houses clustered on a peninsula or hugging the curve of a bay. At one settlement our hopes of refuelling were thwarted when my BBC credit card was declined! Apparently, I owed £1.50 from the previous month's spending that hadn't been cleared and it was enough to bring the whole epic endeavour to its knees. We were stuck nearly 300 kilometres from the nearest settlement with no roads or alternatives to travel on. I wandered along the local beachfront to see if I could sort out the problem. Trying to reach the card company on the satellite phone, listening to their vapid hold music while strolling between icebergs the size of garden sheds, was all oddly surreal. I had just got through to customer services, when a waving local came over and told me not to walk any further, reminding me, 'There's polar bears here, you know.'

Back in the air, we finally left all the bad weather behind us and our journey took us through some of the most incredible scenery and a world beyond imagination. We passed over Kangiqtualuk Uqquqti – formerly known as Sam Ford Fjord, a vertical wonderland of sheer honey-coloured rock that plummets straight down 1,300 metres into the frozen sea. We soared over peaks unnamed that seemed to defy gravity and followed the path of enormous curving glaciers that spilled down from high on the island, before finally reaching the sea. As we travelled north the weather that had so hindered our progress improved beyond all hope. Up here, north of the Arctic Circle, the polar summer meant we had twenty-four hours of continuous daylight every day. With the weather so good, we had arrived in a land where the sun never leaves the sky.

Having flown for seven days we finally made it to our destination, the small town of Pond Inlet. Pond sits on the northern shore of Baffin. It's separated from the icy mountain wall of Bylot Island by a 25 kilometre-wide stretch of water known as Eclipse Sound. It was July and the water of the sound was still frozen solid, but it was starting to thaw and we could see its surface was dappled with ponds of bright turquoise meltwater.

Eclipse Sound is a good place for narwhals. They gather at the southern mouth of the sound where the remaining ice meets the open water. Called the 'floe edge', this is where the whales wait for the ice to split, so they can follow the leads deep into the sound. At the northern edge of the sound was another floe edge where the ice met the waters of Navy Board Inlet. It was here that we had a second crew out trying to film the narwhals. The sea ice had been home for three weeks to our dive crew, who had been working with a family of Inuit guides based in Pond. They had been camping close to the ice and each day headed out to try and find the narwhals. Driving their snow machines while pulling wooden sledges (komatiks) to carry their dive gear, they had been looking for leads in the hope of getting in the water with the whales. So far, they had found it really challenging. Glimpses of the whales seemed few and far between and the animals were very sensitive to the slightest movements on the ice and never came close. As part of the Indigenous community's traditional hunting rights, a quota of one hundred narwhals are shot each year, although many more of them bear the scars of bullets across their backs. Perhaps this had made them super-sensitive to the vibrations of snow machines above them on the ice, but our dive team hadn't been able to get close. They had, however, had more success recording the narwhals' calls. Using a hydrophone lowered into holes in the ice they had captured a beautiful coda of clicks and eerie whistles that were made by the whales.

Researchers in Greenland, using hydrophones dropped from boats and onboard acoustic tags fitted directly onto the narwhals, have discovered that these whales make three distinct types of sounds. The first are whistling calls. These seem to have a social purpose, being used to maintain contact between a mother and a calf, or between pod members. Researchers that listened to 22,000 narwhal whistle recordings have even suggested that these calls may contain elements that are unique to individual narwhals and could be an identifying signature of the individual. More research is required, with evidence from other narwhal populations needed to be sure, but it could be that narwhals have signature whistles just like we also see in dolphins.

Narwhals also 'click'. They are masters of echolocation and can make more than a thousand clicks in a single second. They have poor eyesight and, just like the sperm whale, they dive deep to feed and use these clicks as a 'torch beam' of sound that allows them to build a picture of their underwater world. It's a vital skill when they are diving 1,800 metres to hunt for Greenland halibut, or for finding breathing holes beneath the sea-ice ceiling. The narwhals' rate of clicking will increase as they get nearer to their prey, becoming 'buzzes' that give the whale a more detailed sound 'image' and allow them to be more accurate.

Scan to hear the whistles, clicks and buzzes of a narwhal.

With the ice on Eclipse Sound now melting, it became dangerous for the dive crew to continue their mission and if we were to get any shots of the narwhal migration, it would have to be from the helicopter. Thankfully, from our very first flight out to the floe edge we could see the whales, gathered at the icy frontier and starting to follow the leads into the sound. Being able to cover distance so quickly in the helicopter made the search easier; we could hover high up above them and with our powerful gimbal camera zoom in to shoot without ever disturbing them.

From above, the leads zigzagged across the ice, intersecting, splitting and forming false pathways and dead-ends like a maze. Groups of narwhals – between ten and twenty animals at a time – would head into the leads, keeping their three-metre tusks just below the surface as they swam through the blue-green water. From above we could see them in incredible detail. As they surfaced, the sun would hit their grey mottled backs, their skin being the feature from which they earned their old Norse name. Narwhal means 'corpse whale' and the sailors of old named them this as the hues of their patchwork skin reminded the mariners of the colour of any dead and rotting sailors they found in the water. I could see the spiral of their tusks as they erupted from their upper lip, their left canine grown to extremes, the most remarkable tooth in the natural world. There were tuskless females in the group and smaller olive-coloured calves. As the whales journeyed on with great sweeps of their tails you could see their flukes were scalloped with convex lobes like a gingko leaf. We even saw a few short moments of 'tusking' behaviour, where the male narwhals rub their tusks together in a ritual that looks like a sword fight. As a way of finding the narwhals, Inuit hunters know to listen out for the sound of this jousting, just like two wooden sticks being beaten together.

At one point the highway through the ice closed to a dead end and the whales dived, only to surface again a while later to take a breath. We flew on over the more solid ice and here found a tiny hole, the size of a garden pond. To our wonder and surprise a narwhal suddenly surfaced and it became clear that the whales were using the hole as a breathing stop as they explored the ice, looking for new ways to move beyond the barrier. Up high in the sky, with the fierce sun bouncing up off the ice, it was hard to imagine the narwhal's underwater home. With its icy ceiling, theirs is a world of total darkness in the winter and at best dimly lit gloom in the summer. That they could take a deep breath (a narwhal can dive for twenty-five minutes without coming up for air) and head out under the ice with the confidence to find another small breathing hole, says much about their sonic abilities. But, as for so many whales in today's oceans, their soundscape is rapidly changing.

Scientists using acoustic tags to monitor narwhals have seen that their feeding 'buzzes' were reduced by 50 per cent when human boats made sounds up to 12 kilometres from the narwhal, and that their buzzing stopped completely when those sounds were made 7–8 kilometres away. The study found that the whales avoided deep dives (over 350 metres) and stayed at the surface when exposed to shipping noise. The whales also reduced or stopped entirely their social 'whistles' when human sound was present. And one study showed that ships producing seismic pulses from air guns (used by oil and gas companies to explore the ocean floor) triggered a change in the whales' heart rate, even as the whales swam quickly to get away. They observed increased changes in the narwhals' breathing rate and the beating of their tail flukes as the stressed whales tried to escape. It seems that the sound of a single passing ship might be enough trigger stress in a whale as it swims below. With the dramatic growth in Arctic shipping, as climate change opens up the once frozen sounds to trade and exploration, it's likely that this impact will only increase.

In 1991 a conglomerate of marine scientists led by the Scripps Institution of Oceanography conducted an experiment. They wanted to discover just how far sound could travel underwater, through our oceans. They took a research vessel out into the wild southern Indian Ocean and there, off the coast of remote Heard Island, they lowered ten acoustic sources 300 metres into the water and began to make a series of very loud sounds (each roughly equivalent to a thrusting jet engine). All across the world's oceans were a fleet of other research vessels that had deployed hydrophones to listen for the sound. The sound was made to a repeatable pattern so it would be easily identified by those listening. Incredibly, it was picked up by vessels listening out as far away as Nova Scotia on North America's Atlantic coast and Washington State on the continent's Pacific coastline. The listening station at Whidbey in Washington State first picked up the signal three and a half hours after it had started, meaning the sound from Heard had travelled 18,000 kilometres through the ocean. This remarkable experiment proved two things.

Firstly, that sound can travel a very long way underwater, and secondly, that humans are the noisiest animals on Earth.

Just over 200 years ago in the era before industrialisation, the ocean would have sounded very different than it does today. There would have been whale song, the sounds of spawning fish, the popping of shrimp on the coral reef, the sounds of storms, icebergs calving and deep-sea volcanic eruptions. But today, this most vibrant of natural soundscapes is being crushed under the increasingly forceful uproar of man-made sounds.

Today's oceans are crowded with ships and boats thanks to the fact that 90 per cent of all global trade is transported by sea. Between 1990 and 2021, the volume of cargo transported by ships more than doubled, from 4 to nearly 11 billion tonnes. In 2023 the United Nations reported that the global merchant fleet numbered some 106,000 ships. About 5,600 of these vessels are huge container ships. Up to 400 metres long, if you stood one on end it would dwarf London's tallest building by 90 metres. Each of these behemoths can carry 24,000 cargo containers, with the combined capacity to move, for instance, 115 million pairs of shoes or 37,000 cars in just one trip.

A single large container ship will make about ten to twelve ocean voyages a year. So, in total, giant container ships alone make somewhere between 56,000 and 67,200 journeys across the ocean every year. Each one of these enormous ships makes a lot of noise. The ships' engines are anchored to the frame of the boat, so when they vibrate, the metal hull and the spaces within resonate, just like the swim bladder in a fish, making the sound louder. As well as this, the rotating propellers create millions of bubbles that cavitate (collapse) just like the bubbles created by snapping pistol shrimp, adding to the noise. This means that every container ship crossing the ocean, rammed with new trainers, flat-packed furniture and cucumbers, will be making 190 decibels of noise. To put that into context, each ship is making a noise as loud as the call of a blue whale, although each vessel makes noise constantly and there are many more ships than there are blue whales.

Whales and dolphins are reliant on sound to communicate with friends and family, compete with rivals, search for food and navigate through the water. The fact that they 'hear' their world in the way that we 'see' ours means it's hard for us to grasp the impact that the noise pollution from all this boat traffic has on them.

The North Atlantic right whale is known for its docile nature, its slowness and its tendency to feed in shallow coastal waters. Its body has a thick layer of insulating blubber, meaning it floats when dead and produces a high yield of whale oil. All these factors mean that, for historic whalers, this species was the 'right' whale to hunt and the name stuck. These 16 metre-long gentle giants were so easy to catch that you could do so with just a wooden rowboat and a hand-held harpoon. By the early 1890s tens of thousands of these whales are thought to have died on the end of a whaler's harpoon. With only a hundred individuals left alive, hunting was banned in 1937, but even after the threat of whaling disappeared, the whales were still in trouble.

Unlike their southern right whale cousins whose populations are bouncing back after whaling, the northern whales are classed as 'critically endangered' with only 366 remaining. So why haven't the northern whales experienced the same recovery as their southern relatives? The answer would appear to be that there is much more shipping in the northern ocean than is seen in the south. Between 1970 and October 2006 humans were responsible for 48 per cent of all northern right whale deaths. Getting entangled in fishing gear is one problem, but by far the biggest threat is from accidental collision with ships, which caused a staggering 37 per cent of all deaths. And a scientific study in 2011 discovered that it wasn't just collisions threatening the whales. International shipping lanes pass right through some of the whales' prime habitat in the Bay of Fundy and this creates a lot of noise. By collecting faecal samples from right whales and analysing them for hormones, scientists could see that the whales were experiencing a high level of stress. The link with shipping became more apparent in the period after 9/11. With the world gripped by heightened security, there was a marked reduction in shipping traffic through the area. The researchers measured a 6 decibel reduction in shipping noise during the period post 9/11 and analysis of the whale excrement from this time also found a decline in stress hormones for whales. So, it would seem that shipping is causing high levels of stress for northern right whales.

Imagine being a mother right whale nursing a calf, only for a ship to pass creating so much noise you struggle to stay in touch with other whales. It's so loud, you can no longer find your bearings or even stay connected to your baby and it becomes lost. It's not hard to see how this could be stressful.

Having somehow managed to survive the relentless slaughter of industrial whaling, these ocean giants seem to have gone out of the frying pan and into the fire. As they rely on sound as the primary way to experience their ocean world, all this noise pollution is now a major threat to their future survival. A blue whale's hearing is likely so acute that it is thought to be able to hear a ship coming towards them when it's still twenty-four hours away. Orcas in the Salish Sea are having to increase the amplitude of their calls and 'shout louder' to be heard, and the noise from ships has been proven to affect their hunting efficiency. North Atlantic right whales lose 80 per cent of their ability to hear other whales when a ship passes by them. Mass strandings of whales in the Bahamas have been linked to brain injuries caused by navy sonar sweeps, and seismic prospecting for oil creates a sound so invasive that it's proven to harm the hearing of marine mammals.

With the oceans full of overwhelming human noise, whales can become disorientated and collisions with ships are becoming more frequent. Along the west coast of America there can be more than eighty whales – fin, humpback and blues – killed by collisions with ships every year. But there are actions we can take to make ourselves quieter. New ships with more efficient engines create much less noise and analysis of ocean-going container ships reports that when they arrive at port, they often have to wait up to three days just to unload. So why the rush to get there? If they slowed their voyages down, they would make less damaging noise, be less likely to have a negative impact on any marine life and save money on fuel. And with emissions of greenhouse gases from global shipping up 20 per cent in the last decade, there is another strong argument to take things just that bit slower.

On the way home from our narwhal adventure, our pilot crossed over the frozen waters of Cumberland Sound on the southern end of Canada's Baffin Island. We had refuelled the chopper in Pangnirtung, a small outpost of 1,500 people far beyond the reach of any road network. Ahead we needed to cross the sound to reach the next peninsula of land, where we would find the island's capital of Iqaluit. It was late in July and the sea ice had largely broken up, but here in the sound it had drifted back in again and the broken chunks had refrozen into a jumbled pile. As we headed out over the sound, far below the helicopter and among the relentless blinding whiteness, I suddenly spotted a flash of black. I looked again and could see a patch of blue open ocean, about the size of a tennis court, hemmed in by the ice. A huge black shape burst out of the water, like smoke from a sudden volcanic explosion. It twisted in the air and landed with an almighty splash. It was a bowhead whale.

These Arctic giants are the largest whales to travel to the far north. Relative to their body size, bowheads are believed to be the heaviest of all whales. They have a 70 centimetre layer of thick blubber that helps them survive the polar cold and huge heads that are at least a third of their whole-body length. Their skulls are massive and they use them as battering rams to break through ice, up to 60 centimetre thick, allowing them to breathe at the surface.

The bowhead I had spotted wasn't alone. As we circled the helicopter high overhead, we could see a second whale in the pond. It seemed they were both jumping, breaching out of the water again and again. Bowheads aren't known to breach that often, but when they do, they can do so repeatedly, with the record being sixty-four times in just seventy-five minutes. Nobody knows for sure why whales breach. It takes a lot of energy to propel a giant body out of the water, so it's likely the behaviour must have a purpose. Humpbacks, bowheads, right whales, sperm whales, fin, minke, grey and sei whales are all known to breach, with humpbacks being the most dedicated, leaping up to 130 times in ninety minutes when the mood takes them. Making a big splash could just be the whales having fun or even trying to remove parasites, but one theory suggests this dramatic behaviour could be a way of communicating.

There are times when ocean conditions make it harder for animals to call over long distances. High winds and storms can disturb the upper layers of the ocean surface, meaning sound waves are broken and don't travel so far. It's in these conditions that whales might need another form of communication beyond their vocalisations, and they have developed some of the most spectacular of all ocean signals. Humpback whales with their long pectoral fins 'pec slap', repeatedly beating their fins on the surface of the water. They also 'tail lob', to generate huge splashes on the ocean surface, which, being higher frequency, may have a greater chance to cut through the noise. However, breaching is the one signalling behaviour that is likely to make the biggest impact. A breaching humpback will swim up to the surface with powerful beats of its huge tail so that on occasion they can even generate enough power to totally clear the water. To do this a 36-tonne whale needs to be travelling at 30 kilometres per hour and the resulting splash is considerable. It's thought that the bigger the splash, the further the impact signal will travel. A recent study has found that humpbacks are more likely to breach when they are separated from each other by more than four kilometres and when conditions are windy. So, it looks like this spectacular behaviour might just be a long-range communication method when conditions are too rough to make a call.

It was hard to know just why the two bowheads were leaping again and again. While there were no storms disrupting the ocean surface, at least the top two to three metres of the sea was frozen solid. Could the sea ice itself influence the acoustics? A recent study of bowhead whales vocalising in the Chukchi Sea between Alaska and Siberia found that bowhead calls were three times more likely to be detected in open water than when it was covered with ice. A frozen sea presents a sizeable barrier to sound transmission and acts to dampen the sound as it spreads from its source. This could limit the distance over which the whales can communicate and may affect their chances of finding food or mates or even their ability to avoid predators. The ice also makes its own sound as it splits and cracks and drifts together again, and this likely creates a background interference that would also limit the range of a calling whale. While scientists have shown that whales don't breach because of the sonic interference of the sea ice, a changing climate might create circumstances where the ice conditions shift. This could mean that the whales need to communicate more, and breaching might be one way they try to do so.

Watching the whales leap again and again, I was excited to try and film this amazing behaviour and was already dreaming of the most exciting opening shot of any film ever, as the giant whale flew up into the air from the frozen sea. But while I had been babbling excited exclamations across the cockpit comms system, our camera operator had remained surprisingly quiet during the whole spectacle, and it was now he informed us that the camera system was dead. Dumbfounded, I wasn't sure how this could be happening and we desperately tried to convince the pilot that we should land on the sea ice and try and fix the camera. At first, he was rightly cautious; this was not the environment in which to be taking risks and it was impossible to tell just how thick the sea ice was, but then the whales started jumping again and you could see in his eyes he knew we had to go for it.

We backed the helicopter far away from the whales so as not to disturb them with the vibration from our landing and, very slowly, our pilot took us down until finally he rested the floats gingerly on the ice. Our camera operator jumped out and rushed to fix the camera, taking off the protective housing and seeing if he could somehow reboot it. The pilot, still not trusting the ice, kept the rotors spinning. I half-expected the ice to crack apart and swallow us all but it seemed to be solid and held firm. After an age, our camera operator looked up at me sheepishly through the cockpit window and slowly shook his head. There was no way to fix the camera. By the time we were airborne again and had headed back over to look for the whales, their pond had become calm and they had gone.

It is thought the bowhead whale is the longest-lived of all marine mammals. Scientists have found the tips of Inuit stone harpoons, dating back over a hundred years, embedded in the whale's flesh, and by using laboratory-based aging techniques analysing tissue from their eyeballs, they have even estimated that some individuals may be beyond 200 years of age. That means it's possible there are whales out there that were already teenagers when the SS *Great Western* made the first purpose-built steam-powered crossing of the Atlantic in 1838. Perhaps the two whales I saw jumping in their sea-ice pond were the oldest creatures I had ever met.

Nobody spoke for the remainder of the long flight home, even as we passed over some of the most beautiful broken shapes in the last of the sea ice. In all my travels as a filmmaker this was definitely 'the one that got away'. But as we flew on from the frozen sea and finally made it to the rocky coast, passing over the endless browns and greys of the rolling tundra, the empty spaces seemed to absorb my disappointment. The Arctic was unfathomable in its scale, so a chance encounter with such an ancient and near mythical creature shouldn't really have happened at all.

When we talk about the lives of our elders, we often use the phrase, 'They must have seen a lot of changes.' The same must surely be true for the oldest of whales, but when it comes to reflecting on a life in the ocean, it would be more correct to say, 'They must have heard a lot of changes.'

If we continue to flood the deep with our noise, we may soon discover the silence that comes with a lifeless ocean.

Scan to hear how noise pollution from a passing boat drowns out orca conversations.

6. Music from the Sun

THE WONDER OF BIRDSONG

Dawn chorus

IT WAS AN hour before sunrise and the streets were still eerily quiet. As I climbed the concrete steps, I could feel the wild closing in until the haunting cycle of a far-off siren reminded me that I was only a stone's throw from the centre of Bristol.

I was up early, fighting off the pull of my warm, comfy bed to step outside. It was the start of May but the sharpness in the air still carried the memory of winter. It was due to be a hot day but, so far, I was regretting my decision to wear shorts. Walking through the city I'd felt my excitement building. I've always believed the best adventures start before the sun rises. Although I had been here before, it was always a surprise when the brutal fences and ugly squat buildings of the industrial estate suddenly fell away, leaving me to scale the steep steps up into the woods.

The Northern Slopes is the name given to an island of green in a sea of bricks and concrete. Just a couple of kilometres south of the centre of Bristol, this patch of disorderly thicket was originally farmland, before it became a rifle range in the build-up to the First World War. After this time much of the area was given over to huge estates of council housing, the residents historically drawn from the clearance of the slums in the city centre.

During the Second World War, some of the slope's steep woods and rolling meadows were converted into allotments. One section of the slopes, known locally as the 'Bommie', earned its name from the German bombs that fell there, including one dropped on nearby houses that weighed more than 2,000 kilograms. Luckily 'Satan', as it became known, failed to explode and was paraded through the streets of London during the VE Day celebrations in 1945.

As I stepped out of the last spot-lit pool from the streetlights, I could just about see an opening in the shadowy green that crowded the steps. The path snaked off into the woods, impossible to resist. Turning on my head torch, I plunged into the trees. After a few bends, past the final discarded beer cans and bonfire remains, the path narrowed and I felt as if I had left behind the human world and ventured into an undiscovered wilderness.

The first bird I heard was a robin. These tiny bundles of energy are regularly voted Britain's favourite bird, largely on account of their perceived 'friendliness' and their cultural connection to all things Christmas. They may seem cute but there is nothing Christmassy about robin behaviour. These birds are fierce and males will spend a lot of time and effort aggressively defending their territory. I've seen them divebomb starlings at a bird table and disputes between male robins can account for up to 10 per cent of all adult robin deaths. Male robins have even been seen attacking their own reflections in the window. It makes sense that this feathered ball of hostility is often the first bird you'll hear in the morning, its sweet song defending its territory, long before the sun appears. A singing robin works long hours as they are also one of the last birds to be heard after the sun sets, still performing late into the darkness. Such is their desire to protect their patch, robins can be heard singing all year round.

I wandered further, breaking through countless strands of invisible silk spun across the path by unseen spiders. The sudden sting of a nettle on my bare legs triggered a familiar sensory memory from childhood. Rounding a corner in the path I came face to face with a fox. He stared at me, his head tilted, his expression almost quizzical as if to say, 'You're not supposed to be here yet,' before he trotted off into the woods. It was spooky in the darkness and my imagination ran riot. Close by, but concealed by the trees that leered over the path, came a shuffling sound among the leaves. Whatever it was, the ruckus was loud enough to instil a steady fear into my half-sleeping brain. Something large was stalking me. The innate fear of predators deep within me was imagining a bear or a big cat. I had to laugh as a blackbird flitted across the path and up into the overhead branches. This was Bristol, after all.

Soon after, the blackbird, or one of his neighbours, began to sing. I've always thought a blackbird's song was more of a feeling than an actual song. These birds start singing in the middle of February when it's still winter. Those first performances are like the warm spark that starts the long thaw and gently rouses the distant thought of spring. They sing, then pause, then sing again, on repeat. This slow pace, unhurried and relaxed, is so familiar to us that it's become comforting and the bird now singing above me chased away any lingering thoughts of urban big cats. Each verse lasts just two to four seconds before a long pause, then another verse. And each male blackbird may have thirty different verses in his repertoire, but he will never sing the same verse back-to-back, always keeping his output changing, keen to show off all his variations. If you imagine all other birds singing like a jaunty flute, or an effervescent piccolo, then the laidback blackbird feels more like a mellow clarinet. Blackbirds don't just sing the first song of the spring season; they also jump the gun when it comes to the daily performance. They will often start singing in the darkness and, along with the robins and thrushes, they are the earliest to begin the dawn chorus.

As the first peeking rays of the sun hit the tops of the trees, these early birds were joined by a growing choir. Watching the sun climb and listening to the different singers as they shared the woodland stage put me in mind of something naturalist and birder Mark Cocker once said on the radio. The sun powers photosynthesis in plants to produce the new growth of spring, feeding the hordes of insects, which in turn feed the birds, who themselves turn it to muscle and energy, which they transform into sound. So, birdsong could be considered as 'sunlight that's been turned into music'.

Scan to hear the dawn chorus in a British woodland.

There were diminutive wrens singing way louder than would seem possible for such a small bird, their songs punctuated by machine-gun bursts of rapid-fire trilling that made me think I had somehow wandered into a turf war between some Lilliputian gangsters. There were soprano blue tits and great tits and deep bass wood pigeons. I could hear the formulaic three-note call of a collared dove, alongside the undefined scribble of a dunnock. They were joined by the songs of summer migrants: the jumbled rambling of a garden warbler and the repetitive tick-tock of a chiffchaff, perhaps the easiest of all bird calls to remember (the clue is in its name). It was wonderful to think that some of these small birds, singing so heartily around me, had flown all the way from Africa to be here, even crossing the mighty Sahara Desert on their journey.

They may look plain and unassuming, but their presence here added a sense of the tropical to the overall performance. It soon felt as if the whole woodland was alive with songs. Like the cacophony of beeps and horns at an Indian road junction, it was all so loud and so confusing that I wondered how any of it made sense at all. But if you can listen beyond the chaos, there is a scientific pattern and reasoning hidden in the dawn chorus.

Courtship and conflict

To our ears, birdsong might seem like an expression of joy, but for the bird it's a serious business. Typically, the singers are male birds and they sing to defend their territory from rivals or to attract females with which to mate. Making so much noise, so early in the morning, sends a very clear signal. The best males make the loudest calls. It takes energy to perform in the cold when you haven't yet been able to forage for insects or seeds. Only the strongest males could hope to make such a din, a warning to any rival to stay clear and an invite telling any listening female that *this* singer is strong, healthy and therefore owns a territory with plenty of food. The perfect partner with which to raise chicks.

But why did I have to drag myself out of bed so early to hear all this? For the birds, starting early has plenty of advantages. Singing drains lots of energy, but it's best done in the early hours when it's too dark for foraging and it doesn't get in the way of finding food when the sun is up. Singing also sends a clear 'come and get me' signal to any predators. Before sunrise it's harder for enemies to spot you in the gloom, so you can sing away with less chance of a sparrowhawk ending your performance. The morning air is still and cold, meaning sounds travel about twenty times further, so your song will broadcast far and wide and have the biggest impact.

It's also thought that many of the UK's summer migrants arrive at night. They tend to travel through the darkness, as the colder air helps prevent them from overheating. These new arrivals increase the competition, so resident birds, like our robin, blackbird and thrush, like to get up early to sing and steal a march on their overseas rivals.

The type and variety of birdsongs and calls we hear during the dawn chorus are astonishing. But how on earth do birds make these sounds in the first place? What is the instrument behind their performance? When humans speak to each other, air is forced out of our lungs and up between our vocal cords: two flaps of tissue at the top of our windpipe. These vibrate and we can change the shape of the space between them, allowing the passing air to make different sounds. We then modify this air flow again with movement of our lips and tongue.

Birds do things differently. The noises that they make come from deeper down the windpipe, originating right at the point where it splits into two bronchi to enter the lungs. This upside down Y-shaped tube is called the 'syrinx'. Here too, birds have flaps of tissue just like our own vocal cords, which create vibrations. These are surrounded by rings of muscle allowing them to make rapid and minute adjustments to their shape. Unlike humans with just one set of vocal cords, birds have these flaps in both branches of the Y-shaped tube and they can work them independently, meaning they can even make two different sounds at the same time! If humans make sound through a recorder, then you could say that birds make their sounds through the twin outputs of a panpipe. In fact, *syrinx* is the Greek word for panpipe. The syrinx is also surrounded by an air sac, which resonates and makes the calls louder. Scientists have looked to the differing structures of the syrinx for birds all across the globe. They discovered that some of the simplest of these organs are found in the wrens of Aotearoa New Zealand. Wrens such as the rifleman don't have any modifying muscles in place and their simple squeaking calls recall the original sounds of birds from the distant past, before they evolved into the complex repertoire we hear today. Listening to the complexity of birdsongs and examining the singer's physiology gives us clues as to where and when birdsong might have started. And, backed up by evidence from fossils, it is now thought that birdsong first appeared around 50–70 million years ago in the part of the ancient super-continent of Gondwanaland that went on to become Australia and Aotearoa New Zealand.

The songs of today's birds are incredibly complex in comparison. For us humans, the machine-gun trill of a Eurasian wren's call is so rapid that it's an incomprehensible blur of sound containing notes so minute that our ears cannot pick them up. But it's likely that birds hear things very differently too. In just a single second, a wren can sing sixty-four notes; if you take their call and slow it down to a quarter of the original speed, our slower ears can begin to appreciate their song at a pace and pitch that we can register. Listening at this slower pace, we discover that their song is full of dazzling improvisations and creative flourishes that point to a surprising sophistication. But this is just the start. By recording and analysing birdsong, scientists are making all kinds of surprising discoveries about the information that birds are sharing when they sing.

A new study from Australia's Flinders University looked at the relationship between songs and 'personality traits' in superb fairy-wrens. The males of this species have an eye-popping headdress of black and vivid electric blue. Both the males and the more subdued brown females sing complex songs and it was discovered that, regardless of sex, individual wrens that were more 'exploratory' in their behaviour (that is, they tended to travel further and faster) had more elements to their songs, showing more complexity. Individuals who were more aggressive produced songs made with fewer syllables. It seems that both male and female fairy-wrens advertise their personalities when they sing, so it is likely that they will be relaying important information when it comes to choosing a mate.

In 2014, it was discovered that female fairy-wrens sing too and our perception of birdsong was radically changed. Charles Darwin in his *Origin of Species* wrote, 'All those that have attended to the subject believe that there is the severest rivalry between the males of many species to attract, by singing, the females.' These days we hear things differently.

Perhaps our outlook was skewed by the historical dominance of male scientists, or the fact that more colourful male performances are easier to witness, but it took a remarkable female ornithologist to set the record straight. Professor Naomi Langmore, from Australia's National University, recorded the first ever song of a female superb fairy-wren. She went on to discover that females sing in 64 per cent of all songbird species. Her analysis found that in the past all female birds would have been singers. But what was it that led to the decline in females singing? The surprising answer was migration. As the continents drifted apart, migration came to play a bigger part in the lives of some birds. With migration, it's almost always the males that arrive first. They will establish a territory and defend it, so that when the females arrive later, their role is to select a male and there is less need for them to sing at all. Many songbirds in the northern hemisphere migrate, and so most of our scientific knowledge of birds comes from North America and Europe. This northern hemisphere bias could be another reason why female birdsong went unnoticed for so long. Backing up this idea is the fact that Professor Langmore found that there were more female singers in the southern hemisphere, where female birds sing in competition with other females, over nesting sites, for food and also for mates. They often stay hidden and are less showy than males, but they sing nonetheless.

If scientific analysis can tell us that birds can use their songs to identify the sex and personality of individuals, what else might we learn? Researchers from Duke University studying swamp sparrows in Pennsylvania discovered that a sparrow's song changes, degrading with age. These changes were imperceptible to human ears but, by analysing spectrograms of sparrow songs, they found that older sparrows sing less often and are more inconsistent than younger birds when they sing repeated notes. By first playing back the songs of young two-year-old birds and then older ten-year-old birds from speakers positioned in the swamp, they could analyse the response of other sparrows. They discovered that these sparrows were more aggressive to the speakers when they played the younger bird's song. So, it seems that swamp sparrows are more threatened by younger birds, who are more likely to provide competition for mates and territory. If you are an old sparrow, it appears that your shaky song is a give-away of your age to any younger birds listening.

The study of birdsong has even proved that birds have regional accents. I remember on a family holiday to Italy, my dad pondered whether Rome's sparrows speak with 'Italian' accents? It seems there might be a small degree of truth to his idea. While Rome's sparrows don't speak Italian any more than London's sparrows speak with cockney rhyming slang, it's been proved that birds of the same species, living in different locations, do have marked variations in their songs. Researchers in Bristol looked at the songs of wrens living on three Welsh islands: Sully, Flat Holm and Skokholm. They found that birds on the remote Skokholm sang for significantly longer periods, longer by 66 per cent compared to the other wrens. They also found that peak frequency (the moment when a sound reaches its maximum amplitude or power) was different across the three islands, with the wrens on Sully recording the highest level. The scientists thought these differences might be best explained by a 'cultural drift' leading to local populations of wrens developing local dialects.

Learning the notes

IDENTIFYING BIRDSONG HAS long been a skill that I coveted. As kids, my sister and I would visit our grandparents in the country. These were days full of wild adventure and I remember my 'Nandad' – a nickname for our grandad – teaching us how to play conkers and showing us the slow worms that hid beneath the corrugated tin in the nettlebed at the end of their garden. He was raised in the countryside and could show us all the trees and wildflowers, but it was his ability to identify the birds singing in the woods and hedgerows that impressed me most. He would hear a tweeting in the trees and gently proclaim 'great tit' or 'there's a wren'.

As a greenhorn nature lover, this was an ability I aspired to but never seemed to have the ear for. I wished there was a short cut to remembering all the various changes in pitch, pace and volume that make up even the simplest of songs.

The RSPB's *Guide to Birdsong* does an excellent job of trying to 'translate' birdsong into human words, using mnemonics to describe the individual phrases, so that the 'shimmering trill' of a blue tit becomes zip-zip zizizizizi zip zip zizi zip. These 'translations' would be genuinely helpful if only I could remember them and even then, sometimes, they struggle to sound akin to anything like a bird. The 'quack quack' of a duck seems pretty simple, but it's not easy to interpret the RAAAARRRHG of a black-headed gull or the WEE-Jee, WEE-Jee Chu, WEE, Chu WEE, Witz-U, Witz-U, Chu-a-dee, Chu-a-dee of a coal tit.

Decoding birdsong into onomatopoeia is another favourite way ornithologists have sought to describe it. There are phrases that are centuries old and have become a fundamental part of our countryside heritage. The earliest white settlers arriving in North

America named the bobolink for its call they heard as 'bobolink, bobolink, spink spank spink'. While a walk down a country lane in Ireland might lead you to hear 'a little bread and butter no cheese please' from a yellowhammer or a lazy 'just two bags Nancy' from a woodpigeon.

Flick through any pile of field guides and you'll come across some wonderfully absurd examples. I would love to hear the 'quardle oodle ardle wardle doodle' of an Australian magpie or the 'chip, chip shop, chippy chip shop, chippy chip shop' of a Cetti's warbler.

One way I have found to remember certain bird calls is to attach my own memories or associations to help remember them. The repetitive hooting of a collared dove always sounds to me like football supporters chanting, 'United, united, united' and the slightly camp, 'Awwww' of an eider duck has always brought to mind the comedian Alan Carr.

Some bird calls are so unique that it's easy to remember them. Each summer the islands of the eastern North Atlantic ring out with one of the strangest of all bird calls. During the day, thousands of Cory's shearwaters gather together in rafts floating on the ocean offshore. Then, an hour or so after sunset, they will descend *en masse* to land, where they nest in burrows dug into the clifftops. It's one of Europe's most impressive bird spectacles and the sounds of the birds all calling as they come into land is quite barmy. Their calls have been variously described as a 'sobbing wail' or a low-pitched 'bleating', and have led to stories that sailors would mistake them for the voices of ghosts or sirens luring them onto the rocks.

Researchers have discovered that these calls play a vital role for pairs of birds attempting to reunite in the chaos of thousands of others arriving out of the darkness. They may also play a role in defending nest burrows from newly arrived birds looking for a place to lay, and unpaired males will often call to attract females. Their call certainly is one of the most distinct and unusual of all bird calls. But for me it will always trigger an entirely different memory. If you have kids and know the excruciating pain from stepping on a piece of sharp Lego, you'll recognise the manic 'Oww, oww, oww' of a Cory's shearwater.

Scan to hear the 'anguished' call of a Cory's shearwater.

These days, bird identification apps on our mobile phones have changed everything. Suddenly, on any walk in the countryside, we now have an instant translator to tell us who is singing, even when the deepest thicket means we can't see a thing. Cornell University's Merlin app has been a game-changer for me, although I do sometimes wonder what Nandad would think. You could argue that this new tech is reconnecting us with nature, but being so reliant on an app does make you acutely aware of all the wildlife knowledge we have lost. I am always careful to actually listen to the birds to enjoy the atmosphere and not just stand there staring at my phone.

Like many, my 'reawakening' to the wonder of birdsong happened during the Covid pandemic. The start of our first national lockdown coincided with one of the most glorious springs in living memory. When I think back beyond the endless Zoom meetings, the challenge of home schooling and the paranoid weekly disinfecting of the groceries, my memories are also of sunny days exploring the local woods. My family were so lucky that our South Bristol home was within reach of Ashton Court, 300 hectares of council-owned woodland, meadows and ponds on the southern fringes of the city. I swung like a gibbon through the rhododendrons with my eight-year-old son and named all the giant oak and beech trees, making a fantasy-style map to guide our explorations. The grandest tree of all had branches that bowed like the limbs of a giant octopus, low enough to skim the ground. Held in its boughs, my wife and daughter spent many happy hours reading, while I listened to the goldfinches in the flower meadows, their elaborate songs tinkling like a fast-flowing brook.

The long days of the pandemic lockdowns in 2020 and 2021 changed our relationship with the natural world. In May 2020, 36 per cent of people responding to Natural England's 'People and Nature' survey said they were spending more time outside than before. This rose to 46 per cent in July 2020. Nature-based charities saw big increases in visits to their websites during the pandemic. The RSPB saw traffic to their online pages increase by 69 per cent, with over 70 per cent of those visitors finding them for the first time. Their webpage on how to build your own birdbox recorded a tenfold increase in views.

So what effect, if any, did the pandemic have on the birds? It's long been known that the relentless din of human activity has made urban birds sing louder. In order to be heard above the drone of the traffic they are in effect 'shouting' and singing at an increased frequency. This can lead them to damage their syrinx and even their hearing. The result is that the songs themselves are becoming messy and less diverse. This is likely making male songbirds less attractive to females, reducing their chances to breed. Scientists have speculated that the songs of city birds and their rural cousins could have become so different that the two groups may no longer be able to communicate. The noise pollution is so bad, that in some European cities songbirds are choosing to sing at night just to be heard. This can leave them stressed, exhausted and more vulnerable to predation.

But for many birds, the Covid pandemic gave some much-needed respite. For one short summer, the world seemed quieter. Sitting in your garden (if you were lucky enough to have one), jogging in the park or exploring the local woods, many of us recall how the birdsong seemed more vibrant. It was as if the natural world had gone *a cappella*, stripped of the unnecessary accompaniment of rush-hour traffic or passing jet planes. Now we could focus on the pared-down performance of nature's lead singer and, for the first time in ages, really notice how lyrical it was. It's often remarked that the birdsong sounded 'different' during lockdown and the science supports this, just not in a way we expected.

By comparing the sounds of birds recorded before and during the pandemic, biologists have been able to discover just how birdsong changed. The white-crowned sparrow is a handsome bird with a striking skull cap of black and white stripes. Found across North America, they like to forage for seeds and insects on the ground and in winter form flocks of up to twenty birds. Their song is a long sweet single note followed by a jumble of whistles and a blur of staccato cheeps.

Because of their widespread abundance across America, this species is among the most studied of all birds there. So much so that one scientist described them as the 'white lab rat of ornithology'. The sparrows of the San Francisco Bay area have been recorded in the field since the 1970s, giving scientists there a sizeable historical back catalogue of their song repertoires. Using this history allowed ornithologists from the University of Tennessee to compare the sparrows' songs during the pandemic to the time before. They found an obvious change in the birds' vocalisations during the period when the city went quiet. In this new peaceful world, where the traffic on the Golden Gate Bridge was reduced to levels last seen in the 1950s, the sparrows actually improved the quality of their songs. While to our ears lockdown birdsong seemed louder, San Francisco's sparrows began to sing more quietly. Male sparrows singing to attract a mate and defend their territories improved their vocal performance, reducing the amplitude (level of vibration) of their notes to sing 37 per cent more quietly. These softer songs would have carried further given the lack of background noise. By closely analysing the Covid recordings, the scientists discovered that the songs also featured new characteristics. They found novel changes of frequency within the songs that subsequent experiments have revealed could make these 'softer' males more attractive to females. This research is part of a growing body of evidence that human activity has a powerful influence on the way birds sing.

The sun was now high enough over the city of Bristol to send fiery torch beams through the thicket. A speckled wood butterfly flitted between the patches of burnished orange, where the sunlight hit the leaves of the oak saplings. It was still too cold for any sign of life from the numerous mounds of yellow meadow ants. Now I could begin to see more of the world around me. The narrow path was lined with nettles and bramble patches, the kind of terrain that developers often mislabel as 'waste' or 'scrub'. I was reminded that this haven of wonders in the heart of the city was recently under threat of destruction. In 2022 the city council gave itself planning permission to build thirty-four new homes right in the middle of the slopes. It took fierce resistance from the locals to see off the decision. Less than a kilometre away, the 'Western Slopes', a similar patch of green and a vital link in a chain of wildlife-friendly habitats, now faces a new menace from development. Once again there is a well-organised group of volunteers fighting to defend 'the slopes'. These last urban wild spaces aren't just green lungs for human residents, they provide a refuge for a whole host of natural neighbours who share our cities.

I took a deep breath and continued to explore. Closing around the path was an understorey of hawthorn, its branches weighed down by clusters of sickly smelling white flowers. In places it bent over the top of the path, making a tunnel that I couldn't help but follow. This dense impenetrable tangle is great cover for birds. Here and there taller oak and ash trees emerged like giants above the confusion, providing the perfect perching spots for singers. As the sun came up, a new cast of performers could be heard, with my bird app picking up a jay, a nuthatch, a greenfinch and a passing flurry of long-tailed tits.

The path split in two and I followed a steep offshoot that led up through a tricky tangle of brambles that made me yearn for the machete I used the last time I was in the Peruvian jungle. A woodpigeon panicked and burst out of the hawthorns, the sudden clap of its wings making my heart lurch. Beyond the brambles the path became a darkened subway through dead wood and walls of thorn, before emerging into a secret glade bathed in sunlight that was overlooked by the tallest oak in the woods.

Far below, through a gap in the trees I could see the city. A bird began to sing from right above my head. The app told me it was a blackcap, sometimes called the 'northern nightingale'. These birds typically migrate from Germany and north-east Europe; however, more recently, due to climate change, many blackcaps don't fly south for the winter at all, so this bird was most likely a year-round UK resident. Their song has always been heard as a true herald of spring. I couldn't see the singer as it was lost in all the scrub, but its solo was tantalising. First came a jumble of scratchy, low notes, weak and messy. Then, like a seasoned pro, it found its form and the notes came loud, clear and clean: a melody, sweet and tuneful. This change in 'confidence' partway through the blackcap's song is a key identifier and the kind of trait my Nandad's generation would use to identify songs before we became reliant on apps. It was a little like the vocal warm-ups of an opera singer before they take the stage for the main performance. I leant into the brambles, trying to catch a glimpse of this singer. And there it was, a small bird, grey with a smart black hat, framed in a peep hole in the thicket. It was perched high on the top of a dead ash tree, its body bolt upright and singing its heart out. I put down the phone and just listened.

Tropical troubadours

LOOKING UP AT the tower swaying gently in the breeze, it was hard not to feel a bit wobbly myself.

The narrow stairway, enclosed in a flimsy metal skeleton, ascended far up into the canopy like an improbable pillar of Jenga that disappeared into the early morning mist. I am usually okay with heights, but something about this insubstantial structure, oddly incongruous in the middle of a rainforest, made me nervous.

A few feet from the tower and soaring parallel up into the sky was an altogether more robust structure: a 300-year-old kapok tree. From its huge base, supported by wide buttress roots, this giant rocketed straight upwards. Its grey bark was scratched and lined like an elephant's skin, but as you went up it became smooth and shiny – like some ancient marble column from a forgotten temple.

The tower seemed to sway more vigorously as we climbed higher. The structure looked impossibly thin and delicate and it was hard to escape the feeling it might tip over any second. The mesh steps allowed for an alarming view, all the way down to the floor. My head began to swim and I decided not to look again. Focused on just climbing, I noticed that the forest was changing as we ascended. The low bushes and short trees of the understorey were now gone and with it the air felt different. As we climbed, the forest opened out: it became fresher and I noticed that I could hear sounds from further away. The guttural roar of a troop of howler monkeys echoed through the treetops, while above us, branches crashed where a pair of clumsy Spix's guans foraged among the fruit trees. Finally, at the top of the tower, 40 metres above the ground, we crossed a small gangplank onto a wooden platform nestled securely between the spreading branches of the giant tree. I could finally relax. The canopy was a whole new world. The crown of the kapok was painted with splotched disks of silvery lichen and lush bromeliads clustered along each limb like hanging baskets. Bizarre square-headed black ants wandered the branches and buzzing hummingbirds flitted between orchid-like flowers. In places this garden in the sky parted and through these windows we could see the forest stretching out to the horizon.

At Ecuador's Amazonian research station at Tiputini, where we were recording the sounds of the rainforest, we took the chance – after days of thrashing around in the humidity of the forest floor – to visit the canopy for an entirely different perspective.

Tiputini is home to a staggering 530 recorded bird species. Of these, 30 are classed as 'threatened' by the IUCN (International Union for the Conservation of Nature) and nineteen species are restricted to this area alone, living nowhere else. Dawn and dusk are the best time to hear bird calls in the Amazon and our early morning climb up the tower didn't disappoint. More familiar with the soundscape from a British woodland, the bird calls in this forest to me seemed both flamboyant and beguiling.

A pair of white-throated toucans sat in the dead branches of a nearby treetop. One began to call, dramatically throwing its head back as it made the first note of its high-pitched three-part tune. Its rather unlubricated quality reminded me of pushing my old bike up the hill, the wheels squeaking with every turn. A busy flock of green oropendola moved low over the canopy, on their early-morning commute from their roosting spot to their favourite fruit tree. They seemed to be in constant communication, with staccato 'yaps' just like an irksome chihuahua. Then one of the blue-eyed males began to sing an astonishing warble, starting with a steep descending slide on an electronic zither and ending with some woodwind hooting. The whole performance sounded just like R2D2 from *Star Wars*. We could just pick out a distant compilation of sounds, so wide-ranging that it seemed hard to believe that any one bird could master such a variety. Our guide told us it was likely a yellow-rumped cacique, a bird that lives in large colonies in shared hanging nests of grass. It's so hard to identify from its song because every single nesting colony has its own distinct dialect. This diverse array of sounds can include whistles, moans, buzzes and the 'pew pews' of a sci-fi laser battle. Male caciques are very territorial, so each colony's unique call acts something like a password, identifying colony members from rival males who don't belong and might be looking to sneak in and mate with a female. The dialects within the colony even warp with time, keeping the password changing and making it harder for any trespassers to get close.

But by far the noisiest birds we could hear were the red-throated caracara. These raucous birds of prey seemed stuck in some perpetual family argument. It was a sound that echoed far and wide all across the forest canopy. As they perched in the tops of a nearby fig tree, they looked intimidating with their smart white trousers, dark black cloak and vulture-like facemask of bare red skin. Caracara are incredibly intelligent, highly social and live in groups of up to eleven individuals. Each morning they will greet each other with a complex group chorus before setting off to hunt. Their targets are the deadly nests of fierce colonies of Amazonian wasps. Drawn by the sound of the wasps buzzing, the caracara use their complex vocal repertoire to coordinate the perfect attack. They utter a strange raucous call: 'cowh-cah-cowh' or 'ah-ah-ah-aou'. Working as a team, they fly in fast and hit the nest with their outstretched talons, aiming to knock it out of the tree. With the wasps in disarray and their nest broken open, the birds can feast on the colony's larvae, plucking them from their cells among the nest fragments on the ground.

To virgin ears like mine, the songs of rainforest birds always sound more exciting and unusual. But there is little evidence that they are in any way more complex than the calls of temperate species. They do, however, represent a number of superlatives in the world of birdsong.

The song of the musician wren is perhaps the most tuneful of all birdsongs for human listeners. When these small rusty-coloured birds of the forest understorey team up to mate, they sing duets to each other where first one sings and then the other. Analysis of their songs has revealed that they use the same harmonic intervals (the difference in pitch between two notes that are played at the same time) that are the common basis for Western music. These 'consonant' intervals fit well together and this makes their song sound more musical to human ears. Researchers even found a striking resemblance to passages from classical composers Bach and Haydn. In Brazil, the song of uirapuru (the Portuguese name for the wren) is seen to share familiar properties to lots of traditional Brazilian music. Is it any wonder that Cornell University's ornithological lab awarded the musician wren the 'best song' award in one of their yearly 'Bird Grammy' competitions? To me, it always sounds a little like someone tuning in a radio.

Scan to hear a musician wren's song.

The rainforests of north-east Brazil, Venezuela and the Guianas are home to the loudest call of any bird. Listening to birdsong is usually a pleasurable activity, but get too close to this bird and you might be sent scurrying with some serious damage to your hearing. The white bellbird looks a bit like a small crow but the males have a bright white plumage. These loudmouths also sport a fleshy grey wattle covered in tiny white feathers that hangs limply from their nostrils and dangles down on one side of their beak. While nobody knows the purpose of this bizarre appendage, it gives the bird a flamboyant air rather like a flouncy scarf on a catwalk fashionista.

Perhaps the male's fleshy cravat is attractive to the olive-green female bellbird. But plumage and wattles aside, it's the male's call that's impossible to miss. Hollered from the treetops, it's a resounding two-note 'klooor, kli', sounding just like the horn on a passing high-speed train, but more metallic, like a panel-beater hammering on a sheet of metal. It's been recorded at a staggering 125 decibels. That's the same volume you would experience listening to a pneumatic road drill or at the front of a heavy-metal rock concert. It's three times louder than the next loudest bird, the aptly named screaming piha. Sitting on top of a tall tree and shrieking 'look at me' is a dangerous strategy for any bird. There are eagles and hawks in the forest just waiting to snatch such an obvious bird from its perch. So why risk being so obnoxiously loud? As with birdsong across the globe, the need to mate is the driving force. It seems as if female bellbirds are attracted to the loudest males, who can even be heard from several kilometres away.

To make their far-flung call, the male bellbird first crouches and then thrusts its body upwards and outwards as if it is launching a sonic shot put. They have a large syrinx, a thickened ribcage, ripped abdominals and a mouth that opens unusually wide, all to help generate such volume. The males seem to have their favourite perches to shout from, spending most of the day calling, with each twenty- to thirty-minute performance followed by a rest of five to ten minutes. Bellbirds are fruit-eaters and it's thought the forest's abundance of nutritious and easily gathered fruit allows males plenty of free time to shout from the rooftops. One great unanswered mystery of the bellbird's record-breaking hullabaloo is how on earth the males don't damage their own hearing while making such an ear-splitting clamour?

Scan to hear a performing white bellbird.

The white bellbird may well be the loudest, but there is one rainforest bird's song that takes 'showing off' to a whole new level.

Dull brown and about the size of a blackbird, you might be mistaken for thinking that MacGregor's bowerbird is a bit boring. If you were to thumb through a field guide for birds of Papua New Guinea, your eyes would be instantly drawn to the numerous showy birds of paradise, with their outlandish feathers and bright colours. You would likely flick past the page with MacGregor's bower on it, to settle on something more glamourous. MacGregor's is the archetypal 'LBJ': the name birders give to the hordes of 'little brown jobs' that always seem so numerous. But what this small bird lacks in elaborate plumage, it makes up for in sound – it is a master of the art of mimicry.

Bowerbirds are found throughout the tropical forests of New Guinea and down into Australia. There are twenty-seven species and they all get their name from the elaborate 'bower' that the males build. Often constructed from twigs and all sorts of colourful material, these structures are used by males to attract female birds. They build their bowers in the centre of a 'court', an area that they've cleared of leaves and other forest debris. This is the stage on which they'll try and draw in a female.

There are some truly impressive specimens among the bowerbird species. The satin bowerbird has vivid blue plumage and bright blue eyes. He builds a bower of U-shaped twigs, which he adorns with anything blue he can collect, from bottle tops to feathers. The great bowerbird is something of an illusionist. He has a head crest of pink feathers that 'appear' when he is trying to attract a female, but this is only the start of his magic tricks. Male great bowerbirds arrange their collection of white shells and pebbles with the smaller items closer to the bower and the larger items further away. This creates an optical illusion for the visiting female that the male is actually bigger and more impressive than his true size. The male Vogelkop bowerbird builds a stick yurt that he arranges with scavenged items, each sorted precisely into neat piles, according to its individual colour. But despite all these wonders, my own favourite still has to be the MacGregor's.

The performance 'court' of a male MacGregor's bowerbird is pretty impressive. He'll build a metre-tall tower of sticks, just like a maypole. Using colourful flowers, fruits and insects, he'll then decorate his tower to make it 'just right' for any passing female. His next move is to reveal his orange head crest, which he saves like a dramatic costume change for the middle of his act. But it's the grand finale of his display that moves his performance into a different league.

MacGregor's bowerbirds are champion copycats. When a female comes to inspect his bower, the male will stand upright, his beak pointed to the sky, and launch into a 'greatest hits' of all the sounds he has heard from the forest. He starts with taking the best part of the songs of other birds and uses them to make his own composition. But he doesn't stop there. He'll borrow any interesting sound he hears, from the grunts of forest pigs to the sound of running water and even dogs barking. His utmost feat of impersonation can be heard in his perfect imitation of sounds from our human world. He can mimic axes chopping wood, motorcycles revving and, incredibly, even human voices.

Vocal mimicry has evolved many times in different birds and often for very different functions. The thick-billed euphonia of

South America copies the alarm calls of other birds to gang up on predators. The chicks of some brood parasites (birds, like the cuckoo, that lay their eggs in the nests of other species) mimic the 'begging calls' of their hosts' chicks, so the unsuspecting parents don't spot them as intruders and will happily keep on feeding them. Mimicry can also happen by accident. In captivity, trained mynah birds can even learn to copy human speech. All these examples show just how primed birds are when it comes to learning and perfecting their songs, and mimicry is perhaps the ultimate expression of this ability.

Birds learn to sing in just the same way that we learn to speak, by listening to and then imitating the vocalisations of their parents and elders. Many birds pick up their own songs during their first year of life, but the best mimics are able to add to their repertoire as they get older. One way a singing male can outcompete his rivals is to broaden his playlist and add sounds that he picks up from the world around him. For females looking to select the best-quality males with which to raise chicks, a male with a wide vocal range may seem more experienced, have better survival skills and could therefore be a preferable option as a partner. For our male MacGregor's bowerbird, adding the sounds of a motorcycle to his performance might just say to a passing female: 'Choose me. I will make the best dad.' When you play the extraordinary recording on the following page, listen out for the impressive vocal range of a male MacGregor's as he performs. Among the strange medley of sounds, some original, some borrowed from other birds, see if you can hear the sounds of a grunting pig, the bark of a dog and even the distant voices of children playing in a nearby village.

Scan to hear MacGregor's bowerbird.

Tiputini is easily the most biodiverse and possibly the wildest place I have ever visited. But even here there are ominous changes. This amazing forest is as close as you could come to a world untouched by humans. Despite the increasing threat from oil exploration on the edge of the forest, for many miles around there is no industry, no logging or mining, no roads and no pollution. But since 2009, there has been a continuous downward trend in the overall bird population. Bird numbers are falling across the world, but nobody expected to see it in such a pristine habitat.

Researchers from the University of Florida recorded Tiputini's bird numbers across a twenty-two-year period. Using a combination of results from catching the birds (temporarily) in nets and results from direct observations, they built a long-term census of the area's birdlife and could track the population levels of over 313 species. They discovered that both the overall net captures and observations fell to approximately half the rate that they were in the first decade of the study. They were both catching and seeing fewer birds. The group of birds that showed the strongest decline were mainly insect-eaters. Many species of birds that feed on insects from the forest floor had disappeared altogether.

The striated antthrush is a small, stout bird with punchy chest feathers of white and brown streaks. Not much is known about its diet but spending its entire life on the forest floor it likely catches insects, possibly benefiting from invertebrates flushed from the leaf litter as they try and escape the raiding parties of ferocious army ants. In terms of its size and its plumage, it's not the most remarkable of birds, but the song of the striated antthrush is a little piece of magic. It begins with a repeated hooting, which starts slow but gets faster and faster, like the puffs of a runaway steam train. It may open with a pace of one hoot per second, which it soon dials up to eight hoots per second, almost as if it is struggling to contain control, before once more it slows the pace and ends with a series of decelerating hoots that feel like they were recorded in comic slow motion. The overall effect is entertainingly daft.

Scan to hear a striated antthrush.

The bird census at Tiputini recorded captures and sightings of this charming stripy clown every single year from 2001 to 2010. But since then, the striated antthrush has virtually disappeared.

Tiputini has seen similar catastrophic declines in other ground-foraging insectivores, including the bicoloured antbird, the sooty antbird and the white-plumed antbird.

There have been similar declines in 'pristine' forests across the world. The scientific consensus is that climate change is the likely culprit. Harsher dry seasons have been shown to significantly reduce the survival of 83 per cent of bird species. A one-degree Celsius increase in dry season temperatures would reduce the average survival of birds by 63 per cent. Harsh dry seasons may change the forest, reducing the numbers of insects. The timing of ripening fruit and the blooming of flowers shifts, putting birds out of harmony with their food sources. With less food, it's harder to raise chicks – and this struggle inevitably leads to declining populations.

The Tiputini census research and other studies like it are incredibly worrying. It shows that our actions, however far away, can affect even the most isolated and pristine of protected habitats. Relying on national parks as 'biodiversity arks' may no longer be enough to save species. A glimmer of hope comes from the fact that forest researchers have been able to identify regions that are bucking this trend to extinction and seem more resilient. Scientists are currently in a race against time, working hard to define just why this might be.

Back up on the canopy tower at Tiputini, the treetops glowed with the rising sun but on the horizon a storm was brewing. A slate-grey wall of clouds was racing towards us. We could see the curtains of rain dousing the canopy, getting ever closer. Thunder peeled and a flash of lightning scorched a far-off tree. As the first heavy drops of rain hit the kapok platform, we decided it was time to retreat. Nobody wanted to be stuck on the metal tower – a lightning rod in the storm. Gathering up our things, we escaped onto the stairs for the long climb down.

The wind rose out of nowhere. Deep in the forest the sound was like a jet engine coming at us, a breaking wave that shook a million trees. We could hear branches falling and it rained twigs and leaves from above. The tower swayed alarmingly, its motion propelled by our racing footsteps. Just a few steps from the bottom I heard a bird. I had no idea what it was but later identified it as the call of a white-throated tinamou. It's ghostly lingering whistle sounded like a lament. As we reached the ground, the rain hit, shutting down all other sounds from the forest.

Lost songs

Listening to birdsong can bring us great joy, but there is one bird's call that is tainted with nothing but sadness. America's Cornell Lab of Ornithology is home to the world-famous Macaulay Library. It's probably the world's largest collection of natural history sound recordings. With its catalogue stretching back to the late 1920s, the library has over 6,000 individual birdsongs from over 2,600 species. More recently it has begun to add the sounds of mammals, amphibians and reptiles to its collection, so now the library has well over a million recordings. With a catalogue stretching back almost a hundred years, the library has seen many new species of birds added. But sadly, the Macaulay has now become home to an increasing number of recordings from extinct species.

Among these calls that haunt the Macaulay, one is particularly poignant to me. The kaua'i 'ō'ō (pronounced 'kuh-wai-ee oh-oh') bird was a small black bird only 20 centimetres long. Its plain plumage was highlighted by white flashes on the edge of its wings and a pair of bright yellow feathery trousers. Endemic to the Hawaiian island of Kaua'i, this little bird survived on a diet of nectar, fruits and occasional invertebrates. It nested in tree holes among the subtropical forests that grew in the deep canyons of the island.

The kaua'i 'ō'ō declined due to a number of factors. Insect-transmitted disease forced the birds to retreat, clinging on in the high-altitude montane forests of the Alaka'i Wilderness Preserve. Deforestation and the introduction of mammalian predators that raided the bird's nests led to further losses. The trees in the high-altitude forests lacked suitable tree holes for nesting, adding to the pressure on the bird. By the early 1960s, the population was estimated at just thirty-four individuals. By 1981, surveys found only one surviving pair. The final blow was Hurricane Iwa (a Hawaiian word meaning 'thief') which, on 24 November 1982, devasted the island with 145 kilometre per hour winds. It destroyed many of the last large old-growth trees, so limiting new nesting opportunities, and it was sometime around the hurricane that the last female bird disappeared.

The last lonely male kaua'i 'ō'ō was spotted in 1985 and recorded for the Macaulay in 1986. The very final sound recording of the bird was captured by local biologist David Boynton in 1987, who also claimed to witness a lone male bird tending to an empty nest. These last recordings captured the beautiful flute-like call of the male bird, but the saddest parts are the gaps he leaves between his calls, where the female would have responded. Imagine being the last of your kind, calling with all your energy and waiting for a reply that will never come. Between 1989 and 2000, several expeditions surveyed the island in the hope that somehow, somewhere, the birds had survived. But in 2000, the IUCN finally declared the kaua'i 'ō'ō extinct.

The little black bird with the yellow trousers joins other species such as the ivory-billed woodpecker, the bridled white-eye and Bachman's warbler, to now only exist as digitised fragments of songs, time capsules from the past, each in their own way priceless.

Thanks to libraries such as the Macaulay, these recordings now have a new life, being played to conservation students and school pupils to teach them about our role in the growing loss of species. There is hope that by listening to these voices from the past they might become less a requiem for what we have lost and more an inspiration to save what we still have.

Scan to hear one of the last recordings of a kaua'i 'ō'ō.

As far back as 1962, Rachel Carson's book *Silent Spring* told us of the growing threats to bird species and warned that one day, with all the birds gone, we might wake to a silent dawn chorus. Fast-forward to 2022 and a report from BirdLife International reported that globally 49 per cent of bird species are in decline. The expansion of agriculture alone is putting pressure on 73 per cent of avian species. Since 1970, 2.9 billion individual birds in North America have been lost directly due to human activity. In Europe 57 per cent of farmland birds have disappeared, while in Australia, between 2000 and 2016, almost half of all seabird species have seen declines. It seems that Carson's warnings of a silent spring are becoming true. But in places there is still some hope.

Joy ascending

I USED TO RUN regularly, although, these days creaky knees and a lack of youthful fitness make me reluctant and often stop me pulling on my trainers. However, one sure way to get me out of the house is a trail run through the woods in search of birdsong. Bristol's Ashton Court Estate is my go-to. It has a network of exciting mountain bike trails that twist and turn through the trees and, as long as you are up and out before the biking brigade, it makes for an adventurous jog. On one early morning run on a narrow bike trail, I came flying fast around a corner and barrelled straight into a roe deer buck. I thought my heart would pop and the buck was equally surprised. He jumped out of his skin and leapt in a high arc, off into the ash thickets.

Luckily, on today's run through the forest there had been no such alarms. Although it was early, there was a stifling warmth in the damp air that promised it would be a hot day. A squad of jackdaws bickered in their roost high above. The wrens were busy firing their sonic Uzis. Despite being a stone's throw from the city, this early in the morning I often had the forest to myself. But today I bumped into another soul who had also come for their nature fix. I had met the old man before. He pushed his bike along the steep forest paths, stopping every now and then to scatter a handful of bird seed from his rucksack, before retreating back into the bushes to watch with his binoculars. He once showed me a nuthatch hole hidden high in a tree and told me about the time he had seen two rare marsh tits. He couldn't hide his excitement as a confident male great tit appeared on the log. I recognised the glimmer of joy that flickered in his eyes. Not wanting to crowd his time with the birds, and keen to head onwards to my own flight of passion, I ran on. As I reached the edge of the woods, I could already hear them singing in the distance beyond and the sound alone was enough to make me smile. Even the prima donna performance of a thrush, imploring me to stay in the wood and listen, wasn't enough to stop me and I emerged from the trees and up onto the plateau, drawn to the distant song.

Ashton Court's Plateau and Barn Field areas sit at the very top of the estate, with fine views out over the city. They are an open area of grassland, covering around two square kilometres, popular with picnickers and joggers. There is a mini-golf course squeezed in and several small coppices, where gangs of kids like to play hide and seek and build dens. But the biggest area of the plateau is given over to meadows and it's here that I had come to listen to the skylarks. Eyes peeled to the sky I scanned for them, following their trail of notes, and it wasn't long before I had pinpointed a singer, hanging high up in the blue.

It's almost impossible to find new words to describe the wonder of a skylark's song. It's probably best left to the literary greats who, throughout history, have queued up to make their attempts.

William Wordsworth expressed how a singing skylark would 'leave to the nightingale her shady wood; a privacy of glorious light is thine; whence thou dost pour upon the world a flood of harmony, with instinct more divine'. Ted Hughes described their song as being 'Like a breaker of ocean rolling the shingle'. Even William Shakespeare had a go, in his Sonnet 29, expressing how a skylark 'sings hymns at heaven's gate'.

But my favourite human interpretation of a skylark's song comes from the poet George Meredith, whose 1881 poem 'The Lark Ascending' pretty much nails it as a 'silver chain of sound':

Of many links without a break,
In chirrup, whistle, slur and shake,
All intervolv'd and spreading wide,
Like water dimples down a tide.

In less poetic terms a skylark's song is a rambling monologue of frequently repeated notes and subtly varied trills. The RSPB's *Guide to Birdsong* calls it 'a pleasing, burbling doodle poured out without pause for breath'. Each performance can contain as many as over 300 individual syllables, making it one of the most complex of all birdsongs. Skylarks are also excellent mimics and will include elements from the songs of other birds. I was astonished as I listened carefully to the bird singing above me. Among the 'burbling doodle' I was sure I heard the plaintive cry of a buzzard, squeezed in for fun.

I had the excuse I needed to stop running and fully tune in. To me, the song of a skylark captures emotion beyond any other birdsong I know. It's a sound that makes me nostalgic for long, halcyon summers. There is a homely, calming, almost meditative quality to it, yet at the same time it floods my heart with joy. It feels exactly the same as when, after a long, hot dusty hike, you discover a cold, clear mountain stream in which to dabble your feet. When I hear it, all of life's worries and baggage melt away and for a short time the world is truly wonderful. Skylarks famously sing on the wing, ascending rapidly up to over 120 metres up and hovering, their wings fluttering madly to keep their position. Each song usually lasts between two and four minutes, although some birds have been recorded singing for over half an hour! I became aware that my nearest singer was not alone; other voices were tumbling from above, although it wasn't easy to spot them so high up. One bird was obscured, hidden against the brightness, and looking up it was as if his distant song might have been coming from the sun itself, the whispered voice of our nearest star. But, one by one, I managed to pick out the tiny singers and I counted at least six birds dotted against the sky.

A skylark's performance is something of an endurance event. It takes huge amounts of energy to fly, your wings beating fast, and stay singing at the same time. This public display of stamina gives a very clear signal to other males to stay away from this patch of field and sky. Sometimes rivals will compete more directly in a sing-off, performing just a few metres apart to determine who is the strongest. It's unclear what qualities of the song decide which bird is the winner, but the loser will retreat and leave the winner singing in place. The skylark's extraordinary song also acts as a sonic dating profile, allowing female skylarks to pick the strongest males with which to raise chicks. The female seems particularly keyed in to the part of the display where the male hovers and sings; if she likes his performance, they will perform a courtship flight involving a high-speed game of 'catch me if you can'. Research suggests that the male's song flights also send an important signal to would-be predators. The study indicated that singing skylarks were able to escape the attack of a merlin more frequently than birds who weren't singing. If pursued by a merlin, the strongest skylarks will sometimes sing while being chased – sending the predator a clear signal that they should look for a weaker victim elsewhere. Just like gazelle that 'stot', leaping high to tell a big cat they are too strong to be worth chasing, the skylark's song also tells predators hoping for an easy meal they may as well give up and look for an easier target.

Skylarks are beings of two worlds. They inhabit the wide flat places where horizons meet the sky. Their twin realms are both the arcing dome of blue above and the tangible dirt of the field. They are equally masters of each, for as well as we know them for their aerial displays, they are magicians when it comes to camouflage on the ground. With their plumage the colour of dry grass, they can be very hard to spot. Once paired together with a male in his territory, the female bird will scrape away a shallow depression in the earth and line it with woven grass, creating a snug nest bowl, hidden deep beneath the grass stems. She will commonly lay around four olive-green eggs, speckled brown to break up their shape against the nest. Skylark nests are notoriously hard to spot and you can be standing right next to one and not even know it's there. But, despite their cryptic ways, nesting on the ground makes skylarks vulnerable and they are very careful to land a distance from the nest and approach on foot, creeping through the grass like a mouse so as not to give the position of the nest away.

According to the RSPB, skylark numbers have fallen by 67 per cent since 1967. A bird that has been the soundtrack of British summers for as long as there have been people here to listen is now suffering a steep decline. In the last twenty-five years alone, we have lost 1.5 million pairs. This crash has coincided with the rise of intensive agricultural farming. Skylarks are now 'red listed' among Britain's other most endangered birds. Since the 1930s, 97 per cent of Britain's hay meadows have vanished and things have got a whole lot more challenging for skylarks nesting on British farmland. Skylarks like to nest in fields where the grass isn't too short or too high. They prefer fields with vegetation around a metre in height. But in the past few decades, the shift to planting cereal crops in winter rather than spring (to give their growth a head start) means that when the birds come to breed in late spring, the crops are already too high for the birds to nest in. They may have a short period where they can raise a brood, but there is little chance for them to rear a second or third before the crop makes the job challenging for them. Crops are now also sown more densely than in the past, making things even more inhospitable and leaving the skylarks crowded out. Winter fields left fallow once the crop was harvested also provided winter roosting and feeding grounds for ground-nesting birds, but these 'stubble' fields are now sown again in winter, removing a vital refuge for the birds. Combine this with frequent cutting of hay meadows and grassland habitat and the skylarks are increasingly left with nowhere to go.

With skylarks disappearing from our skies, it was time for conservationists to take action. When I first moved to Bristol thirty years ago, the meadows of the plateau were mowed flat each summer. The barn field was used as a huge outdoor concert venue, trampled to muddy oblivion by thousands of human feet, and the plateau served as a giant open-air car park. If there were skylarks back then, I have no recollection of them. But in 2017, the estate managers at Ashton Court decided not to mow the plateau, transforming the area into a sea of bright flowers. Now the place is alive with colour. Swathes of ox-eye daisies turn to follow the sun. The clustered globes of yellow rattle erupt from the ground and bright buttercups line the edges of narrow pathways mown through the swaying grasses. These meadows created the perfect habitat for skylarks and they came in numbers. One count in 2019 recorded thirty-two birds on the plateau.

In 2021, the estate started to give further protection to the skylarks by fencing off their nesting area from spring through into August. This gave their fragile nests added protection from walkers and wandering dogs, who might do damage to eggs and chicks. The new skylark paddocks also gave protection to vulnerable green-winged orchids and common spotted orchids, which have now appeared growing among the meadow flowers. According to the RSPB, at their Hope Farm reserve in Cambridgeshire, creating small skylark plots among the cereal fields have increased the birds' numbers by 50 per cent in just ten years.

Far above me, the light of the climbing sun touched the white fringes of the skylark's wing and tail feathers, shining through them like stained glass, giving the bird a glowing aura. An angel against the blue sky. It stopped its whirring beats to glide on open wings, and its song seemed to slow and slur as if its energy was finally draining away. Suddenly it stopped singing altogether and dropped like a stone, folding its wings back and plummeting down. This dramatic climax to its display has always been my favourite bit and I couldn't help but exclaim my excitement with an awestruck 'Oooh' as if I was watching a firework display. These dives have been recorded at speeds of over eight metres per second and, as the streaking lark fell, it looked for a moment as if it would hit the dirt, only to pull up and float serenely down to disappear into the grass.

Charles Darwin wrote that birds sing for 'their own amusement'. Listening to the rippling verses of the skylark, it's not hard to imagine that singing would in some way be an enjoyable activity for the birds themselves. There is some recent science that supports this notion. Studies from the University of Wisconsin looked at the levels of endogenous opioids (natural chemicals, made by the body, that act to induce pleasure or limit pain) in starlings that had flocked together in winter. Both male and female birds in these flocks sing a song that is associated with their social grouping (called the 'gregarious' song). They discovered that the presence of other birds in the flock and the safety that provides may lead to the release of opioids, reducing anxiety and creating a positive state that would be more conducive to singing. They also found that the singing itself triggered opioid release. So, you could say that singing can give a bird a natural high.

But it's not just the birds getting positive vibes from singing. Research from King's College in London showed that seeing birds or hearing birdsong was associated with an improvement in our own mental wellbeing. They asked over a thousand people from across the world to tune in to a mental health app three times a day. If they could see or hear a bird, they would have to answer a series of research questions about their mood. The researchers discovered that just listening to five minutes of birdsong every day can reduce your blood pressure and calm you down. The positive benefits can even last up to eight hours after the encounter. These improvements were also seen in people suffering from depression. If daily encounters with birds improve our mental health, could we see a time when doctors prescribe us a dose of 'nature' to boost our mood and leave us feeling chirpier?

In the First World War, birdsong had the power to raise the morale of the 'Tommies' fighting in the trenches of the Western Front. Skylarks in particular filled them with hope and joy. Nothing seemed to dent the spirit of the larks, who even sang throughout the seven days of continuous bombardment before the Battle of the Somme, where 1.7 million shells exploded across no man's land. The war poet Private Leslie Coulson put his appreciation of this small brown bird into poignant and beautiful verse:

From death that hurtles by
I crouch in the trench day-long,
But up to a cloudless sky

From the ground where our dead men lie
A brown lark soars in song.
Through the tortured air,
Rent by the shrapnel's flare,
Over the troubleless dead he carols his fill,
And I thank the gods that the birds are beautiful still

Skylarks were seen as courageous spirits; their constant singing reminded the soldiers of summers at home and the birds were commonly thought of as 'one of the boys'. Birds and their songs have shown they have the ability to lift our hearts, even in the darkest of times.

Scan to listen to a skylark's song.

As the larks continued their rippling 'silver chain of sound' it was time to go. But I knew that as long as there were larks here singing, I would always come back and listen. Running down through the woods on my way home, I thought about how much pleasure the simple act of listening to birdsong now gives me. Just like learning a new language, it had opened doors to novel experiences, adventures and emotions, leaving me stirred beyond measure. It is hard to imagine a future world where our woods, jungles and meadows might become empty of birdsong. With the silence spreading, our responsibility grows louder: we can save the dawn chorus, but only if we act to protect the birds that give it voice.

7. The Living Heartbeat

LISTENING AS A TOOL FOR CONSERVATION

Pulse of the planet

THE NIGHT TIME soundscape of Australia's desert can be really beautiful. Here, the landscape is vast. The wind blowing through the dry vegetation is the most common sound and then there are the crickets. As soon as the sun sets and the heat of the day dissipates, the crickets start their chirping, trilling their repeated rhythm, 'chirrup, chirrup, chirrup', that always makes me think of endless open spaces under the stars. You may sometimes hear a frogmouth hooting in the gum trees or the plaintive howl of a dingo, a little like a wolf but longer and much less familiar, making it seem all the wilder. You might see something scurry across the sand, but its movements are silent. As the night goes on and the insects lose their energy, it becomes eerily quiet – and when the sky is moonless, only the wind gives any scale to the darkness.

On the rarest of nights, you could be incredibly lucky and hear a haunting whistling drifting on the wind, like the voice from a wandering desert spectre. It's the evocative call of one of Australia's rarest bird species, the night parrot. Once found throughout Australia's arid lands, this small green and gold parrot lives a furtive, nocturnal life, sneaking like a footpad between the clumps of spinifex grass. It can fly when alarmed or when it needs to travel to water, but prefers to keep its feet on the ground. However, the bird's terrestrial lifestyle has made it vulnerable to introduced predators such as foxes and cats, and with the spread of sheep and cattle farms destroying its habitat, the parrot's numbers have crashed. Like its ghostly whistle, the parrot faded on the desert wind to become just a memory. It wasn't to be seen alive for a hundred years.

Then, one remarkable night in 2015, two ornithologists surveying in south-west Queensland, captured a live individual. The night parrot was back. They nicknamed the bird 'Pedro', but were careful to keep the exact location of the rediscovery under wraps. *Birdlife* magazine described the find as the 'birdwatching equivalent of finding Elvis flipping burgers in an outback roadhouse.' With the world awake to the fact that the night parrot wasn't extinct, efforts were made across Australia to discover more. But with just a handful of sightings across the continent, the parrots remained one of the most elusive and mysterious birds anywhere in the world.

Australia is huge and the desert covers an area of close to six million square kilometres. Where do you start to even look for a small secretive parrot that only comes out at night? The answer was to look for the right habitat. It's a little-known fact that half of Australia's threatened vertebrate species occur in areas that are owned and managed by Australia's First Nation peoples. Of those threatened species, 32 per cent are being protected under conservation agreements. Indigenous rangers are involved in projects to help protect 31 per cent of Australia's threatened bird species, so all in all Indigenous management is integral to the conservation of the continent's declining species. The Ngururrpa IPA (Indigenous Protected Area) is a 29,000 square kilometre reserve in the Pilbara region of Western Australia's Great Sandy Desert and was a perfect place to start a search. Between 2020 and 2023 the Ngururrpa Aboriginal rangers surveyed the desert for signs of night parrots. But finding a parrot was never going to be easy. In the project's report, Ranger Clifford Sunfly describes their approach. 'We as Rangers are working together with scientists to learn two ways – the science way and the traditional way.'

The traditional way involved reading the country, searching the areas around water and looking for the plants the parrots might want to eat. The science way included using technology to 'listen out' for the parrots. The team deployed remote acoustic monitoring units called 'songmeters' to listen out for any parrot calls. Placed in rugged weatherproof boxes, the recorders can survive the worst of the desert conditions. They staked out thirty-one likely locations with the units, each for a minimum of twenty-one days. Some of the sites were so remote they could only be accessed by helicopter. The recordings gathered by the songmeters were then analysed by a computer to search for calls within the parrot's range of vocalisation – a frequency between 1,500 and 3,500 hertz.

Next, the rangers listened to the recordings of any potential night parrots to manually verify them by comparing them to a library of historic parrot vocalisations. The parrots are known to have a wide range of calls, from the eerie whistle to a 'didly dip, didly dip', like a telephone, and a 'dink, dink, dink' just like a tinkling bell. They call predictably around their roost sites in the first hour after sunset and then again in the last hour before sunrise. So, by recording a parrot's whistle it was possible for the rangers to pinpoint potential roosting sites that might need further protection. After recording thousands of calls, the project indicated that there could be at least fifty night parrots in the Ngururrpa IPA, which would be the largest known population in the world. As one ranger, Samuel Galova, said, 'We didn't know about night parrots before but now we know about it and want to protect it.'

The rangers' next steps are to build a long-term conservation plan to manage the land for the parrots. This would include controlling burning around the parrots' favoured locations, as the birds depend on old-growth spinifex grasses, which form a protective dome under which they can burrow. Burning of the land – from wildfires, to clear the land for ranching and land management burns by Indigenous communities – can leave the spinifex too short and destroy the parrots' nesting and roosting opportunities. The rangers can also monitor and control the sites to keep an eye out for introduced predators such as foxes and cats, giving the parrots the best chance to successfully rear their chicks. By combining Indigenous knowledge with the latest technology to listen in on the desert, the Ngururrpa rangers are ensuring that the night parrots are part of the landscape's song, to be passed on to the next generation who walk the land.

Scan to hear the ghostly whistle of the night parrot in the Australian desert.

Today, remote listening tech has become a vital part of the conservation tool kit. Some listening devices can go further than identifying rare species, they can even raise the alarm when a habitat is under threat.

I know from visiting the Amazon the sickening rattle of a distant chainsaw. Few sounds have the same capacity to drain the blood in an instant. In 2011, while volunteering at a gibbon sanctuary in Sumatra, Topher White went for a walk through the rainforest.

During his time there he had fallen in love with the natural sounds of the jungle but, on this occasion, he heard the threatening rasp of a chainsaw and the crash of falling trees. White knew he wanted to do something to help so, leaning on his background as a software engineer and physicist, he used Kickstarter to crowdfund for a new monitoring system that could help protect the forest. White quickly realised that if the project was to successfully monitor large areas of rainforest it would have to rely on listening: 'We could put up cameras in the forest, but all you're going to see is the tree that's twenty feet in front of you. If you really want to capture what the essence of the forest is, it's sound.'

He formed a small tech start-up called Rainforest Connection and began to design and build the first generation of remote listening devices that he christened 'Forest Guardians'. The devices would be installed by climbing into the canopy to fit the tech up in a tall tree where it could listen over the forest. The first generation repurposed old smartphones, powered by solar panels, but the system evolved and today the latest generation of guardians are at the forefront of remote listening technology.

The RFCx Guardian runs on a solar array that charges a battery pack and means the system has the power to be listening for twenty-four hours a day. The Guardian connects to the Rainforest Connection Cloud Platform using the global mobile network or satellite connection in remote areas. Each device has a sensitive external microphone that can detect chainsaw noise from up to one and a half kilometres away. The sounds sent to the platform are analysed in real time by AI and can be programmed to pick out specific sounds such as chainsaws, gunfire from poachers, logging trucks or the sounds of road-building. If these danger sounds are detected the system sends a mobile phone alert to forest rangers or Indigenous authorities, raising the alarm in time for them to intercede.

Ednaldo Tembé is a tribal chief in Brazil's Alto Rio Guamá Indigenous land. His community were one of the early collaborators with the Rainforest Connection project. Interviewed for a documentary on the project's website, he explained the challenges facing Indigenous groups trying to protect their land from the scourge of illegal loggers. 'We used to patrol the territory on foot, sometimes we would run into invaders, which would cause a lot of conflict. This became a huge problem in our lives.'

The Alto Rio Guamá is a 280,000-hectare triangle of preserved forest surrounded by a flattened wasteland of stumps and blackened burn scars. It's home to 2,500 of the Tembé, Timbira and Kaapor peoples. But it is also often occupied by some 1,600 non-Indigenous settlers, many of whom are there to clear the forest to make space to grow cannabis to sell. The local Indigenous people regularly patrol the area, but its huge size makes it difficult to find every illegal incursion and often the loggers pay for hired gunmen to protect them. Some of Chief Tembé's people have even been shot and killed. The Tembé have only thirty warriors who act as rangers patrolling the forest, and the size of the land means it's a huge drain on their resources. The Guardians have given them the ability to listen in to remote parts of the forest night and day, allowing them to learn about new incursions and inform the authorities without putting their own lives at risk.

Brazil's latest government has promised to help expel the trespassers in the Tembé's forest, but until then they must work alone to protect their land, so the Guardian monitors have been a huge help. White knows the importance of this kind of collaboration: 'People on the ground in these places, they're the solution, they're the ones that can really fight off deforestation, but technology can play a really big part in helping them do it more safely and more effectively.'

The people of the Alto Rio Guamá are on the front line, protecting their homes and risking their lives – not only for their own survival, but to save their beautiful forest for the benefit of the rest of us. For Chief Tembé, the Guardians have been a huge positive for his people: 'The system pinpoints exactly where the problem is so we no longer need to spend many months patrolling the land like we used to. That means we have more time for our culture, for our family and for survival. A society without culture is nothing.'

In rainforests across the world, illegal deforestation is seen as a 'gateway' activity that starts the grizzly process of clearing a forest. If you can stop these early activities, then you stand a chance of keeping the forest intact. If you can protect the trees, then you stand a good chance of protecting the whole forest community, maintaining biodiversity and limiting carbon emissions that fuel the climate crisis.

At the time of writing there are around 600 Guardian systems helping protect forests across thirty-five different countries. They are monitoring and protecting 726,000 hectares of forest. But these 'intelligent ears' aren't just listening out for chainsaws. They can be programmed to keep an ear out for animals too, making them the perfect tool for the remote monitoring of biodiversity. To date they have detected and identified 4,126 different species, tracked the populations of 310 threatened species and recorded over 300 million minutes of audio data that is a vital resource for conservation. They even have an app that allows you to livestream the real-time sounds of the rainforest. As I write here in rainy Bristol, I am listening to a soundscape of night-time frogs and crickets coming live from a forest in Ecuador and it's wonderful. But it's also comforting to know that by the simple act of listening, there is also a better chance that the forest might be safe in the future.

Toad phones and frog saunas

On 14 May 1964, Californian herpetologist Jay Savage was walking along the ridge top of Costa Rica's Monteverde cloud forest when he stumbled upon a hoard of golden treasure. The dark shadows of the root crevices and the puddles of rainwater were scattered with hundreds of bright flashes. It was enough to stop him in his tracks. But these were no Spanish doubloons. This trove was a living treasure. Savage had discovered a new and remarkable species of amphibian, which he named the 'golden toad'.

A year earlier, Savage had been visiting a Quaker colony in Monteverde where he was told stories of a wonderful orange toad that appeared during the rainy season. He had even been shown some recently preserved specimens and these had piqued his interest, making him determined to search for the animals in their forest home. But nothing could have prepared him for the wondrous sight he encountered on the mountain.

The toads were about five to six centimetres long and there were hundreds – maybe over a thousand – of them across the ridge top. There were males, sitting around the pools, their warty skin ranging from bright yellow to satsuma orange. The females were a little bigger and just as impressive, their jet-black skin painted with vivid red circles, bordered by swirls of gold.

In November 1965 Savage published his paper announcing this new species to the world. Even today it is somewhat unusual for a scientific paper in that the excitement readily seeps off the pages. The title itself reads like a thrilling proclamation: 'An Extraordinary New Toad'. He named it *Bufo periglenes* from the Greek 'periglnzes', meaning 'very bright'.

The toads' forest home was a cold, sodden ridge called Brillante. Up on the top of the mountain the terrain narrows to a crest. Exposed to the elements, the trees grow short and twisted, defining the forest as 'elfin'. A forest lost in the clouds. Orchids grow on the branches, and mosses and lichens hang from the low canopy, flourishing in the moist air.

Once a year, this fairy-tale landscape played host to a biological fantasy that, for those lucky enough to witness it, felt just like make-believe. With the rains in late March and into April, the toads would emerge from beneath the damp tropical soil to mate in the pools of rainwater that had collected between the tree roots. As many as 1,500 toads were counted on one occasion. The males would arrive first, often clasping onto any other toad that moved, regardless if it was male or female. When a female did appear, the males would jump on her back and hold her in 'amplexus' (the favoured mating position of frogs and toads, where the male clings on to the female's back, often holding her tightly with his fore limbs) until the female released her spawn. There were always more males than females, with the golden boys outnumbering the spotted girls by as many as 10:1. This often led to males attacking pairs already in amplexus in an attempt to wrestle their way to the female, and at times the forest floor was dotted with 'writhing masses of toad balls'. Some of these wrestling matches contained as many as twenty-three individual toads. In one pool alone, just the size of a kitchen sink, 133 mating toads were recorded. With the fierce competition, only fourteen out of every one hundred males obtained a mate. One scientist who studied the spawning event described it as 'one of the most incredible sights I've ever seen'.

But while the toads provided an obvious visual spectacle, what, if anything, did they sound like? During his initial observation Savage remarked that the toads were 'voiceless' and that no sound could be attributed to them. But work by biologist John Vandenberg and Susan Jacobson in 1982 revealed more detail. Vandenberg remembers how tough it was working up on the ridge: 'Recording at night was quite scary. Way up on the trails, I had a very close encounter with a hissing jaguarundi!'

Jacobson recalled, 'A tropical storm was flooding the cloud forest when I first heard the call of a golden toad.' It had rained non-stop for eleven days and 'this stimulated their mating binge'.

Sitting upright alone by the side of a pool or when holding a female in amplexus, the males would occasionally make a gentle 'tep-tep-tep' call that Jacobson described as 'like the beat of wooden spoons knocking together'.

More frequently heard was a low intense trill, often accompanied by vibrations of the toad's body. Vandenberg identified this as a 'release call' performed by males that had been disturbed or grabbed hold of by other males. A kind of, 'Let me go – you've got the wrong toad!', if you like. Compared to many courting amphibians, the vocalisations of golden toads seemed to play a smaller part in the mating game than the visual signals coming from the male's glorious colour. But with so many toads trilling, it still made for a wonderful soundscape.

The discovery of the toads and their magical spectacle sent ripples around the world. Their picture appeared in *National Geographic* magazine and on the cover of *Nature*. They were transformed into characters for a children's cartoon and they spawned a whole tourist industry of global visitors to Monteverde. They gave their name to hotels in the town and such was the impact of their discovery that in 1973 their mountain was given national protection, becoming the world-famous Monteverde Cloud Forest Reserve – perhaps Costa Rica's best known, with up to 70,000 visitors each year. In 1979 the toads even starred in David Attenborough's seminal *Life on Earth* series, appearing before a global TV audience.

The existence of the golden toad was made even more improbable in that it was only ever recorded over a total area of no more than 8 square kilometres and, at any one time, over an extent of just 0.5 square kilometres. It was also to be found at a narrow average elevation of 1,500 to 1,620 metres. So despite all the attention, the fact that this toad was only found in such a small place and on only one mountain left it vulnerable.

In 1988 the spring was drier than anyone in Monteverde could remember. The landscape was desperately thirsty and there was no sign of the toads. In May the rains finally came and American herpetologist Marty Crump would hike up the mountain to the ridge top each day to check out the familiar breeding pools. But still, there were no toads to be seen. Then, at last, at the end of May Crump spotted a solitary male toad sitting on the edge of a pool. She continued along the ridge top, unaware that this would be the last golden toad she would ever see. With her field season ending in July, she returned home to the US thinking that perhaps the toads had sensed that, after the drought, conditions for breeding weren't at their best, and had decided to sit out the mass spawning for a season.

Crump returned to the mountain the following year with her graduate student Frank Hensley to look for the toads again. But once more they found nothing. At the start of May Crump had to return home for a family emergency, leaving her student to continue the search. On 15 May 1989, Hensley scaled the mountain alone. Checking every pool and every hollow he suddenly spotted a bright orange toad sitting off the trail. For Hensley it was a thrill to finally see a golden toad, even if it was the only one he could see in the forest. He pulled out his camera and took a photo before moving on, still hopeful of finding other toads on the ridge. Perhaps the toads were just starting to emerge and he had spotted an early riser? Hoping to see more tomorrow, he headed down, but the next day he couldn't find even the single toad from before and the ridge was eerily quiet. He couldn't have imagined it at the time, but Hensley's encounter with that lonely individual was the last ever confirmed sighting of a golden toad and his photograph, the last ever taken of the species.

Years passed and with each rainy season, eager herpetologists would scale the ridge hoping that the toads would return. Each time they would descend, their hopes crushed. Finally in 2004 the IUCN declared the golden toad extinct.

Sadly, they weren't to be alone. All across the world scores of frog and toad species were mysteriously disappearing and it took considerable effort for scientists to discover the culprit. They finally were able to point the finger at a chytrid fungus that they named *Batrachochytrium dendrobatidis* or *Bd* for short.

The fungus infects the frog's skin, which is crucial for their breathing and the regulation of internal levels of bodily water and salt. Infection causes a thickening and shedding of the frog's skin, leading to a loss of vital electrolytes. The frogs would end up skinny and weak, and those that weren't easy pickings for predators would eventually die of heart failure. A mutation of the *Bd* fungus called *Bd*GPL (short for Global Panzootic Lineage) has been able to spread around the world, possibly given a leg up in the 1940s by the global export of African clawed toads. These strange amphibians were once commonly used as a reliable pregnancy test – if a pregnant woman's urine was injected under the toad's skin, it would quickly go on to lay eggs. Shipped around the globe in their thousands, nobody knew that the clawed toads carried a deadly stowaway. *Bd*GPL was living on the toads' bodies and, while its host had adapted to the fungus and had become largely immune, they were giving a free ride to a potential killer.

If there is one thing you can say about African clawed toads it's that they are slippery customers. I know this from personal experience of trying to catch one during a frog survey in Tanzania. Even for a frog, their skin is incredibly slimy and trying to hold one in your hands is like gripping a bar of wet soap in the shower. Added to this, the toads have hugely powerful back legs for swimming and these can propel them surprisingly quickly when needed. Soon after they had been shipped around the world in their role as amphibian pregnancy tests, the toads were managing to escape.

From their original home on the African continent, they can now be found across North America, Europe, South America and Asia. The frogs have become so ubiquitous that they were even selected for experiments on the International Space Station, making them one of the few amphibians to go into outer space. The spread of this successful species and the deadly fungus that it carried is thought to have led to the catastrophic decline in many amphibian populations throughout the 1990s.

But the clawed toad wasn't the only carrier of the *Bd* fungus. A burgeoning international trade in amphibian 'pets' is likely to have helped the fungus move around and, in a heart-breaking twist, it's also been theorised that the fungus may have been unknowingly introduced to some isolated and pristine frog populations by well-meaning scientists carrying the fungus on their shoes or equipment as they moved from one study site to another. In one example, conservationists trying to boost the declining population of rare Majorcan midwife toads inadvertently released captive-bred toads that were carrying the *Bd* fungus back into the wild to mix with the endangered toad population. Mass tourism is also a plausible way in which the fungus may have been able to spread. It's not hard to imagine when you remember the thousands of tourists that came from all over the world to see the golden toad. Whatever the method, human-caused transmission of the fungus led to catastrophic declines in frog populations across the globe. In some places herpetologists reported dead frogs littering the forest like fallen leaves. To date the fungus has led to declines across 500 different frog species and the sad extinction of at least 90.

But was the fungus the only culprit? Did it have a willing accomplice in the slaughter? It's still an area for lively scientific debate, but there are many who believe that climate change might have played its part. When it comes to the golden toads, it's been doubly hard to be certain exactly how they met their end. Unlike many amphibian mortalities due to *Bd*, there were no dead frogs that were ever found. Like a whodunnit without a body, it makes proving the murderer all that bit harder. What we do know is that climate change has led to much drier conditions in Monteverde.

For a toad dependant on rainwater pools to breed, less rain could present a challenge to survival. Could the stresses of a drought make the toads more susceptible to infection? It's been observed that, counterintuitively, the drier springs came with increased cloud cover and less sunshine. "*Bd* is known to thrive in cool, wet conditions, and less sunshine may further aid the fungus by limiting opportunities for frogs to bask and raise their body temperatures – a natural defense that can help them rid themselves of the infection."

In Australia, conservationists have had success helping rare green and golden bell frogs fight off infection with *Bd*. By putting out 'saunas' for the frogs to shelter in – black masonry bricks with round holes big enough for a frog to sit in – they were able to turn the tables on the fungus. The dark bricks absorb the heat of the sun and this raises the body temperature of any sheltering bell frogs enjoying the 'spa treatment', helping them to fight off the chytrid fungus. The study found that infected frogs recovered after spending time in the brick saunas, and those that used them as refuges showed less severe levels of *Bd* infection. In addition to this, frogs who had used the saunas and recovered from the infection were then twenty-three times more likely to survive should the fungus return to infect them in the future. So there seems to be a clear link between temperature and infection. Could the drier springs in Monteverde have forced the golden toads to seek out damper places, which would in turn be cooler, leading them right into the path of the deadly fungus? Without the evidence of tissue analysis from any dead toads, it's unlikely that we will ever know for sure. While the lack of corpses adds significantly to the mystery of the disappearing golden toads, it also raises doubts about their extinction. Without knowing for sure why they disappeared, can we honestly say that they are gone forever?

Amphibians have some form when it comes to 'de-extinction' – the process describing the rediscovery of a species that was once thought to be gone forever. In Monteverde the golden toad wasn't alone. During the late 1980s and early 1990s, about twenty other frog species disappeared from the mountain. One species – the green-eyed treefrog – was commonly seen and very abundant. But surveys in 1991 and 1992 didn't find any of these pretty little frogs at all. The species went unrecorded beyond the millennium and was on the verge of being classified as extinct when in 2002 a British naturalist called Mark Wainwright sat on a log in the forest and a bronze-coloured frog with vivid green irises suddenly jumped out next to him. He knew immediately it was a 'missing' green-eyed treefrog and further investigations found a whole pond full of green-eyed tadpoles. It seemed this frog species had come back from the dead. Across the world, there have been plenty of other examples of so-called 'Lazarus frogs'.

In Borneo the multicoloured rainbow toad was rediscovered in 2011, after being 'missing presumed dead' for eighty-seven years. In Ecuador the stubfoot toad popped up again after being lost for fifteen years. Israel's endangered Hula painted frog came back from extinction in 2011 after last being seen fifty-six years earlier, and in Columbia the beautiful starry night toad reappeared in 2019, having disappeared during the peak of the *Bd* pandemic in 1991. Could the golden toad one day be added to this list? Many of those who were lucky enough to see them in their pomp and those who studied the toads up close would admit to hoping that this is the case.

And their hope isn't without some foundation. In 1991, two years after Frank Hensley's last confirmed sighting of a golden toad, a Costa Rican naturalist and guide claims to have witnessed a gathering of about twenty golden toads on a mountain ridge in the Children's Eternal Rainforest, far beyond the toads' previous limited range on the ridge at Monteverde. This forest, known to locals as the BEN (El Bosque Eterno de los Ninos), is a huge 23,000-hectare reserve close to Monteverde. Could it be that the toads were more widespread than scientists had once thought? Could they have survived the *Bd* pandemic in a place unvisited by humans, deep in the forest? The guide who spotted the toads didn't get any pictures and, while there is no reason to doubt his discovery, the encounter remains officially 'unconfirmed'.

The biggest difficulty in studying rare frogs in the wild is how to monitor them. At Monteverde, the terrain is often steep and challenging to move through. The frogs there can be hard to spot, with some only occasionally appearing during spawning. At these times the forest can seem alive with their presence. Every pool and every leaf can be dripping with frogs. But arrive too early and you will miss them completely; come a day later and they could all be gone. Their remote mountain-top homes are hard to reach and you have to be incredibly lucky with impeccable timing to get a glimpse of what you came for. So, knowing how hard it is to find them, how on earth could we ever hope to 'rediscover' the golden toad if it is out there? One answer might be to listen to the forest.

Researchers from Australia were pondering this challenge over a glass of wine when they came up with the idea of a remote listening device that would allow them to eavesdrop on amphibians in remote locations. By the second glass of wine, they had agreed to try and build it, and soon after the 'FrogPhone' was born. Powered by a solar panel, the system consists of a remote microphone in a weatherproof box that can use 3G/4G cellular data networks to transmit real-time audio directly to a user's mobile phone. This allows the scientists to 'dial-a-frog' and listen in to any frog calling at the site within a 100–150-metre radius.

Frogs and toads have species-specific calls, so by listening in during the mating season it was possible to tell which species were there. This helped minimise the human impact on the location, saved money on travel and logistics, and allowed the researchers not to miss the main event when the frogs were spawning. They could also survey several key ponds in a huge area of national park in only fifteen minutes, just by making a few phone calls. During one trial, a researcher who was on holiday in Spain was able to phone into a pond in Canberra and listen in on the frogs there.

One problem, though, is that frogs and toads often breed after the onset of the rains and all at the same time so you can get a mass spawning with lots of frogs calling at the same time. How do you tell if your rare frog species is present and not being drowned out by the calls of more abundant frogs? Once again, listening technology has come up with an answer.

In California, populations of red-legged frogs have long been on the decline. A small sleek frog, they are named after the red colour that can sometimes be found on the underside of their thighs. These frogs used to be so abundant that they were a common food source for prospectors in the gold rush of 1849. The frogs have since become threatened due to the draining of their traditional wetland habitat for agriculture. They are also on the menu for the 20 centimetre-long, 1 kilogram behemoth that is the American bullfrog, a species that has been introduced into California from the eastern United States and has gone on to decimate populations of the smaller red-legged frog.

Luckily, the endangered red-leg is still to be found in ponds across the border in Mexico. So in 2024, with help from Mexican conservationists, a team from the San Diego Natural History Museum translocated eggs across the border, in the hope of re-establishing the rare frog back in California. But how could they tell if the frogs were successfully breeding? The team deployed remote microphone recorders around the release ponds to listen for the frogs' calls. Unfortunately, red-legged frogs have a very subtle call. It's a low-key grunting sound that has been likened to someone rubbing a finger gently on the surface of a balloon. Compared to the bellowing calls of the bullfrogs and the din from Pacific treefrogs, the red-legs are easy to miss. With California's last remaining breeding pools often surrounded by urban sprawl, it makes for a noisy atmosphere and the calls of the red-legged frogs just get lost. But by analysing the recordings with AI trained to focus on the wavelengths specific to the endangered frog, the conservationists were able to hear beyond the din and pick out the whispers of the red-legged frog. The presence of these more subtle calls confirmed where the frogs were breeding and, soon after, the team found that the rare frogs had successfully laid eggs. Remote listening to vocalisation is becoming a useful conservation tool, increasingly used to track rare species around the world – from northern spotted owls to African forest elephants and big cats such as mountain lions.

It took me some time to track down sound recordings of the golden toad. John Vandenburg sent me a recording from 1977 and the Macaulay library has a recording made by a Dutch ornithologist in 1981. But the last ever recordings of the calls of golden toads were made by Susan Jacobson in 1982. Sadly, just like the toads, these precious recordings have disappeared, lost among the archives of the museum she donated them to. Looking back is bittersweet for the scientists studying in Monteverde in the early 1980s. Jacobson remembers, 'It was magical to see them. Now it's just profoundly sad that they are extinct.'

In 1982, the golden toads were one of only four frog and toad species internationally recognised as 'endangered'. Today the number of 'endangered' and 'critically endangered' frog and toad species is 1,778. Much has changed in the way that we measure and record how much trouble a species may be in. These days there is a lot more data that goes into assessing extinction risk, so it's hard to draw too many conclusions from modern comparisons, but it does at least show us how the threats that amphibian species face have been growing.

Listening in on the golden toad recordings for myself, it's hard not to feel incredibly sad at what we might have lost. But, like many others, I cling to the fragile hope that, somewhere out there on a wilderness mountain in Costa Rica, the species could somehow have survived. As I listened, I could begin to imagine how a recording just like this one might one day pop up on a remote listening device, transmitted to the mobile phone of an excited scientist. A glimmer of hope that the golden toad might just have come back from the dead.

Scan to hear what is likely the last recording made of the golden toad.

The quietening of giants

Over the last century, the animal with one of the biggest and deepest voices of all – the blue whale – became much rarer. According to figures from the International Whaling Commission, the greatest number of blue whales killed on the end of a whaler's harpoon, occurred in the first half of the 20th century. In the 1930–1931 season alone, nearly 30,000 of these ocean giants were butchered. Over 300,000 blue whales were killed in the Southern Hemisphere and a further 20,000 in the North Atlantic and North Pacific. Thankfully humanity saw sense and since 1966, the whales have been given full protection from hunting. Today some populations are recovering at rates of up to 7% a year and it's thought their numbers now range somewhere between 10,000 and 25,000 individuals. Their slow but steady recovery should be a reason to celebrate, but just as these mighty whales bounce back after the wholesale slaughter of whaling, they face new threats to their continued recovery.

Oceanographer John Ryan from the Monterey Bay Aquarium Research Institute led a long-term study that listened in on the ocean. The study began in 2015 and it coincided with the occurrence of a marine heatwave. 'The Blob' as it became known, saw ocean temperatures in the northeast Pacific rise by around 4 degrees Celsius. These conditions lasted for about two years – from late 2014 through to 2016. During this time the increased temperatures had a devastating impact on the marine ecosystem, with one study reporting the death of 62,000 seabirds.

Blue whales feed almost entirely on krill, which could make them highly vulnerable to warming oceans. Krill in the California Current ecosystem feed largely on phytoplankton and algae which thrive in nutrient rich waters brought to the surface by coastal upwellings. When the surface of the ocean gets warmer, it creates a barrier to these upwellings and a decline in the abundance of nutrients. The warmer waters also increase the krill's metabolic rate, leaving them energy hungry in an ocean with less food. It causes them increased stress, reduces their growth and reproductive capacity and kills off their larvae. So, warmer water can lead to a decline in the numbers of krill and this in turn can make life much harder for blue whales.

The California study found that the detection of whales' songs, rises and falls with their food supply. With less and less krill, the whales have to spend much more of their time looking for food and put less effort into looking for a mate. 'In the case of blue whales especially, they can't switch prey, so they simply have to search farther and wider for the only prey they eat – krill,' explains Ryan. 'We can imagine that if they have to dedicate much more time and energy to foraging, then there will be less time and energy available for other behaviours.'

As a consequence, during 'The Blob' the researchers found that the blue whales were singing less and becoming noticeably quieter. A similar pattern was also seen in a separate study with blue whales off the coast of Aotearoa New Zealand during their own ocean heatwaves in 2016 and 2018.

It seems that different whales react differently to ocean warming. Ryan's team observed that the lowest levels of both blue and humpback whale songs were detected during the climax of the 2015 heatwave. Both whale species then saw a similar increase in song detection over the next few years until they diverged after year three of the study. At this point humpback whale songs detection continued to rise while the detection of blue whale songs fell for two years in a row. This separation is likely due to the different foraging strategies of the two whales. Humpbacks have a more diverse diet than blue whales, so were able to adapt to the changes. But blue whales feed almost exclusively on krill, so it was their songs that were heard less during the warmer period. 'As the ocean changes, some species will be more affected than others,' says Ryan. 'Compared to humpback whales, blue whales in the eastern North Pacific may be more vulnerable due to not only a smaller population size but also a less flexible foraging strategy. These findings can help scientists and resource managers predict how marine ecosystems and species will respond to climate change.'

Thankfully the Californian whales soon started singing more when the ocean waters returned to normal temperatures. After the heatwave the detection of whale song for both blues and humpbacks increased notably.

It's too early to say just how periods of ocean warming may go on to affect blue whale populations, however, with marine heatwaves occurring more frequently, the future could be challenging. But Ryan believes that by listening to the whales, we have the chance to inspire people to help protect them: 'We can only care for something, and we can only find a sense of caring within ourselves, if we feel some connection to it. And I think sound naturally does that for people when they listen to the powerful voices of whales.'

The Santa Barbara Channel is a 110 kilometre stretch of ocean separating mainland California from the Northern Channel Islands. It's a busy international shipping route leading in and out of the ports of Los Angeles and Long Beach. Further up the state's coastline is the mega-port of San Francisco, supporting shipping at Oakland, Redwood City and San Francisco itself.

These waters, so busy with huge cargo ships, are also home to several endangered whale species, including blue whales. Tragically, many whales die after being run over by these ships in violent collisions. The National Oceanic and Atmospheric Association (NOAA) brought in a voluntary speed restriction for ships making their way through the sensitive whale habitat. Research proved that slowing the cargo ships to ten knots significantly reduced the risk of fatal whale collisions. But sadly, whale–ship collisions are still on the rise off America's west coast.

To change this requires the commitment of both port authorities and shipping companies. One project, off the coast of California, is setting a good example for others to follow. Scientist Ana Širović from the Norwegian University of Science and Technology, has been studying blue whale vocalisation in the Santa Barbara Channel for ten years. A major feeding site for blue whales, this stretch of water 'is very interesting acoustically, with lots of anthropogenic noise and a high density of animals'. However, as a global shipping lane serving the port of Los Angeles, Širović knows the Santa Barbara Channel presents challenging conditions for any whales.

Širović and collaborators from Woods Hole Oceanographic Institute, NOAA and the University of Washington, researched ways to stop these deadly collisions. Their ingenious solution relies on the sound of the whales' underwater singing. The project began trialling a new remote acoustic buoy, which aims to give ships advanced warning of whales in the area. The 'Whale Safe' detector listens out for whales calling in the channel. With acoustic buoys fitted with hydrophones and a small computer using AI to interpret any sounds, it records and differentiates whale song from shipping noises. But because sound travels faster and further underwater, the system can only point to the presence of whales in the area and cannot pinpoint their exact location. That requires some extra help.

Experienced observers aboard whale-watching tour boats or on aircraft can record information of whale sightings on a mobile app, adding to the information on whale activity, where they are and where they are heading. The system also adds oceanographic data to predict where blue whales are most likely to be, based on their known historic habitat preferences. A message is then relayed via satellite to a scientist for verification, before a warning is sent to shipping in the area. Any ship that receives the message knows to keep watch for whales and to dramatically slow their speed, giving the whales a much better chance of avoiding collision. The information is also combined into a daily 'Whale Presence Rating' on the project website, which indicates the likelihood of whale encounters from 'Low' to 'Very High', so skippers can plan the voyage ahead. Širović is amazed by the technology: 'It is really exciting to know that there are whales in the channel now, within an hour or two of them making the vocalisation.'

The tool also tracks ships using GPS and ranks the individual vessels and shipping companies according to their rates of cooperation with NOAA's voluntary speed restrictions. Looking at the 'report card' data for this on the Whale Safe website shows that many companies are reaching high compliance, while some can still do much better.

Ship collisions are currently the leading cause of death for large whales, and it's been estimated that over eighty blue, fin and humpback whales are killed by vessel collisions on the USA's west coast every year. Research has shown that speed limits can reduce the number of collisions by 80–90 per cent. So having a system that helps warn shipping of the whale's presence, but points the finger when they fail to react appropriately, has the potential to help save the lives of many whales. Whale Safe has proved to Ana Širović the importance of listening as a conservation tool: 'With improvements in acoustic monitoring technology, this is the perfect time to collect the kind of data that gives valuable insights into marine habitats and the behaviours of endangered animals.'

A boat closes in on a blue whale as it comes up for air. A figure leans out over the bow platform holding a long pole, directing the skipper to steer in closer. It's a scene that recalls a brutal history, but this is no harpoon and these pursuers are not whalers. They have not come to take the whale's life, but they *are* looking to capture its heartbeat.

The moment when a blue whale surfaces gives us a glimpse into an incredible world. For a few seconds, the largest animal that has ever lived on this planet crosses the line between their world and ours with explosive drama. Its presence slowly rises. Seen above from a drone, its huge stretched shape is surprisingly elegant and hydrodynamic. These giants aren't slow and clumsy, they are streamlined athletes of the ocean, albeit on a colossal scale. As the whale closes in on its intended breath, we see that underwater its skin appears as blue. But as it threatens to break the surface, it becomes a mottled silver-grey. This unique pattern on each blue whale's skin can be used by scientists to identify individual whales, a lot like a human fingerprint. The surfacing whale may show a glimpse of the yellowish hue sometimes found on its underside – the colour coming from remnants of microscopic algae called 'diatoms' that grew on the whale's skin as it fed in colder polar waters. Its yellow hue once earned the whale the nickname 'Sulphur Bottom' with the early whalers. As the whale finally surfaces, it expels a vertical cloud of pressurised water vapour from its twin blowholes. This can rise nine metres into the air and create a sound so forceful that it can help us locate the whales in the vastness of the ocean. The giant then takes a deep breath, closes its blow holes and points its head down beneath the water, dipping as gently as an aircraft nose touching down after landing. Sometimes it aims to dive deep and its whole body will bend and arc over the surface until its huge tail flukes finally appear, before slipping once more beneath the waves. These dramatic brief encounters, when blue whales come up for air, give researchers a narrow window of opportunity to get closer.

A team from Stanford University's Hopkins Marine Biology department were keen to discover the mechanisms that allowed these huge whales to regularly dive to depths of over 100 metres. They built a special remote monitor, about the size of a lunchbox, and attached it to the whale with suckers. To fit the device, they had to steer their boats carefully alongside a surfacing whale and, using a long pole, deliver the box neatly onto the side of the animal. The suction cups contained electrodes that allowed the device to record the whale's heart rate as an ECG (electrocardiogram). This was the first time ever that scientists had been able to measure the heart rate of a blue whale and what they discovered was extraordinary. They found that the whale's heart rate during a dive was typically 4–8 beats per minute and even dropped as low as just 2 beats per minute. (For a human adult it's usually somewhere between 40 and 100 beats per minute.) At the surface, the whale's recorded heart rates increased to between 23 and 37 beats per minute, which is thought to be the maximum rate possible.

It has long been known that whales experience a state of 'bradycardia' – a slowing down of the heart rate – when they dive. This is a physiological adaptation that allows them to conserve oxygen, reducing the amount needed by the heart itself and keeping it for more vital organs such as the brain. It's an adaptation that allows the whales to spend so long underwater. A blue whale has the capability to dive for up to thirty minutes on a single breath. But the fact the whale's heart can slow to just 2 beats per minute was a real surprise. The researchers now think that a blue whale's heart is performing near its limits and that this may help explain why no other animal has ever evolved to be larger than a blue. It's unlikely that any heart could ever be efficient enough to pump blood around a body bigger than a blue whale. It would struggle to generate the necessary pressure, beat efficiently and avoid structural failure. So, the heart of a blue whale is operating on the very edge of biological capacity. The whale's surprisingly low heart rate could be due to a 'stretchy' aortic arch – the part of the heart that pumps blood out into the body. In blue whales this structure might contract more slowly, to give some additional blood flow in between the infrequent beats.

After a day, the whale's tiny sensor-filled backpack detaches, ending its ride on the world's biggest ever animal. With a GPS tracker inside, the researchers can then retrieve the device as it bobs on the surface. Their next goal is to add more capabilities to the tags so they can learn more about the whales' secret underwater lives. By listening to the blue's extraordinary heartbeat, biologists are hoping to learn more about the physical limits of whales and have a better chance to understand how they react to stress and disturbance. Just like we use wearable fitness monitors to tell us about our sleep patterns and to track our health, tuning in to the whale's own physical wellbeing could help tell us exactly how individual whales are affected by noise pollution and a changing climate.

There is no sound more intimate and more fundamental to an animal's life than its heartbeat. The heartbeat of a blue whale is a wonder of nature that is both powerful and fragile, each beat is a single sound that represents all that we may so easily lose. It is the living rhythm of an extraordinary life, one that we are privileged to share our planet with.

8. Silence and Storm

THE SOUNDSCAPES OF MOUNTAIN AND ICE

The sea bear

Of all the wild animals I have encountered, the one that really sets my heart racing is the polar bear. The Canadian Inuit have a word – 'ilira' – that describes the powerful emotions you feel when coming face to face with a bear. Its approximate translation is 'the fear that accompanies awe'. First up, they are huge. The largest on record weighed over 1,000 kilograms and when standing up on its back legs was reported to measure over 3.3 metres tall. One record has the same bear at 1.5 metres tall, even down on all fours. Our film crew followed bear tracks in the snow, where each footprint was the size of a dinner plate. The wooden walls of the hunters' cabin where we were based were scarred by deep claw marks, higher than you could reach.

It's not just their size. Meeting a polar bear also inspires awe because they are beautiful. Not in the traditional way that a leopard is beautiful. Polar bears don't have the feline grace of a big cat or the catwalk aesthetics of a peacock. A polar bear's beauty is more visceral. It shows itself when you spot a distant bear wandering over the frozen sea, through the haze of shimmering blue icebergs. You'll spot it when, lit by the low sun, a bear's dirty yellow fur will suddenly glow like a fleece of gold. It can be seen when a bear, walking into the blowing snow and biting wind, closes its eyes and gently turns its head to keep its nose out of the cold. It can be seen in the red bloodstains of a seal kill, corrupting the clean white ice. A polar bear's beauty is all about power and all about the ability to survive in a hostile frozen world.

But half of the feeling described by 'ilira' is fear. This comes from the fact that polar bears are the largest of all land predators and that they have been known to hunt humans. I had felt this fear when a big male bear came off the sea ice and made directly for our cabin. This bear had the number 23 sprayed on his side, an identifier left by scientists of the Norwegian Polar Institute. The number led us to nickname him 'Beckham' after the footballer with the same number. He came right at us without any doubt, his head lifted, tasting our scent with his nose. We threw snowballs, banged pots together, waved our arms and shouted, but still he wasn't deterred. It's an odd feeling to have an animal look at you as its prey, fixing you directly with its eyes. We were ready to abandon our defence and run back inside the cabin when our guide fired a bright red flare that whistled over the ice and went off with a bang. At this the bear finally turned and went to find another meal elsewhere. But as the bear moved off, the feeling of 'ilira' flipped again. I had been afraid, but the bear was such a magnificent creature that I was sad to see it leave and, awake to its wonders, I felt a curiosity that begged me to follow. It took all my rational mind to stop myself running after the bear. Fear and awe can be addictive.

Polar bears live in a world of constant change. In winter they wander out on the platform of the frozen sea, hunting for seals. They can travel huge distances and for this reason the Inuit sometimes call them 'Pisugtooq', 'the great wanderer'. Polar bears tagged in Svalbard have shown up a year later in Greenland, over 3,000 kilometres away across the ocean.

Then, as the seasons swing, their world out on the frozen ocean begins to melt away, leaving the bears facing a whole new set of challenges. It was into this shifting world that I ventured with a small crew to film hunting polar bears. We began our journey on a chartered Norwegian fishing vessel and this was our home on a summer circumnavigation of the Svalbard archipelago. Each day we would go out in a smaller boat, searching the maze of broken ice for a bear. Days had passed with barely a glimpse of anything at all. The ice that year was less than in previous seasons and it seemed the whole of the Arctic was being pressed down by a heavy grey cloud that showed no sign of shifting and seemed to go on without end. Looking at the satellite ice charts with our vessel's skipper, it seemed that there was more ice to be found further north, so we headed up the coast of Spitsbergen Island following the broad waters of Storfjorden until, after a day or two of travel, the fjord narrowed into a bottleneck at Heleysund. Here the tidal currents can flow at ten knots, charging through the gap between two islands. I was woken from my sleep in the bowels of the ship when the whole vessel tilted scarily over as we rode the tidal flow like a paper boat in a bath after the plug has been pulled out.

The world beyond this cataract was immediately more austere and frozen. Bits of broken ice sailed out of the fog, drifting lost on the ocean. We headed north until the huge island of Nordaustlandet filled the horizon. As the skipper cut the engine and the vessel dropped anchor, we could hear a distant roaring. Finally, after days of gloom the sun broke through and we awoke to an Arctic wonderland. The enormous 7,800 square kilometre ice cap of Austfonna met the sea in a towering sheer cliff of ice that snaked on and on beyond sight. Countless cascades of falling meltwater plummeted from high on the ice, straight into the ocean, columns of backlit silver against the turquoise-blue ice. To the west, the rocky bay of Vibebukta was nestled in the lee of the ice cap and it was here that we finally found the broken remains of the winter sea ice and our best chance of finding bears.

Polar bears are not known for their wide range of vocalisations. This makes sense, as they lead largely solitary lives and only rarely encounter other polar bears. While on a film shoot to Churchill in Arctic Canada, I was lucky enough to watch two huge male polar bears sparring. It was autumn and the bears were waiting on the land to be ready for the sea ice to refreeze. At this time of year, the biggest males will seek each other out and, rearing up on their hind legs, they will mock fight, pushing and swinging at each other. These bouts may play a role in sorting out a dominance hierarchy before the more serious battles over females still to come. Even so, these sparring sessions were pretty physical and we could hear the heavy panting of the bears as they fought and occasional 'snorts' and even a short plaintive roar.

On the rare occasions that wild polar bears meet, their vocalisations can range from growling to hissing and 'jaw-popping' (a kind of exhaled snort). During courtship, males have been heard to make a low coughing 'chuff' sound in the presence of a female. But the truth is we don't often get close enough to the bears to hear any subtleties in their vocal communication and they are largely quiet. Polar bears are definitely the strong silent type.

The one time when the bears are surprisingly chatty is in the maternal den. After a female bear mates in the spring, she will work hard to catch as many seals as she can through the summer months. The fat she accumulates must see her through a long fast ahead. Sometime in the early days of autumn, she will come ashore and seek out any remaining snowdrifts from the previous winter. These are often the favoured places for the bears to dig their dens, a cosy 2×1.5m chamber linked to the surface by a short entrance tunnel.

Very brave (or foolish) scientists have probed these dens to take their temperature and have discovered that inside the den it can be around 10 degrees Celsius – that's about 21 degrees warmer than the outside air. Female bears will have mated in late April or May, but their fertilised egg remains in a state of suspension until August or

September when it finally implants into the wall of the bear's uterus. This process is called delayed implantation and is how the female can ensure that her cubs are born when conditions are optimal for their survival. The cubs are born between late November and early January. During the whole period of three to four months in the den, the female does not eat, drink or defecate and relies solely on her fat reserves. She feeds her cubs with rich milk, 35 per cent of which is made up of fat. The mother polar bear will focus all her attention on keeping the cubs warm and fed, giving them the best chance to grow, and it's during this intimate time that the polar bear is at its most vocal.

Denning polar bears are vulnerable to disturbance, so it's too risky to intrude into a wild den to place microphones. What we know of the bear's vocal exchanges in the den comes from a study of captive bears denning in a zoo in Holland. If adult polar bears are largely silent then – to quote the study's lead researcher – their cubs 'didn't get the memo'. Listening in on headphones the researchers were overwhelmed with constant noise, but after hours of observation and listening, patterns began to emerge. The cub's vocalisations could be placed into five different groups. 'Distress calls' took the form of crying and screaming when a cub wanted Mum's attention or simply 'didn't get its way'. 'Discomfort' was a moaning call when the cub couldn't find its mum's teat or was squashed, while 'comfort' was a contented 'mmm' when the cub had finished suckling or was asleep. 'Nursing attempt' was heard when the cub was trying to get on its mother's teat but lost it. These sounded like a gulping 'uh uh' and were always heard before or after nursing. The final sound was in relation to 'nursing' behaviour. When suckling, the cubs would make a rather strange humming that sounds almost exactly like someone trying to start the engine on an old reluctant car.

The study discovered that it wasn't just the cubs making sounds. The mother bears too were surprisingly noisy and the microphones picked up the stressful panting of Mum when the cubs were crying and the soft licking of her grooming them. They even recorded the mother bear's heavy snoring as she took a well-earned rest.

Scan to hear the humming of a polar bear cub as it suckles.

Scan to hear the snoring of a mother bear.

I couldn't hide my excitement as our skipper lowered our small filming boat, an open 4.5 metre-long aluminium vessel with an outboard motor, off the big ship and into the water. Our small crew climbed down the ladder, jumped in and waved goodbye. Soon we were travelling through a strange yet beautiful world. The last traces of the winter sea ice, known as 'drift ice', collected by tides and wind, had ended up in the bay of Vibebukta. It made for an incredible seascape and our guide steered our small boat through an endless maze of floating chunks of ice, infinite in their size and shape. They turned and rolled on the current, blue gems in a sea of deep green. Every now and then we stopped the boat to scan for bears through our binoculars. All seemed quiet except for the background rhythm of dripping coming from the melting ice. We heard the occasional splash of a seal, but the only other thing to break the silence was the distressed cries of the kittiwakes, as pirate mobs of Arctic skuas harassed them to surrender the fish in their crops.

Then we spotted a bear. It was being mobbed by a pair of Arctic terns as it walked along the pebbly beach. It slipped silently into the water and we slowly followed in the boat. She was a female, about six years old and in her prime. She swam through the icy water, her head an island of dry white fur, leaving a long V-shaped wake behind her. Through the glassy water we could see the powerful strokes of her long front paws and her stumpy back legs trailing. It wasn't hard to see how her species had earned their Latin name: *Ursus maritimus*, meaning sea bear. Climbing up onto a piece of drift ice, barely making a sound, she stood with her wet fur blue-grey and dripping before she shook herself like a dog, sending sparkling drops of water flying like a shower of diamonds. She sniffed at the air, trying to detect any seals. The bear crossed the ice, her huge paws making no sound and she launched low and smooth into the water on the far side, her rump hitting the surface with the slightest 'ploop'.

Watching her hunt through the ice, it made sense that she would be so quiet. Polar bears are ambush predators, and nothing gives the game away more than the clumsy crunch of a misplaced paw in the snow, or the explosive splash of a belly-flop into the water. Their sense of smell is world famous, being able to pick out the scent of a seal's den beneath the snow from nearly a kilometre away and reportedly able to pick up the smell from a seal resting on top of the ice from 30 kilometres away. While this incredible sense of smell allows the bear to locate its prey from a distance, when it gets closer it also has to rely on its sense of hearing. Research has shown that polar bears have sensitive hearing over a wide frequency range and that it is likely similar in sensitivity to that of a dog. There is some evidence too that bears may even be listening to the underwater sounds of seals to help find them.

Aside from 'aquatic stalking' of their prey through the drift ice, polar bears also practise 'still hunting'. I've watched them stand completely motionless at a seal's breathing hole for almost an hour, but they can last even longer. Then, should a seal pop up for air, they will explode into action and try and hook it with their paw or dive straight down to grab the seal with their jaws. A fidgeting bear would make sounds that would likely give them away, so the bears know that staying still means staying silent.

We lost our female bear in the maze of ice, but later that day we spotted another, this time a young male. A gentle breeze had pushed the ice further into the bay, and close to the beach it had piled up packed tight with only small patches of open water in between. It was harder to navigate the icy jumble with the boat, but it was here that we found the young male bear hunting. We watched as it stealthily lowered its body into a small pool between two chunks of ice. It would disappear from view for minutes at a time and, just like the bear itself, we had to stay patient and focused to keep eyes on it. Every now and then it would surface, its head rising up slowly like the periscope on a submarine, to peer low over the ice.

Suddenly it burst out of the water, a small ringed seal in its jaws. It dragged the seal back and forth over the ice and circled it almost as if it was either celebrating its success or was surprised at its own skill. It began to tear into the seal, peeling off long strips of pink blubber, using its incisors to pull it away. The bear was eating the seal's energy-rich fat and seemed to be ignoring the meat, which soon had drawn a flock of hungry ivory gulls. The bear would swallow huge chunks of blubber, lifting his head high to gulp them down. With the seal stripped bare of its fatty coat, the bear disappeared off into the rubble piles of ice – where we couldn't follow – and abandoned the rest of the carcass to the gulls. The long scarlet smear of blood left behind came as a sudden shock in a world of white, the only sign of our encounter with the Arctic's silent hunter.

Emps

There is a place at the end of the world where you don't see the sun for a whole month. Scoured by storms with hurricane-force winds, temperatures have been recorded at –70 degrees Celsius and everything, even the sea, is frozen. There is no dry land, no vegetation and no rock. The only thing here is ice and a deep penetrating cold. And yet one incredible animal survives here.

The breeding cycle of Antarctica's emperor penguin has to be the most dramatic 'story' in the natural world. You could lock a coachload of Hollywood screenwriters in a room for a month and they still wouldn't pitch you a script with as much drama, as much pathos and with such an achingly beautiful ending as the story of a pair of penguins, struggling to raise their chick. Natural sound is at the very heart of this extraordinary tale and whether there is a happy ending or not all comes down to one 'call' given in one short moment in time.

Emperor penguins, or 'emps' as the biologists like to call them, at just over a metre tall, are the largest of all the penguins. They are excellent swimmers, reaching speeds of up to 14 kilometres per hour when in pursuit of fish. They can dive to depths of over 500 metres and hold their breath for twenty-seven minutes underwater. They are truly aquatic birds, but once every year these sleek torpedoes of the Southern Ocean leave the water to stand upright on their two feet. In the southern hemisphere, autumn falls in April. As temperatures drop sharply it becomes cold enough for the surface of the sea to freeze solid. The sea ice starts to grow, advancing northwards at about four kilometres every day. In just a few short weeks the continent of Antarctica effectively doubles in size. Once the ice is thick enough to support their weight, the emperor penguins appear, often dramatically shooting out of the water as if they were jet propelled, before crash-landing on their bellies. While other animals fly and swim north to escape the oncoming cold, the emps are just arriving. They will waddle upright or sometimes toboggan along on their bellies, propelled by alternating kicks of their huge webbed feet. The journey south over the ice can be as far as 160 kilometres and the penguins form long lines of birds, all of them heading in convoy to their chosen breeding sites. These are often areas that are sheltered by the towering walls of grounded icebergs, frozen into place by the sea ice.

Around the coast of Antarctica there are some sixty-six emperor penguin colonies, including four that were discovered in 2024, having been spotted by analysing satellite images. The birds' 'guano' stains the sea ice pink and black, making them easy to spot on the pure white sea ice. The largest colony is found at the Dawson-Lambton glacier and is home to nearly 15,000 breeding pairs. It's likely that these breeding sites are the very places where the adult birds themselves were hatched.

Top of the agenda for any penguin arriving back at their colony is to find a mate. Emps show 'serial monogamy', finding a new mate every year, although 15 per cent of birds may team up again with their partner from the previous season. Their elaborate courtship is lots of fun. The males will call, serenading the female, starting with their heads down on their chest and tossing them into the air, bills pointed skywards, giving their repeated honking call. If she likes the male's proposition, the female will answer in kind and the pair will spend time in close attendance, standing still and posed like statues as if they are admiring each other. This is the vital time when both penguins become used to the voice of the other. They need to form a vital vocal connection that will see them through the challenges ahead. As the birds start to sing to each other, the colony is soon alive with sound. Each pair will now spend lots of time preening one another, then, to confirm their bond, they will take a walk together, one following the other. At this time of year both penguins are in good condition, having fed well through the summer. Their bodies are rather rotund and this can make the act of copulation more than a little awkward. With the female lying on her belly on the ice, the male will gingerly wobble his way up onto her back. It's all a bit precarious and he could slide off at any second and often does, but if all goes well, a few days later the female will lay a single white egg about the size of a grapefruit.

By late May and into early June, the female, having travelled over the ice and invested so much in making her egg, is now running low on energy. There is no chance that she could incubate it throughout the winter. That job will be for the male alone. But first she must transfer the egg to him for safekeeping. Other penguins that breed in Antarctica in the summer months do so on bare rock. For the female emp, there is no option but to lay her egg straight onto the ice. The male must quickly scoop up the precious cargo, as it could soon freeze solid. He carefully shuffles it up on top of his toes and then covers it in a fold of skin where he can keep it warm. Cradled by Dad, the egg is kept at a snug 38 degrees Celsius, while outside in the cold temperatures can drop to –35 degrees Celsius. The female will now leave the colony, using her last reserves of stored energy to repeat the epic journey all the way back to the open sea. With the females now departed and without the calls of duetting pairs, the colony suddenly becomes a much quieter place. The only sound is the relentless wind and the occasional lonely cry from a male emp.

Throughout June and July, the males must guard the eggs on their own. During this period, the sun will set below the horizon and it will be mostly dark except for just a few short hours of twilight. Polar night brings fierce winter storms and these can scour the colony with winds of over 100 kilometres per hour for days at a time. The temperature can sit at around –40 degrees Celsius and has been recorded even lower. It seems impossible that anything can survive in these conditions, but the male emperor penguins must stand firm.

The experiences of the first explorers to Antarctica give us an idea of what life must be like for the male penguins. In June 1911, three members of Captain Scott's final Terra Nova expedition set out from their base camp on Ross Island, heading for the emperor penguin colony at Cape Crozier some 110 kilometres away. Henry Bowers, Apsley Cherry-Garrard and Bill Wilson headed off with two sledges laden with food and equipment. Their goal was to bring back specimens from the colony for zoologist Wilson to help prove the evolutionary link between birds and reptiles. At the time it was believed penguins were 'primitive' birds and that their embryos might just show signs of their reptile ancestry. Their journey, trudging through the darkness and the freezing gales, was unimaginably tough. The snow was so thick they had to resort to pulling just one of the sledges at a time, running relays to retrieve the second sledge. For every kilometre of progress, they were forced to walk three kilometres. They survived intense blizzards where temperatures dropped to −60 degrees Celsius. In the dark of the polar night, they had to find their way by navigating by the stars and by candlelight. They fell into hungry crevasses and were so cold that poor Cherry's teeth chattered so violently they cracked and shattered. As they finally reached the penguin colony, a storm blew away their tent and the men retreated to their sleeping bags, lying down on the ice without shelter for two days. With a gap in the weather Bowers somehow found their tent. 'Our lives had been taken away and given back to us,' wrote Cherry.

To finally reach the penguins, the men had to scale huge walls of ice. They took five eggs but Cherry managed to drop two of them. On 1 August 1911, the three men staggered back into base camp on Ross Island with their precious cargo of three emperor penguin eggs. Their quest had come at a heavy cost; each man returned a physical shadow of his former self. Their clothing was so frozen solid that it had to be cut off them. Their eyes were sunken, faces scarred and noses blackened by the cold. Cherry's fingers were frost-bitten and he had lost his toenails.

His injuries played a part in him not being chosen for the five-man party that Scott later led aiming for the South Pole. Sadly, his Cape Crozier companions Bill Wilson and Henry Bowers famously perished in the attempt, alongside Captain Scott, Lawrence Oates and Edgar Evans.

Back in the UK, Cherry took responsibility for delivering the precious eggs to the Natural History Museum in London. Initially he was met by a junior research assistant, who didn't want them. He was made to wait out in the corridor before someone finally took the eggs from him. 'I handed over the Cape Crozier embryos, which nearly cost three men their lives and cost one man his health, to your museum personally and your representative never even said thanks,' Cherry complained in a letter to the museum.

Sadly, the eggs remained unstudied until 1934 and even then it was admitted that they added little to the advancement of penguin embryology and evolutionary understanding. In 2012, I was lucky enough to visit the centenary anniversary exhibition of Scott's last expedition at the Natural History Museum in London. There was a collection of artefacts from the time: diaries, ski boots, shaving brushes and even Scott's famous farewell note from his fatal last camp. But in one cabinet there were three white eggs, cracked from where the embryos inside had been sampled. More than just eggs, they told a story of exploration and adventure that is hard to match. They were also a reminder of the miraculous survival skills of a remarkable bird. To me they were as precious a treasure as anything in the museum.

Cherry later wrote about the mission undertaken with Bowers and Wilson in his book *The Worst Journey in the World* and it seems he had developed a deep respect for the penguins of Cape Crozier: 'Take it all in all, I do not believe anybody on Earth has it worse than an Emperor penguin.'

Just how the male emps are able to withstand the longest and coldest of winters is a wonder of the natural world. To keep the egg safely in place, they must stay on their feet. They cannot lie down for a moment and even sleep standing up. They are wearing a double-layered coat of feathers, waterproof on the outside with an insulating layer of down on the inside. Beneath this there is a jacket of three centimetre-thick blubber, but without food they are still surviving on their summer fat reserves and their blubber layer is getting thinner every day. In order to stay warm, they gather together in 'huddles', forming groups of over 5,000 birds at a time. They will spend 90 per cent of their time in these huddles. With their heads tucked down they will stand close together, backs outwards to the wind. The huddle is 50 per cent warmer in the centre, but for birds on the outer edge things aren't so toasty.

It was previously thought that these males on the edge of the huddle were at a huge disadvantage, but researchers from Germany discovered that the penguins have found the best way for every bird to keep warm. By setting up cameras that took a still photo of their study colony every 1.3 seconds, they were able to build a timelapse of the huddle and work out what was really going on. If the huddle is too loose the penguins begin to freeze, but if it's too tight they can't move at all and, locked in place, those on the edge will freeze. The researcher's videos revealed that the huddle didn't ever remain still for long. Individual penguins would move every thirty to sixty seconds and this movement would spread like a wave through the huddle. With every wave, penguins would waddle out of the group and rejoin in another position. So, after several hours the huddle would shift about and each penguin would get an opportunity to be at the warm centre and keep out of the wind.

French researchers fitted male emperors with temperature monitors and discovered that the huddle didn't just help the penguins stay warm, it even played a role in saving them precious energy. Their results found that penguins in the huddle saved 26 per cent more energy than penguins in smaller groups, and birds that had gathered together saved 32 per cent more energy than individuals standing alone. The only way the male emperors can survive the coldest, darkest of winters is to stand together.

About a month after it last set, the sun finally reappears. At first it stays low on the horizon, but with every day its power grows. With the males having carried their precious cargo for between sixty-five and seventy-five days, it's around this time their eggs finally hatch. The males are in a terrible state. It's been four months since they last ate. They have lost around 45 per cent of their previous body weight, as much as 20 kilograms. By facing out the Antarctic winter, their energy levels are seriously depleted and now they have a hungry chick to feed. The chicks are very small and vulnerable when they hatch, weighing only about 150 grams, and with just a thin layer of down they cannot regulate their own body temperature and so are still susceptible to the cold. With their chicks still balanced in the warm fold above their feet, the males don't have the option to head to the sea and find food. Their chicks would fall and freeze to death on the ice. So, the males' ordeal isn't over yet. But incredibly, they are still able to offer one small, first meal to their chick. The male produces a single feed of 'crop milk', a high-protein, cottage-cheese-like substance secreted from his oesophagus. This buys some time for the chick, allowing it to survive for about another week.

For the emaciated males and their hungry chicks, things aren't looking too good, but one day hope appears on the horizon. In late July or early August the females finally return – and they are just in the nick of time. Convoys of well-fed females march over the sea ice in long lines. The colony, which had remained largely silent during the harshness of winter, now erupts with sound. Waves of excited honking rise among the waiting males. With both males and chicks running on empty there is little time to lose. It becomes imperative to the penguins' survival that the pair are reunited as quickly as possible. But as the first females reach the colony chaos breaks out, with thousands of penguins wandering around honking, desperate to find their mate. Unlike other birds, the emps do not have a stationary nest making them easier to locate. The huddle will have moved about a great deal over the winter, and the sun is low enough that it's hard to pinpoint anyone through sight alone (and let's be honest – all the penguins look pretty much the same, at least to us!). To our ears there would seem little chance that the birds could hope to locate each other in such chaos and cacophony. That they do so is all down to the honking calls they make.

Researchers from France have discovered that when it comes to finding your partner, for emperor penguins, two voices work better than one. Like all birds, penguins have a paired tubular syrinx. Here there are a series of membranes that open and close, meaning the penguins have the ability to call with 'two voices' at the same time, as sound is produced from controlling the air flow in each of the two parts of the Y-shaped tube. Emperor penguins can call from each tube of the syrinx simultaneously, producing two different notes. The penguins can manipulate these notes, making a sound that is unique to each and every individual penguin. The researchers played back manipulated calls to the emps, finding that they would respond to the 'two voice' call, but if they modified it to play only one half of the call, the birds showed no response.

Not only do the calls help the birds work out who is who, it was also found that these 'two voice' notes propagate well through obstacles such as the huddled bodies of other penguins. The researchers found that other penguins that have fixed nests do not have the same elaborate acoustic coding that helps the emps to identify individuals in the colony. So, with their energy on a knife edge and with the survival of their hungry chicks hanging in the balance, emperor penguins are able to find each other by using sound to save the day. Recognising their partner's call, both male and female emperors are able to locate each other and are reunited after months apart.

The females are all big and beautiful having spent the winter out at sea; they have built up their fat reserves and carry stomachs full of squid and fish. In contrast, the male penguins are thin and desperately in need of food. So now it's the turn of the female to take over parenting duties. Perhaps understandably, such is the bond between the male and his precious cargo, that he is reluctant to hand over the chick and the female has to gently convince him. It's a dangerous transition as the male must spill the chick onto the ice and the female must scoop it up without delay. Now finally the chick gets its first proper feed from the female and the male, having not eaten for 115 days, is free to walk the 160 kilometres or so to return to the sea, where he will get to fill up on fish before returning to his partner and chick.

As the chicks grow from balls of downy fluff, the male and female will continue to swap their feeding shifts, and with each turn the distance to the ocean will get slightly shorter as the sea ice starts to melt away. Too big to fit in their parents' pouches, the chicks become toddlers – wandering here and there across the colony, their watchful parents in tow. Growing fast, they start to hang out in creches with the other chicks and sometimes it's easy to get lost. But once again their parent's 'two voice' call comes to the rescue. The chicks whistle their endearing call, which the parents can recognise, and they give their own unique response, which then helps bring the two together. Life for a penguin chick is tough, with only about 20 per cent of the young emps surviving their first year. So, facing the hardest conditions on the planet, emperor penguin parents use their voices to give their chicks a fighting chance. In the most brutal wilderness of all, this extraordinary sound can make all the difference between life and death.

Scan to listen to the whistles of emperor penguin chicks and the 'two voice' honking call of their parents.

Windy walruses and singing seals

My stomach muscles clenched with every impact of the small boat as we bounced over the waves. It felt like we had been searching for hours. Our guide was following his GPS, steering us left and then right as if following a set of signposts the rest of us couldn't see. Surrounded by ocean and with no hint of land in any direction, it was beginning to feel a little bit like we were lost. This feeling wasn't helped when the engine suddenly spluttered to a halt and we drifted silently on the current. A fulmar passed overhead checking us out, while our guide hunted through the storage trunks, finally emerging with a plastic bottle of oil to top up the thirsty engine and have us on our way again.

We were looking for Svalbard's Tusenøyane or 'Thousand Islands', a rarely visited remote archipelago south-east of the mainland of Spitsbergen. This mysterious group of low-lying, rocky islands has done little to earn its name, as there are in truth only about forty islands and none of them has been discovered to be the source of the world-famous salad dressing. When at last we spotted land, it was veiled in shifting curtains of fog and as we closed in on the first island, we were treated to only occasional glimpses of a barren stony beach through the sea mist. Gangs of little auks whizzed overhead, their stubby wings beating so fast that they hummed like a cloud of fireworks. We could hear the eerie whistle of a purple sandpiper and then, rounding the final headland to complete our circumnavigation, we spotted a polar bear, sleeping in the hazy sunshine. We had come all this way to try and find one of the Arctic's largest residents, the walrus, and having seen nothing on the first island we had little choice but to press on to the next and hope for better luck.

We could hear them before we could see them. A distant choir of moans and groans, grunts and snorts. With the drifting fog, we could even smell them before we could see them, a heady mix of on-the-turn seafood and wet shoe leather. Then the clouds parted and the sun burnt through and we could finally set eyes on them. About forty individuals lay hauled up on the beach, their bodies turning a raw-sausage pink in the growing sunshine. About another twenty walruses were swimming in the water. We slowed the boat to a stop and watched. So far on our journey to Svalbard, filming these giant tusked seals had proved to be challenging. They were hard to work out, being both a mix of frighteningly curious but then instantly flighty. On the first day of our filming trip around Svalbard, we had struggled to squeeze ourselves into our insulated neoprene float suits, bright dayglow orange with their own welly boots and emergency lights built in. These would hopefully keep us alive if we should accidentally fall overboard into the freezing water. Wanting to test if the 'float' suits actually worked, we decided to take a stroll down the beach for a quick dip into the Arctic Ocean. With the hoods up we waddled into the water like a family of orange teddy bears, to discover that our suits did indeed 'float' and that we couldn't feel the cold water at all. Then suddenly a small herd of about five walruses popped up out in the bay and upon seeing us began to come closer. They would rear up, heads clearing the surface, and bark at us before diving below with a dramatic splash. Then a few seconds later they would pop up again, this time even closer. We got out of the water pretty fast for a gang of inflatable pumpkins.

On another occasion, we had been in the small outrigger, scouting along Svalbard's remote northern coastline, exploring bays, beaches and headlands on the lookout for polar bears. Coming around a corner we found a huge walrus colony, sleeping on a narrow beach at the bottom of a tall cliff. Upon hearing the boat engine their heads were up and they lolloped into the water, the undulating fat in their bodies rolling them in waves down the beach. They were none too pleased to see us and surrounded the boat, bursting up out of the water. With their red eyes glaring and their dagger-like tusks, they made for an intimidating sight and would come straight at our small boat snorting their annoyance, before diving beneath us at the last second. Looking over the edge into the clear water, the walrus would pass beneath the hull and I got the perfect view of just how huge they were. Not wanting to cause them any more disturbance, we quickly turned the boat and left them to their bay in peace.

Big groups of walruses were still quite a rare sight on Svalbard. For about 350 years they were hunted for their oily blubber, their thick skins and their ivory tusks. In the early 17th century, whalers visiting the Tusenøyane were so taken aback by the abundance of walruses that they shifted away from hunting whales to focus on this new quarry. When, finally, the animals were given full protection in 1952, there were only a hundred walruses left in Svalbard's waters. Thankfully, their numbers have been slowly recovering. A survey in 2018 counted 5,503 walruses found across ninety-eight different sites where they like to haul out. It seemed that Svalbard's walruses still held an innate fear of humans in boats and we were always mindful to give them the space they needed. Hauled out on the beach is where the walruses feel most vulnerable. This is the place a polar bear will try and catch one and their calves are the most likely to get snagged. They will stampede into the water in order to find safety, even if the disturbance is in the form of a boat.

Coming into the mouth of the small bay where we could see the haul-out, we stopped and planned our best approach. The beach shelved gently into the sea and, beyond the piles of blubbery bodies, the interior of the small island stretched out. Largely flat, there were no trees or bushes for cover, but we did spot some piles of bone-white Siberian driftwood, behind which we might be able to set up a small filming hide. We decided our best approach would be to drive the boat back out of the bay and around the far side of the island, slowly creeping our way on foot across the interior in hope of finding a safe spot to view the walruses. Hugging the coastline, our guide had to steer our small boat through churning eddies, skirting over shallows with spiky reefs.

On the far side of the island all was quiet and we jumped out of the boat and walked it in towards the beach. With no way to get in past the rocks we had to wade through the chest-deep water, carrying the cases of camera kit above our heads. Once on land and still in our bright orange float suits, we stood out like satsumas in a tray of kitty litter, so decided it was best to finally take them off. Then we began the long trek over the island, hauling the rucksacks full of camera gear. It started to get quite hot in the sun, and looking through the binoculars I could see that more and more walruses were hauling themselves up the beach to join the snoozing pile-on. You could see that their bodies, shiny and brown from being in the sea, quickly turned bright pink as they soaked up the warmth of the sun. We found a position hidden behind a small pile of boulders and filmed the contented walruses as they slumbered. They appeared very relaxed, so we crept a bit closer and filmed them again.

As the afternoon wore on the sky became even clearer and the animals were bathed in light, their wet brown bodies flecked with bronze as the sun hit them. Slowly, carefully, we moved forward again, but it was becoming apparent that the walruses weren't in the least bit bothered about our presence. As long as we stayed quiet and kept low they paid no heed, and the gentle breeze was blowing onshore, so kept our scent away from their nostrils. Again, through the binoculars I watched the animals still swimming out at sea. They seemed to be frolicking in the glassy water and having a great time.

These walruses swimming offshore would dive and disappear for a while and I guessed they were probably feeding. With the summer retreat of the sea ice, vast areas of Svalbard's coastal waters are opened up for them. Walruses feed predominantly on marine invertebrates, but bivalve clams are their favourites. They dive down, sculling along the sea floor with their paddle-like flippers, faces down in the silt, grazing and searching out buried clams with their sensitive bristly whiskers. When they find a clam, they hold it in their rubbery lips and pull their tongue into the back of their mouths, like a rapid piston, creating a vacuum with enough suction to pull out the clam. They can dive down to 100 metres and hoover up around 4,000 clams in one feeding session! As they forage like this, the walruses stir up the sea floor, sending up great clouds of sediment that help make the Arctic summer seas even richer.

Walruses have a complex repertoire of acoustic communication. In the wintertime, as they shelter among the drifting pack ice, males will display to attract a female. When they find a herd of females, the male will present a series of vocalisations both above and below the water. The males inflate the pharyngeal muscles in their throats, helping them both amplify any sounds and stay afloat and upright in the water at the same time. They will make lots of sounds, from clacking their teeth, to whistling, in order to draw the females into the water. The highlight of their performance is their 'knocking' song. Males will make these songs following complex patterns that include a rhythmic knocking, punctuated by occasional metallic 'twangs' like the sound from a country and western mouth harp. These songs are made up of hundreds of short repetitive pulses that are delivered to a set cycle and can go on for hours or even days at a time. They are among the longest and most complex vocal breeding displays of any mammal. Male walruses in captivity have also been observed to clap their fore flippers to listening females. It seems that this repeated clapping makes sound through cavitation (the displacement of water to create a vacuum), similar to the snapping of a pistol shrimp.

Walruses aren't the only members of the pinnipeds (the family of seals and sea lions) that show extraordinary vocalisations. In the Arctic, the bearded seal is known for its haunting song, but perhaps the most extraordinary singer of all is found at the opposite polar extreme.

Imagine you are walking across the frozen sea ice in Antarctica. It's late October and the temperature is a chilly –20 degrees Celsius. The six months of winter are technically coming to an end, but it doesn't feel like it where you're standing – despite being wrapped up warmly, you can still feel the bitter cold on your face and in your toes. The crunching of your boots resounds over the ice, the only sound for what seems like miles around. The sea is frozen solid as far as the eye can see and it feels a little unnerving to be strolling around on top of the deep ocean. Beneath your feet is another world under the ice. It might as well be another planet. That other worldly feeling grows stronger as you hear a strange and wonderful sound. Lying down, you put your ear against the ice and incredible noises rise up from the depths below.

The sound, a bizarre chorus of buzzes, clicks and weird descending trills, seems just like the intro to an experimental prog-rock album. These fantastic voices belong to the southernmost living mammal on the planet, the Weddell seal.

October, when the mother seals haul out on the ice to give birth, is the best month to see them. On the surface, with their plump speckled bodies, they look a little like huge Cumberland sausages, but with the cute face of a puppy at one end and some flippers at the other. They congregate to give birth close to pressure ridges – the raised barriers of sea ice that are formed by ocean currents and strong winds. These ridges contain many cracks and holes where the seals can get access to and from the ocean. The seals make a living swimming beneath the blue icy ceiling, feeding on fish, squid, octopus and prawns that live on the bottom. They can swim underwater for eighty minutes on a single breath and reach depths of 700 metres beneath the surface.

There are no predators here, so the female seals give birth to their pups up on the surface of the ice. For their newborns, it must be something of a shock to be evicted from the warm surrounds of Mum's body, out into the minus-double-digit world outside. But Mum feeds them with some of the richest milk on the planet, containing a whopping 60 per cent fat (your daily pint of semi-skimmed has only 3 per cent) and the pups put on weight at a tremendous rate, growing a thick blubbery coat to help them stay warm. In just a month, these pups can bulk up from 30 kilograms – the size of a nine-year-old child – to 100 kilograms – the size of a premier league rugby flanker.

The bond between the mother seal and her pup is strong. Pups can even hear their mothers calling from down beneath the ice. Mothers often call to their pups from their breathing holes, to try and encourage their young to follow them into the water. But perhaps the oddest vocalisations here are made by the male Weddell seals and are thought to be related to breeding. From late September to early December, male seals establish underwater territories, focusing on areas where groups of females use holes in the ice to access the ocean. These adult males, measuring about 3 metres long and weighing up to 500 kilograms, are known to fight to defend their territories and the females within them from other males. So it may be that their elaborate songs have a role to play in defending these spaces from rivals; but equally it could be that their songs play a role in attracting the females in the first place. Because all this action plays out under the frozen ocean, it's pretty hard for scientists to study the males' behaviour and know for sure.

To answer some of the mysteries around Weddell seals, scientists from the McMurdo Oceanographic Observatory placed out remote underwater camera and microphone arrays that spied on the world beneath the ice. For two continuous years these remotes captured sounds and pictures from the strange turquoise underworld.

They discovered that the seals regularly vocalise at ultrasonic frequencies, with as many as 17 per cent of their calls made above and beyond the frequency range of human hearing. The recordings showed up nine different types of ultrasonic calls. Weddell seals are the only pinniped that makes ultrasonic calls, so this is a pretty unusual finding. We don't yet know whether it is males, females or both making these new calls, or just what their function might be.

One theory is that they are a crude form of echolocation. It would seem to be much less sophisticated than that seen in dolphins and toothed whales, but it could be a vital survival tool. In the winter months, when Antarctica plunges into four months of darkness and topside temperatures crash, the seals retreat from the surface to spend most of their time underwater where it's warmer. This means they can avoid the worst storms, but they do have to work hard to keep their breathing holes open, scraping away the growing ice with their teeth. Under the ice, without sunshine from above, it will be pitch black, and having a method of finding your way around without bumping into obstacles would be pretty useful. So, echolocation could be the perfect acoustic tool.

There is still a lot left to discover about the extreme lives of these remarkable seals and the role their extraordinary vocalisations play in their survival. But whatever is behind their calling, there can't be many voices as unusual as that of the Weddell seal.

Scan to listen to the extraordinary song of a Weddell seal, beneath the Antarctic ice.

The sun was starting to dip low over the ocean, bathing the Tusenøyane in fantasy light. It wouldn't sink beneath the horizon until late August, making this the land of the midnight sun. A gang of puffins were busy coming and going across the island, and out at sea the Arctic terns hovered over the calm water before diving down to pick off small fish from the surface. We'd had a wonderful day filming the walruses and had got so close we could film their nostrils opening and closing as they snored the day away. The only thing left to do was record some of the amazing sounds coming from the slumbering beasts. Unfortunately, we had left the sound recording kit back on our expedition vessel but, after some gnashing of teeth, a solution presented itself. Our camera kit came with a detachable microphone that we could fit on the top to record sound on the camera. The only problem was we couldn't really risk taking the delicate and expensive camera close enough to record good sound. It was also very bulky and impractical to move without risking disturbing the walruses. Searching through the kit we found a long length of extension cable, which meant we could attach the microphone on one end of the cable and plug in the other end to the camera ready to record from a distance. Now the only problem was getting the microphone in among the sleeping walruses. There was only one thing for it. I would have to crawl.

I shuffled across the black sand on my belly, propped up on my elbows and trailing the microphone cable back to my bemused camera operator. Taking my time, I would pause every couple of metres, just to make sure none of the walruses had spotted me, but they were fast asleep and it didn't take long to reach a point where I was surrounded on three sides by walls of warty pink blubber. I was there to capture the sound, but the first sensation that hit me was the smell. With the walrus living on a diet of clams, the beach was left smelling like a fish market and the sleeping giants were relaxed enough that there was a near constant leak of fishy digestive gases coming from both ends of the animals. It was hard not to giggle, but I didn't want to ruin the recording so forced myself with stoic professionalism to keep a lid on my sniggering and limited my joy to just a smile. Alongside the farting and belching, the walruses made for incredibly noisy bedfellows. There was the constant wheeze of their breathing and their rubbery lips would wobble and smack together with their snoring. Sneezes and snorts occasionally erupted, each throwing wads of salty, snotty water flying. The walrus next to me sighed with deep content, her tummy rumbling as she stretched out a flipper into the air. I could see her tiny fingernails lined up along the edge of the giant paddle-like hand, a reminder of our shared mammalian ancestry.

Although the walruses were huddled close together, it seemed to me that they were reluctantly social. Further down the beach, a sudden argument flared up, raising the volume considerably. Two neighbours reared up and began honking aggressively at each other. Spitting and stabbing with their tusks, it was enough to send a wave of unease through the herd and I realised it was probably time to make a polite exit. As the walruses quietened back down and their soundtrack returned to the steady rhythm of their snoring, I started my crawl back. As I passed the last sleeping giant it lifted its flipper, scratched at the tubercles on its dry flaky skin and let out an enormous fart.

It was 3 am by the time we had packed up, crossed the island, wriggled into our float suits and waded back out to the boat. As we headed home across the endless sea, the low sun turned the ocean to gold.

About a year after returning from filming the walruses, it was time to edit the footage together for the final show. With vivid memories of my time among the herd, and keen to reflect the walruses' true character, I wanted to use some of the more 'uncouth' sound effects that we recorded. At first, I ran into the objections of a rather strait-laced TV executive who thought the whole thing was too 'juvenile' for the BBC. But I stood my ground and, in the end, the walruses in all their vulgar sonic glory made it to the broadcast show. We even got David Attenborough to narrate 'digesting a belly full of clams generates a lot of wind, making walrus colonies *very* fragrant places', perfectly cuing up an enormous walrus fart.

Scan to listen to the impolite rumblings of
Svalbard's sleeping walruses.

The shattered stillness

In 2025 the International Energy Agency predicted that our consumption of oil would rise by 13 per cent from current levels by 2050. It also forecast gas consumption to rise by 50 per cent by 2030. The same report also went on to say that the world is highly likely to fail in its attempts to limit global temperature rise to its 'safety' target of 1.5 degrees Celsius.

Our rapidly warming world is changing the Arctic beyond all recognition. According to satellite data from NASA released in 2024, the previous eighteen years saw the lowest sea ice extents on record. The area north of the Arctic Circle is believed to contain 13 per cent of the world's undiscovered oil and 30 per cent of its undiscovered gas, so it's always attracted attention from 'Big Oil' companies. But with the frozen sea opening up, giving better and more consistent access, the polar north has now become a new frontier to be exploited.

Wherever our species go, we inexorably change the soundscape. Those extra ships, helicopters, planes, bulldozers and trucks all become new sources of ambient noise. Add to these the explosive blasts from mining, drilling for oil and the use of seismic air guns to search for fossil fuels, and the change can be dramatic. In the still and silent world of the Arctic, these new sounds can have devastating effects.

Walruses are dependent on vocalised sound. It's vital to their courtship displays and to maintaining the relationship between a mother and a calf, and is key to social communications of aggression and sharing the threat of danger. As their polar home gets noisier, it's likely that their lives will be affected. A clue to their possible future comes from a study in Scotland that found that the noise from shipping can be so loud it's enough to cause temporary hearing loss in harbour seals. I know from my own observations that walruses are sensitive to noise. The airborne noise of a low-flying helicopter or plane has the capacity to cause a terrible stampede for the water, putting small calves at risk of being crushed or drowned. And it's not just the walruses at risk.

The IUCN's Polar Bear Specialist Group are rightly concerned about this new industrial Arctic soundscape and its potential effects on polar bears. They state that noise pollution from seismic surveying activities and from aircraft can be heard within 300 metres of known polar bear denning sites. They fear that any disturbance at this sensitive time for the bears may cause them to abandon their dens, and in one study den disturbance has been linked to a lower birth weight in female cubs, which is likely to have a negative effect on their future survival.

The concern of the world's leading polar bear experts is backed up by the science. One study in Alaska by scientists from San Diego Zoo built four artificial polar bear dens in the snow. Each had a variable depth and thickness of roof in order to mimic the differences seen in the bears' own dens. The den sites were fitted with recording devices and then subjected to sounds from nine different human sources, including aircraft, tracked vehicles and wheeled vehicles. Then, comparing the levels of sound recorded to the known hearing range of bears, they were able to estimate the ability of denning bears to hear human sounds. The research discovered that aircraft noise was detected 75 per cent of the time when the sound originated from a range of 1.6 kilometres or closer. Sounds made from ground-based human activity had the highest probability of being heard by bears when made inside a 0.8 kilometres distance from the den. Conservationists are now pushing for buffer zones around known polar bear den sites to help keep things quiet during this vital time for mother bears and their cubs.

But it's not just bears in dens that are vulnerable to our noise. A study published in 2024 looked at aircraft disturbance in polar bears in the South Beaufort Sea north of Alaska. It found that the noise of aircraft led to abrupt changes in polar bear activity and movement, and that the probability of disturbance increased with a decrease in the aircraft's altitude. Another study, this time in Svalbard, attempted to measure the distance at which a polar bear can detect an approaching snowmobile and their different behavioural responses. The research discovered that, on average, the bears were alerted to the snowmobile at a distance of 1,164 metres. At a distance of 843 metres most bears responded by moving away. So, it's even possible that bears can be disturbed by the sound of snowmobiles before they can likely see them. The study observed that female bears with cubs showed a more intense response to the intrusion and were especially vulnerable to disturbance.

Polar bears are classified as 'vulnerable' by the IUCN. In America they are classed as 'threatened' under the US's Endangered Species Act. In Canada and Russia, they are considered as a 'species of special concern'. Unfortunately, the bears are under attack from a number of threats, noise pollution being just one. Many bears show high bodily concentrations of polychlorinated biphenyls or PCBs – a type of persistent pollutant that accumulates in the bears' fatty tissues. These are known to cause reproductive abnormalities, interfere with the bears' hormones and weaken their immune system. Beyond our poisoning of the bears, we are doing our best to destroy their homes. By 2100 the Arctic will see more days where the sea ice retreats enough to leave open water. This will greatly reduce the bears' ability to hunt for seals. We have entered a new era for Arctic sea ice. These days the ice is thinner and there is less of the thicker multiyear ice that would survive from one season to another. This new young ice is more vulnerable to melting and is more easily pushed and pulled by the currents, turning the bears already unpredictable world into a living chaos where it's harder to find food, find a mate or rear cubs. A recent study shows that if we fail to meet the goals set out by the Paris climate agreement and limit warming to 1.5 degrees Celsius, the polar bears of Canada's Hudson Bay could become extinct as soon as the 2030s.

On one of our last days filming in Svalbard we came across a mother polar bear and her two cubs swimming out in the open sea. They were miles from land and all the ice had gone, but somehow, they found a lonely iceberg drifting on the current and they had soon scaled their way up its fluted blue walls to lie together in a warm fuzzy pile on the top. All the bears were panting heavily from their exertions. Seeing the bears taking a rest from their long swim made me wonder at their extraordinary ability to survive in such a harsh and shifting environment. But it also made me fearful for their future in a world without ice. Polar bears are truly spectacular animals and to encounter them in the wilderness of their Arctic home is a sort of biological epiphany. The Inuit have many names for the polar bear, but my own favourite is 'Tornârssuk' – 'the one who gives power'. Through their encounters with bears, Inuit hunters would test themselves to the limit and, if they survived, their feelings of strength and joy were seen as a gift from the bear. But this relationship between human and bear has shifted and now we are the ones wielding great power. Our way of life is on course to annihilate polar bears, with one study suggesting that with the sea ice gone, only a handful of bears will survive beyond the end of the century. Nothing makes me as sad and angry as knowing that this animal's fate won't be decided by its own legendary strength, but by our own weakness and refusal to change.

The grey ghost

FROM THE WINDOW of the aircraft all I could see were mountains. An endless procession of snowy peaks and deep valleys that filled the small oval window and stretched away to fade in a haze beyond the horizon. It was beautiful. Looking down I started to scan every precipitous ridgeline with my eyes. Somewhere in this vast wilderness there were snow leopards. Faced with the impossible, I began to worry how on earth we could expect to find one, let alone film one, in such a daunting landscape.

I had come to the Indian Himalaya with a small crew to try and film snow leopards, the 'holy grail' of wildlife filmmakers the world over. Snow leopards are hard to film for three main reasons. The first is that they are secretive creatures, active only during a few hours of daylight at the beginning and the end of the day. Their luxuriant silver-grey fur is painted with dark rosettes that perfectly mimic the pattern of shadows among the rocks. They roll in the mountain dusts and take on the background colour of the landscape. Few creatures 'do' camouflage as well as a snow leopard.

The second reason is where they live. Snow leopards make their home in some of the toughest terrain on Earth. They are commonly found between 3,000 and 5,4000 metres altitude. They think nothing of moving over the steepest terrain, jumping from ledge to ledge, using their long tails as a counterweight to help their balance as they flow over the tortured mass of rock with liquid ease. Living in this most extreme of worlds makes the snow leopard a tough animal to get close to.

The final reason is that there aren't that many of them. According to the IUCN, as of 2017 there were between 7,446 and 7,996 snow leopards in the world. These figures may seem oddly specific and yet are presented as a wide range. This is entirely because snow leopards are so hard to count. Biologists are reliant on statistical models that can only really provide us with an estimated range, albeit with figures that sound incredibly precise. Surveys tend to rely on extensive camera-trap work and digital identification of individual cats caught on camera. In Nepal, scientists have analysed the DNA found in snow leopard scat to give estimates of numbers. But these cats are found across a range that adds up to 2 million square kilometres..

How on earth do you survey a physical space this large, especially one so remote and mountainous? The truth is that we don't really know for sure how many snow leopards there are out there.

In Ladakh, the region of northern India where we had come to film, the density of snow leopards can be relatively high. By relatively, I mean that in Hemis National Park, our chosen destination, there can be around two snow leopards per 100 square kilometres. Across some of their range in Mongolia, these big cats can be as sparce as 0.1 cat per 100 square kilometres. So, as one wildlife photographer once told me, filming snow leopards can be like looking for the only fast-moving, hay-coloured needle in a haystack the size of a football field. I had spoken to others who had tried to film these elusive cats, to be told stories of them sitting in the cold for weeks and not even seeing a single snow leopard. Was it any wonder that across their mountain homeland, from the mighty Himalaya and Karakorum, the desert peaks of Tibet and Mongolia and on into the mountains of China, these cats were often more legend than reality. In the high-altitude desert of Spiti in India, it was once believed they were a vampire cat that sucks the blood from its prey. While in northern Pakistan it was thought the leopard fed on the life-giving blood of its victims and left the flesh and bones behind. In the Pamir Mountains there are stories of people transforming into snow leopards and in Tibet there is a well-known legend of the 11th-century poet Milarepa, who transformed himself into a snow leopard to escape from the Great Cave of Conquering Demons when he was trapped there by heavy snow. In Russian Tatarstan the people are protected by Aq Bars, a legendary winged white leopard carrying warriors into battle. Across Asia there are many stories of winged leopards. Could this be something to do with the cat's remarkable ability to vanish and reappear again on a far-distant mountain?

So, with all this in mind and having suffered sleepless nights worried about the task ahead of us, it came as a complete surprise that we saw a snow leopard on our first day in Ladakh! It was a moment I will never forget, but one that nearly didn't happen. One of our guides spotted it from our mountain camp. 'Shan!' he shouted (the Ladakhi word for snow leopard), and everyone dropped what they were doing and raced over. We all queued to peer at it through the spotting scope and I waited my turn, tingling with anticipation. As everyone got a glimpse of the cat, they let out a deep sigh, or an excited 'wow' or even a giggly 'yelp'. It was wonderful to see how just the hazy sight of one distant animal, still hundreds of metres away, could cause so much happiness. Those who had taken their turn stood around clapping and dancing, smiles as broad as the Indus Valley. When it finally came to my turn, I squinted one eye and leant down to peer into the scope. Nothing. Just rocks, endless rocks. Feeling a bit awkward and not wanting to ruin the celebratory atmosphere, I looked up and smiled at our guide and for a moment considered faking it. But he could see through my conceit and invited me to look again. This time giving instructions. 'See the tall rock on the right, scan above until you see a ledge and then …'

'Bloody hell!' I interrupted, 'It's a snow leopard!'

It was like seeing some ancient magic, still alive. I couldn't have felt more astonished if I had been looking down the scope at a dragon. We watched the cat as it climbed higher up the mountain, bounding over the steep terrain as if it was floating rather than climbing. At the top of the ridge, it sat for a while, its outline framed against the blushing sky, a creature belonging more to heaven than among us mortals on Earth.

While getting lucky enough to see a glimpse of a snow leopard was one thing, being close enough to film one was a whole different challenge. But we had a hidden advantage in the form of an incredible team of Ladakhi spotters. Every morning they would get up before the sun and be ready to head out on the hill, scopes in hand, to look for any movement. Our camera crew would be primed and ready to rush out should the excited call of, 'Shan, Shan, Snow leopard!' crackle through on the radio. On foot, our team might get lucky enough to see and film a wild cat, but it would always be from a big distance away and filming them would take an 800 millimeter lens as long as your arm. If we were to get up close and personal with a snow leopard, we would need another way of closing the distance. For this we relied on the knowledge of our guide Khenrab Phuntsog, who knew the cats here better than anyone else. He had been studying the park's snow leopards using camera traps and had worked out the best spots to place them if we were to win a shot of a cat. We set off early to one of Khenrab's secret locations, climbing higher and higher up a narrow twisting valley that led us right up into the mountains. Over the course of many visits to Ladakh this path would become my favourite.

As the route ascended, the mountain walls started to close in around us and we followed the course of a stream coming down from high above. The water was frozen solid and where it had once poured over waterfalls it had been suspended in time as dramatic sculptures of white marble. It looked somewhat alien against the bright colours of the rocks, rusted orange with lichen and the thorny bushes of wild rose, dotted with the red splashes of rosehips. As the valley wrapped around us, leading us into a gorge, the path had to cross the frozen stream again and again. Each time, we teetered across the polished white floor of slippery ice; Khenrab threw down handfuls of dirt to help our boots keep their grip.

Further up the gorge Khenrab found the pugmarks of a snow leopard on the frozen river. He bent low reading the ground, telling us the cat was an adult and pointing out a sprinkling of dark ruby-red ice crystals on the imprint of one of the cat's toes. Snow leopards sometimes leave blood in their footprints, as the snow crystals get stuck on their paws and cut the pads of their feet.

Higher and higher we went; there seemed to be less air to breathe and the walls of the gorge closed in ever tighter. We passed a big waterfall, a turquoise wave petrified by the cold. The going got harder and harder and I felt a real shortness of breath and a degree of clumsiness in my movement. The altitude was starting to take its toll. It was hard to escape the feeling that we were being watched. As with all wild mountain ranges, the soundscape was largely silent. On clear cold days like this one, the air seemed to quietly hum but the atmosphere was spread so thin it was barely perceptible. I became increasingly aware of how loud we were as we journeyed ever higher, our every move intrusive, like a bunch of circus clowns gatecrashing a wake. The huff of our breath in the thin air, the endless talking, the crunch of our boots on the snow, the clatter of our walking poles on the rocks; we were simply incapable of being truly quiet and it added to the feeling that we could only ever be visitors here and never truly belong. The enclosed walls of the gorge amplified our presence, announcing us to all around. As we rounded a bend in the river, we must have disturbed two snowcocks up on the ridge, as we heard their wonderfully eerie rising whistle, followed by an outburst of 'bubbling', clucking that echoed back and forth above us.

Scan to hear the call of a Himalayan snowcock breaking the mountain silence.

Around another bend and we spotted some bharal, or blue sheep, the snow leopard's favourite prey. They were high up on the sides of the gorge, crossing the slope. As they walked, small stones dislodged by their hooves skittered down the mountain, tinkling like spilt coins. I realised that mountain animals rarely seem to make a noise.

Here every loose rock could give away your location and I wondered if, as predators, snow leopards are keyed into the silence, looking to pick up on the occasional bursts of sound from potential prey?

Surprisingly there is very little scientific evidence that big cats listen in on their prey. Most comes from studies with captive cats showing an alert response to sounds of their favourite species to hunt, played back to them over speakers. There is, however, plenty of anecdotal evidence. In India, national park guides use the phrase 'When a sambar calls, a tiger walks' to describe the way tigers adapt their behaviour to the sound of their prey. Tigers are also reported to mimic the 'dhonk' alarm call of watchful sambar deer, perhaps in an attempt to cause confusion before they launch an attack. There are accounts of prides of lions stealing the kills of hyenas after hearing the commotion and social calls of the hyenas hunting. And smaller cats such as serval and lynx are known to listen to the rustling sound of rodents to hone in on them. Unfortunately, seeing a snow leopard hunt takes a great deal of good fortune and nobody has witnessed this behaviour sufficiently to know for sure if the grey ghost is listening in to find its quarry. But hearing the sound of the blue sheep moving through the mountains did suggest to me that, in a wilderness where hunting opportunities are few and far between, sound could be a key way to find your next meal.

A little further up the gorge my question seemed to have been answered by the discovery of the partly devoured remains of a sheep. The bones of a dead bharal ram had been scattered by a lammergeier (bearded vulture), the head, with its curved horns, sitting alone and separate from its body, but Khenrab told us the kill belonged to a snow leopard. We could see clumps of the sheep's grey fur scattered over the snow where the cat had pulled it off to get to the meat below. The gorge was a great place to hunt as the sheep were drawn down into its depths to take a drink from the last few unfrozen pools. This gave the cats high up in the gorge a better chance to spot and to hear the movements of the sheep and attack from above. It felt like we were getting closer to the ghost cat and when Khenrab shouted to us from up ahead we knew he had found another clue.

We found him on his hands and knees beneath a low overhanging boulder, just off the path. He sniffed at the rock – 'Oh, it smells strong!' – before inviting us to do the same. Knees in the snow, I craned my neck to get a good sniff of the pungent musty scent coming from the rock. I was smelling the perfume of a big cat. Snow leopards often use the same pathways through the high mountains, sharing the same routes but always a few days apart from the next cat. At certain points along these paths, there are these low overhanging boulders, where any passing snow leopard will choose to lift its tail and spray the surface with urine. These smelly signposts act as community noticeboards and the next cat to pass by can sniff the rock and tell all sorts of things about those that have come before. Scientists studying snow leopards have called these scent messages 'pee mails' and it's thought that the cats can determine the age, health and sexual status of others from just a quick sniff. The leopards also rub scent from glands in their cheeks, anointing the rocks with their own personal calling card.

Khenrab pointed to a spiky point on the overhanging rock. There we could see a small clump of wizened snow leopard hairs. As if examining some rare treasure, I reached out my finger and gently brushed one, taking care not to dislodge it from the rock. I had seen a snow leopard, smelt a snow leopard and now I had touched a snow leopard (well, sort of). All that was left now was to hear one.

This had been one of the rubbing rocks where Khenrab had set up his own camera trap; back at the start of the trip, he had shown us footage of a female leopard with three full-grown cubs as big as she was. It was a remarkable thing to see so many rare and elusive cats all together like this and as we set about installing our own camera rigs, I could only hope we would be so lucky.

*

Excited shouting roused me from our mess tent. As I struggled to get my boots on, I could see our spotters pointing up at the mountain ridge above our camp. Thinking it was a snow leopard I raced over, but the two animals coming across the scree slopes above us weren't cats, they were Tibetan wolves. They came lower past the camp, confidently trotting by without even a glance in our direction. I could see their long winter fur, their sharp muzzles and piercing eyes. These wolves are known for their pale coats, which help them to blend into the dusty mountain landscapes. Across their haunches and thighs, the wolves were coloured with red, picked up from the local soil. A crest of smoky black fur ran from their heads down their backs and their threadbare tails ended with a dark tip. Tibetan wolves – sometimes called Himalayan wolves – are a distinct subspecies of the grey wolf and are thought to be one of the oldest types of wolf on the planet. They live in small packs based around a family group, often with only two adults, and will wander over a huge home range, covering over 20 kilometres in a single day.

I had been lucky enough to see wolves up close before and it was always a real thrill. A whole pack of over ten wolves had once trotted past my pick-up in a remote corner of Alaska. I couldn't believe how huge they were compared to our own familiar pet dogs. Their paws were as wide as my hand and they moved along the road trying to flush out red foxes from the verges. I remember listening to the wolves' distant howling as the light faded from the sky and the darkness crept beyond the wall of forest, out across our campground. Seeing wolves so close is a powerful reminder that the world can still be wild, but hearing them is an encounter with the very essence of a wilderness.

The howl of a wolf is perhaps the most recognisable sound made by any wild animal. To humans it can provoke a primal response that connects us back to our species' own past and elicits both fear and wonder, but for the wolves themselves it fulfils a variety of functions.

Howls are commonly used for long-range communication between pack members. An individual wolf's howl can be heard from up to 16 kilometres away in open terrain and 10 kilometres away through a forest. Over the years, researchers listening in on howling wolves have discovered they have several different howls that are used in different situations and are likely to communicate different things. First there is the 'lonesome howl' given by individual wolves locating their pack when they are separated. These howls sound like a low-pitched, long and continuous sound and are designed to carry over distance. The low frequency of this howl helps it to travel further, but it may have some degree of pitch change that might make the wolf's identity and location easier to pinpoint. The 'rallying howl' is given by all members of the pack and helps gather them together before a hunt, a call to arms for the hungry pack. Again, this call is low frequency so travels far and wide. These howling sessions are often accompanied by excited tail-wagging, greetings and playful close contact, and play an important part in the social bond of the pack.

The third type of howl is known as the 'confrontational howl' and is harsher sounding and lower in pitch again and is used in aggressive confrontations by wolves looking to defend themselves from rival packs. But perhaps the most extraordinary howl of all is known as the 'trick group howl'. Like the rallying howl, it's given by multiple members of the pack howling in unison, but with each wolf howling at a different pitch or volume and for different durations. These group harmonies have the effect of a sonic illusion, creating the impression for listening rival packs that the howling pack is larger than it actually is. By harmonising rather than howling the exact same note all at once, it makes it difficult to accurately assess the number of howlers and may even make it seem like there are more. The trick chorus howl is a vital survival tool, helping packs reinforce their territorial boundaries, protect their vulnerable youngsters from rivals and avoid fights with other packs.

The final type of wolf howl is that made by the pups. The 'pup howl' is used by hungry youngsters to call their parents when they are waiting for food, but also may have a function in practising for being part of group howling sessions in later life. In 2019, a video from a trail camera set up by wolf biologists in Minnesota's Voyageurs National Park became a worldwide viral hit on social media. It showed footage from outside the den of a pack of wolves where a tiny four-week-old pup practised his howling to adorable effect.

Researchers from the University of Cambridge used computers to analyse the howls of a wide variety of wild canids, from wolves to foxes and jackals. They studied 2,000 howls and, based on pitch and fluctuation, were able to identify 21 different types. They found that the howls' frequency – from flat notes to more varied – was different between species and for wolves was even different between the various subspecies. A timber wolf is known for its flat, low howls whereas an endangered red wolf shows a high, looping howl. Being able to identify species from a distance is useful when it comes to determining the numbers of individuals and how they use the landscape. So, listening in remotely could be a vital tool in making plans for the conservation of endangered wolves and other wild members of the dog family.

But it's not just different species that howl differently. Research has shown that the howls of wolves within the pack are also unique to individuals. In 2022, a team of biologists from Denmark, Slovenia and the UK used computers to analyse the acoustic properties of 170 recorded howls from seventeen individual wolves of three different species and not only discovered discernible differences between the species, but that the computer could identify the individual wolves with 80–90 per cent accuracy. More research is needed, but this could suggest that the wolves themselves can tell each other apart from the sound of their howl alone.

Scan to hear the group howl of a pack of wolves.

While it was spectacular to see the wolves come by our campsite, as I watched them climb back up the slope and finally disappear over the ridge line, I was also a little worried. Tibetan wolves can be direct competitors of snow leopards and will steal their kills, chasing the cats off. Our guides told us that seeing wolves might be a bad sign for our chances of finding snow leopards. I couldn't help but wonder if our impossible task had just become even harder.

The Ladakhi people have a saying. A snow leopard is as beautiful as ten women, as strong as ten men and as wise as ten astronomers. It shows just how highly the people here honour and respect their wildlife. But this isn't always the case in the Himalaya and elsewhere across the snow leopard's range. According to figures from conservation group the Snow Leopard Trust, between 2008 and 2016 a snow leopard was killed every single day. That's between 220 and 450 cats every year. And these were only the cats whose deaths were recorded. The true extent of the killing is likely to be even greater. While the international trade in snow leopard trophies is strictly prohibited, there is still demand for their luxurious fur and their bones and other body parts for 'sham' medicines. Even when the snow leopard isn't in the crosshairs or caught in a trap, it still suffers widely from poaching. Many of the cats' favourite prey species are hunted for meat or for their horns. As their populations are driven down, life for the snow leopards gets even harder.

Around 53 million people share the snow leopard's Himalayan home and many of them rely on domestic livestock to survive. In remote mountain communities much of the economy revolves around yaks, sheep and goats, and in many areas human populations are expanding up into the mountains. This can lead to the leopard's historic prey being poached or out-grazed by livestock, leaving the big cats with little choice but to target domestic prey. In some locations in Mongolia as many as one in three of all snow leopard kills may be stolen livestock. This can result in terrible conflicts between the human inhabitants of the mountains and the big cat with which they share their home. Khenrab had shown me upsetting footage of a snow leopard that had got inside a sheep pen one night. Trapped in the enclosure, the leopard's predatory instincts had run wild and it had killed the entire flock. When it was discovered, the cat just sat there, unable to find a way out, surrounded by the bodies of the sheep.

It was a shocking image and, with their livelihoods threatened, it was perhaps understandable that herders might want to kill snow leopards in retribution; in some places, these revenge kills may account for more than half of all snow leopards that are killed by humans. Luckily, in Ladakh there has long been a concerted effort to help mountain villagers live peacefully alongside hungry snow leopards. Community conservation projects offer compensation to herders who have lost animals to the cats. They are also building special anti-predator corrals – a circular stone-walled enclosure with a roof made of chain-link fence – that keep the sheep and goats safe inside and ensure that hungry snow leopards can't get in.

In Ladakh, conservationists such as Khenrab have been working hard to strengthen the bond between the cats and the people who share their home. It's the dream of many people to come to the Himalaya and see a snow leopard, and villagers in Ladakh can benefit by offering authentic 'homestay' accommodation to support tourism. They have also been trained and encouraged to make snow leopard toys out of yak wool, shaped with a felting needle, which visitors like to buy as a souvenir of their time in the mountains.

Our film crew were lucky enough to visit the village of Rumbak on many occasions. The people there showed a level of warmth, hospitality and generosity that is beyond anything I have experienced on my travels. I always loved the welcoming sounds of the village as we came down from a tough day up on the mountain ridges. You could hear the yak bells and the occasional bark of a dog. A donkey brayed in the fields as the children played and a farmer sang gently as he put out bails of fodder for his horses. On one visit we accompanied Khenrab as he showed the assembled villagers some of his camera-trap footage of the cats, and everyone, from the rosy-cheeked kids to the village elders, reacted with curiosity and wonder. I remember he told them to close their eyes and the joy and pride on their faces as they listened to a recording of one of their own snow leopards singing.

Even without the presence of poaching, the cats still face some major threats. Across central Asia the mountains are being increasingly exploited for their coal and mineral content through mining. From the Tost Mountains of Mongolia to the Tien Shan of Kyrgyzstan, snow leopard populations have become vulnerable to disturbance from mining. In 2025 a report by the WWF looked at how expanding infrastructure is threatening the survival of Pakistan's snow leopards. Human activity and road-building is fragmenting the leopard's habitat and disrupting their natural movement. Heavy traffic on the Karakoram Highway has led to increased air and noise pollution that is likely to affect the wildlife. I had seen this type of disturbance with my own eyes in Hemis on one of our visits. A road had been dynamited into the park leading all the way up to the village. I had no right whatsoever to begrudge the people of the village better access to medical attention, schooling and outside food markets, but I was concerned about how much the noise of the blasting might disturb the leopards, as it passed directly through one of their mountain crossing points. On that particular visit we didn't see any cats at all, so at the least it appeared all the noise may have temporarily chased them away.

Climate change is another significant threat to snow leopards and Ladakh is on the frontline of the crisis. The amount of winter snow is reducing and the mountain glaciers are receding. Spring temperatures are getting warmer and during our visits we could increasingly hear the tinkling sound of running water from the river that had always been frozen. No one is quite sure exactly how a warming climate will affect the snow leopards, but as the snow melts and temperatures rise it may change the vegetation of the mountains, compromising the habitat for their favourite prey and bringing them further into conflict with people. One thing is for sure, if these remarkable cats are to have a secure future, they will need more supporters like Khenrab and the people of Rumbak.

Scan to listen to the sounds of a Himalayan village.

The toughest challenge on our quest to capture the sounds of snow leopards came when we set out to place camera traps and remote recorders on the high ridge top overlooking the village. Knowing it would be a long day, we rose early. Stepping into the frigid leather of our boots felt like wearing blocks of ice and I wriggled my toes to get the blood flowing. The ground was frozen and we crunched over a garden of frost flowers, yet to be touched by the sun. It was hard going getting up the hill, I was struggling to catch my breath and my heart was racing in my chest. I had to stop and let my breathing recover then I slowed my pace so as not to get puffed out again. The climb up to the ridge seemed longer today and we paused to rest more frequently. Luckily, the view was worth any delay. From the tiny specks of our orange tents and the village far below, we could see the valley rear upwards towards the high pass of the Stok La, the snowy mountain dome of Parcha Kangri looking down on the valley, the first breaking wave in a tempest of high peaks leading the eye to the mighty pyramid of Stok Kangri, at 6,153 metres the tallest mountain in Ladakh. A lammergeier and a pair of griffon vultures sailed overhead. I was envious of how easily they climbed on the updraughts, soaring up to be with the clouds. What grandeur they must see from their lofty outlook.

Back on our feet, we slogged our way up the final slopes, wading through deep snow before the ground levelled out and we had finally reached the ridge top, a kilometre-long undulating spine of rocky towers, broad saddles, exposed lofty balconies and plummeting drops that was a favourite route of passing snow leopards. Our camp cook suddenly joined us, carrying a backpack full of steaming food. His friends had given him the nickname 'the lunch leopard' and it seemed appropriate as he had climbed the hill in double time. We stopped for a high-altitude banquet of rice and veg, chicken sausages and chapattis, washed down by cups of warm milky chai. With snow starting to fall we got a move on, setting up the camera traps and remote sound recorders at the first of several marking rocks on the ridge. Everyone mucked in, clearing the snow, building a pile of rocks to balance the camera on and pretending to be a snow leopard, crawling on all fours to test that the camera triggers worked and the framing of the shot was lined up properly. A small flock of industrious yellow-billed choughs settled at our lunch spot, hopeful of any titbits. They seemed to be arguing among themselves and their crow-like caws and high-pitched dog barks disrupted the quiet of the mountains.

Scan to hear the calls of a yellow-billed chough.

We worked our way along the ridge, setting up cameras and microphones on paths we knew the leopards favoured and at spots we knew they liked to linger. At one point the ridge became so narrow that, standing upright, I could feel the dizzy pull of vertigo – or the lack of oxygen was playing tricks on me. The fractured ridge of folded brown and bronze rock, spotted with bright orange lichen, formed sharp pinnacles that framed spaces where the world dropped away. With just one more camera to set up, Khenrab directed us to a balcony where the leopards liked to call. It was further down the ridge, now an airy arête of rusty miniature pinnacles. We couldn't get down this sharp rock ridge as it plummeted over dangerously steep terrain, so we had to scree-run down the infamous KC road – named after a famous snow leopard spotter who liked to use it for a thrilling short cut home after a long day on the ridge. It was a wide, steep scree slope of purple red aggregate, that zoomed all the way down to the valley below in one relentless sweep. After an invigorating and occasionally uncontrolled descent, more like powder skiing than walking, we cut across and back onto the ridge, climbing through a desperately broken, shattered terrain of sketchy crumbling ledges and slippery gullies full of scree. The ledge on the ridge itself was incredible, overlooking the intimidating buttresses of the Rumbak Gorge and the frozen river below. How any animal could climb through this terrain seemed impossible to me. But I had learnt that snow leopards are the most improbable of creatures and Khenrab had seen them calling from this spot on more than one occasion. We set up the last camera and microphone on the calling spot and sat watching the afternoon light change over the mountains. The shadows of the clouds played across the snow and somewhere in the gorge below a disturbed rock fell, its clatter echoing far and wide. Straining to listen, we could hear the chatter of a group of partridges, the likely culprits.

I asked Khenrab what it was like to be in the mountains and hear the sound of a snow leopard calling. He replied, 'Like an electric shock passing through your body.' He wandered over the edge of the balcony and, crouching down before the void, lifted his hands to his lips and yowled just like a snow leopard. As the echoes of his voice died among the peaks the mountains returned to stillness. We sat listening to the sound of endless space, waiting in vain for a cat to answer.

For days we climbed up the mountain to check the camera traps and sat and hoped to hear the cats calling but to no avail. Then, one cold night in camp, I was woken by the haunting echo of a snow leopard calling. It was the most otherworldly sound I had ever heard and it was enough to lure me from my warm bed, out into the freezing moonlit night to listen. But once it had faded away and I returned back to my sleeping bag, I wasn't really sure if it had been just a dream. The altitude had been affecting my sleep so that I was experiencing 'periodic breathing'. In the night I would suddenly stop breathing, causing me to awake with a start, gasping for air. Each night unfolded like a surreal story, half awake, half asleep. In the morning, as I listened to the sounds of the camp coming to life, I was left groggy and this made the waking world even more unreal. It had snowed through the night and under this new white blanket the very stillness seemed dampened. The sounds of the mountains, the clatter of rocks and the cawing of the ravens were softened. Even the tinkling bells from the village horses, passing our camp on their way down the valley, were strangely muted. At breakfast I asked if anyone had heard the leopard in the night. Nobody else had. While I was at first disheartened that no one had shared my encounter and could confirm my experience, I knew deep down it was real and the memory felt all the more special because it belonged just to me.

The first time I set out with a team to reveal the secret lives of snow leopards, I never could have imagined what a huge part it would play in my life. Over the years I have been lucky enough to visit Ladakh on multiple trips and have got closer to the cats than I ever thought would be possible. On one occasion I sat huddled and shivering in a cloth hide, stiffened and brittle in the prodigious cold. Peering through a tiny slit torn into the cloth, we waited until at last a male snow leopard crept down the mountain to feed from its kill, just 25 metres or so in front of us. I looked into its pale grey-green eyes and held my breath as it looked back. Even though it couldn't see us, it seemed to know something of our presence. In a world where every footstep made a sound, I was aware of the importance of staying stock still, even when fiery cramps flared up from the discomfort. I wondered if it could hear my heartbeat thumping in my chest.

On another adventure, we had captured on camera an encounter between four snow leopards. I had been told that this was the equivalent of winning the lottery four times in one day! But perhaps the best insights into the snow leopard's mysterious world started with an envelope. I would be back in Bristol, working hard on setting up another film shoot somewhere, and I would suddenly and unexpectedly receive a small brown-paper parcel covered in Indian stamps. Inside, carefully swaddled in bubble-wrap and cellophane, would be a small stack of SD cards from our camera traps that were still running up in the mountains. The parcel had come from Khenrab and his colleague Smanla, who continued to service the camera traps long after our own crew had gone.

I would rip into the envelope, my excited fingers pulling at the cellophane, and race to load the cards onto my computer, anxious to see what we had captured. I was never disappointed. Among the incredible footage captured of snow leopards, there were cats rubbing right up against the camera so you could hear their purring breath. We had mothers followed by their playful cubs. A male leopard that rolled in the dust to camouflage itself before a hunt. Cats spraying on rocks and sniffing each other's secret messages. Unlike my time in the hide, the magic of camera traps is that the cats have no idea they are being watched. You see an animal at ease in its own world and to me it is the purest form of wildlife filmmaking there is.

As we returned again and again to the mountains, we were able to improve and modify the cameras and fit them with sensitive external mics that allowed us to eavesdrop on the cat's lonely soundscape. I learnt that, under their own terms, when no one else was listening, the cats were actually quite noisy! You could hear them coming before they even appeared in the shot and after they had walked out of the frame, as their footsteps would send the rocks tumbling.

Perhaps my favourite ever capture was a shot we ended up using for the starting shot of BBC's *Planet Earth II*, where a magnificent cat walked into the frame and came to a stop with its head lifted. With the snowy peaks of Ladakh as the backdrop it began to sing, yowling its signal far and wide across the mountains. A shot in a million, it was so improbable that I have been asked on more than one occasion if it was generated by a computer. Helped in no small part by Khenrab's knowledge of the cats, we were able to place cameras in spots where it seemed they liked to call. This yielded the most intimate call from a male snow leopard, singing to a female as he stood just out of shot but right next to the microphone. It's likely to be the best ever recording of the call of a wild snow leopard.

We had managed to get closer to the cats than anyone had thought possible, but they had one more surprise. Even though our filming has long finished I occasionally get sent a new recording from Khenrab, these days not in a brown envelope but via WhatsApp. The recording below is very special to me. It takes me back to the time I was on that first flight to Ladakh, flying over the expanse of the Himalaya wondering how on earth I could hope to find a cat in such a huge wilderness. My dream was to get close to these elusive creatures, to know them and come to understand them. So, this recording feels like the culmination of that adventure. It's the sound of a female snow leopard and her two cubs, visiting a scent-marking rock. All three cats are close enough that they almost touch the hidden microphone. It's just not possible to get any closer to the grey ghost of the mountains, and the sounds they make are extraordinary. Their intimate 'purring' sound is sometimes called a 'chuffle'. Its more scientific name is 'prusten' and it's a vocalisation made by four of the big cats: tigers, jaguars, snow leopards and clouded leopards. We don't know much about this sound in snow leopards as, until now, it's only ever been heard from cats in captivity, so to hear it from a wild snow leopard is incredibly unusual. Scientists studying this call with tigers have discovered that the sound originates in the thick vocal folds in the larynx of the cat. It also involves air being blown through the mouth and nose at the same time to make the 'chuffle', the characteristic purring, snorting sound.

Each of the four big cats that chuffle do it slightly differently, but they all tend to make between four and ten pulses of sound for each vocalisation. The cats make the call in a variety of social circumstances. Tigers kept in captivity are more likely to chuffle when housed together in groups than apart. Some cats in zoos are known to chuffle as a type of greeting, when their keeper comes to see them. With captive snow leopards it's been heard when females are looking to initiate mating with a male, and mother snow leopards will chuffle when they return to their cubs in the den. The cubs will also start to make the sound, usually around the age of five weeks. One study on captive clouded leopards found the cats made the sound more frequently when they were content, so it's been theorised that it could even be the cats expressing their own sort of feline 'happiness'.

Listening to this precious recording, I am mindful that it has captured the warmest of family moments between a mother leopard and her two cubs. Its rare intimacy is all the more special when you consider that there may only be two snow leopards found in every 100 square kilometres of the mountains. I am also reminded of the hard work of my Ladakhi companions in getting us so close that we could hope to hear such an unlikely secret, whispered among the peaks. Each time I listen, it makes me grateful for the friendships I have made in the high places.

As you listen for yourself, see if you can hear the leopard's low growling moan before it starts to chuffle. Perhaps the mother cat is picking up the scent of another snow leopard, perhaps she will soon be looking to mate again or perhaps she is gently telling her cubs to keep up. Maybe picking up the smell of other leopards and leaving behind her own scent by rubbing on the rocks is 'pleasurable' to her in some way that we can never understand. As with all encounters with a snow leopard, much remains a mystery. At the end of the recording, as the wind gets up, listen out for the sound of the cats heading off, sending the shattered rocks tumbling as they walk. The sound of a ghost swallowed up by the limitless silence of the mountains.

Scan to hear the rare and unique 'chuffle' of a mother snow leopard.

Epilogue: Learning to Listen

CONNECTING TO THE SOUNDS OF NATURE

A manifesto for listening

IF YOU HAVE enjoyed listening to the sometimes bizarre and often beautiful natural sounds in this book and want to experience more, the next step is to tune in more closely to nature in your everyday life. This is easier than it sounds, but here is a short list of guidelines you might also find helpful. If you like, it's a manifesto for listening to nature. The first step is to begin to notice the nature around you.

Short cuts to noticing nature

1) Engage your senses. Modern life dulls our senses. Here are some simple acts to switch them on.

- Next time you are at home indoors and it rains, stop what you are doing and go stand by the window and just listen to the rain falling. Feeling brave? Go outside and stand in it!
- Never pass a pile of autumn leaves without wading through them!
- That ugly bramble patch on the walk home? Stop and eat the blackberries.

2) Value the small things. An entomologist I met was asked at a conference, 'Apart from bees and butterflies, why do people dislike insects?' His brilliant answer was that the UK is home to 24,000 different types of insects. Anyone who didn't like them just hadn't found the right insect yet. Go find your bug. Our homes and gardens are full of invertebrates. Next time you see one, take five minutes to watch it: How does it move? Where is it going? Find out what you can about its life. Use a magnifying glass and you'll discover you share your home with a miniature masterpiece.

3) Become a seasonal animal. The ebb and flow of the seasons gives us a framework that helps connect us to the natural world. Find a sensation you like for each season and tick them off. It could be swimming in the sea in summer, making a crumble with all those stolen blackberries in autumn and watching the sunset colours in winter clouds. For a deeper seasonal nature connection, you can buy a nature almanac, which gives a month-by-month calendar of all the incredible things going on across the year.

4) Get involved in nature. Getting closer to nature can be a participation sport. In the UK, the first Sunday of May each year is International Dawn Chorus Day. Up and down the country there are organised dawn chorus walks where an expert can introduce you to the wonders of birdsong. Check out your local Wildlife Trust or RSPB group to get involved. There are also excellent opportunities to volunteer for conservation projects on both a local and national level. Even if you don't fancy getting muddy or you don't have much time, from habitat restoration to wildlife surveys there is something for everyone. Contact your local Wildlife Trust or national organisations such as the Conservation Volunteers, the National Trust, National Parks, Woodland Trust, or the National Council for Voluntary Organisations. If you are in Scotland, you can also try the NatureScot's website.

Park life

If, like my own family, you live in the middle of a big city, finding nature can sometimes be a bit of a challenge. About 84 per cent of us in the UK live in urban areas and this can limit our access to nature. But there are green spaces to be found. Seek out your nearest park. Get to know it, visit it for a weekly walk. If you do this regularly, wonders will start appearing before your eyes and sounds will delight your ears. You will see the seasons change. You'll hear the arrival of winged migrants in spring. I had never seen a 'treecreeper' before I spotted one picking its way up a big tree in my local park. This tiny, secretive bird is a hard one to tick off, but there among the buggies, kids' football and joggers it suddenly appeared one day. I watched it hugging the furrowed bark like a climber scaling a cliff and, despite the roar of the traffic on the flyover, I even heard its elfin high-pitched whistle. Many local parks have community groups that help look after the nature there. Check out the park noticeboard for information. Some parks in London even do organised night walks to hear the spooky sounds of tawny owls.

Listen when you travel

Going on holiday or travelling (if you are lucky enough to do so) provides an excellent opportunity for listening. New places come with their own exciting soundtrack. I like to record the sounds I hear on holiday on my phone. It helps me to plug into the unique soundscapes of a place and time. It could be a herd of bleating goats blocking the road in Crete, or the sound of screaming swifts overhead in Devon. These recordings help me be present in the place, but also provide me with listening memories from my travels – a bit like a photo album but with sounds.

When we are on holiday we often rush around, eager to gather new experiences, see new places or eat new food. We should also try to experience new sounds as part of the adventure. When travelling on long journeys listening to music or podcasts helps shorten the journey. Try mixing it up by listening to recordings of natural soundscapes too.

Listening adventures

When you are feeling confident about your listening you could try and set yourself some 'challenges'. Not only will this feed and develop your listening skills, it will help connect you to nature, make new discoveries and have an adventure on the way. Try setting out to record the song of a favourite bird (I am planning such a trip to listen to nightingales in London), or perhaps take a walk along a coastal path to hear the seals talking among themselves. In spring, find a big pond on a map and explore it after dark to see if you can hear the croaking of spawning toads. Challenge yourself to find somewhere wild, where you can't hear roads or aeroplanes or any other human sounds. It's not as easy as you might think!

Tuning in

If you are enjoying listening in to the natural world and want to start capturing your own recordings there is a dizzying multitude of microphones and recorders available. But most of us carry a pretty good recording device on our mobile phones. You can download specialised recording apps and there are now an array of external microphones that can connect to smartphones to improve the quality of the sounds. If you are looking to record sounds remotely and don't want to risk losing your phone, search for AudioMoth, who make a range of small field-ready remote recorders that won't break the bank.

How You Can Help

If you are inspired to help protect nature but aren't sure how to, here are some links that are a good place to start.

If you want to help save the curlew:
curlewaction.org

If you want to help protect wildlife in Africa:
Help local communities value and protect lions – lionguardians.org
An Africa-wide elephant conservation initiative – elephantprotectioninitiative.org
Championing community-led conservation in the Okavango – clawsbotswana.org

If you want to help save the rainforest:
Where you can sponsor an area of forest – rainforestconcern.org
Campaigns to stop deforestation – amazonwatch.org
To help save endangered sloths – slothconservation.org
To support Rainforest Connection listening in on the rainforest – rfcx.org

If you want to help protect the life in our oceans:
To protect whales and dolphins – uk.whales.org
Helping to protect whales from ocean noise – ifaw.org/uk
To learn more about great whales – whale.org
To listen to orca – orcalab.org
To help save the Great Barrier Reef – barrierreef.org

If you want to help reverse the decline in our bird species:

Supports a wide range of actions to protect birds, including skylarks – rspb.org.uk

Take part in surveys and help save threatened bird species – bto.org

Works globally with local communities to conserve bird populations – birdlife.org

If you want to help protect endangered frogs and toads:

Umbrella group supporting frog conservation worldwide – amphibians.org

Help save threatened frogs through captive breeding – amphibianark.org

Runs programmes to help save endangered amphibians – savethefrogs.com

To help protect frogs, toads, newts and reptiles in the UK – froglife.org

If you want to help protect our insect life:

Helps save habitats for insects and campaigns against pesticides – buglife.org.uk

If you want to find out more about climate change in the Himalaya:

Helps mountain communities prepare for climate change – theglaciertrust.org

To help plant trees in the Nepal Himalaya – thepartnersnepal.org/one-day-one-tree

Encourages community conservation in Ladakh – wcbcl.org

If you want to help protect the polar regions and animals such as polar bears:

To help save the polar bear – polarbearsinternational.org

To support conservation of Arctic wildlife and habitats – arcticwwf.org

If you want to help give snow leopards and Himalayan wolves a future:

At the heart of Ladakhi efforts to save the snow leopard – snowleopardindia.org

Supports wolf conservation in the Himalaya – himalayanwolvesproject.org

Glossary of Sound

Amplitude – The magnitude of a sound wave, which is related to its loudness. Measured as the extent of vibration.

Anthrophony – All human-generated sound.

Biophony – The collective sound produced by living organisms in a specific environment.

Decibel – A unit used to measure the intensity or loudness of a sound. The scale is logarithmic so that an increase in 10 decibels is perceived as twice as loud by the human ear.

Echolocation – The location of objects by reflected sound, as seen in animals such as dolphins and bats.

Frequency – The number of sound waves that occurs across one second, measured in hertz. This determines the pitch of a sound: the faster the frequency, the higher the pitch.

Geophony – Non-biological natural sounds of a physical environment.

Hertz – The unit measuring the frequency or speed of vibration of a sound wave. Usually synonymous with cycles per second (CPS).

Infrasonic – Sound waves with a frequency below the lower limit of human hearing.

Pitch – The degree of highness or lowness of a sound. High-pitched would be 'squeaky'; low-pitched would be a deeper sound.

Reverberation – The persistence of sound in a space after the source of the sound has stopped.

Sonification – The transformation of data into sound.

Stridulation – Sound made by the physical rubbing together of body parts.

Transmission – The propagation of sound through a medium (air, solid, liquid).

Ultrasonic – Sound waves with a frequency above the upper limit of human hearing.

Vibration – The force of oscillation around a specific source.

Wavelength – The distance between the beginning and end of a sound wave.

Sound Recordings

Thanks to the following who supplied sound recordings for the project.

Chapter 1) Call of the Wild

Snow leopard calls – Wounded Buffalo

Soundscape 1) Indri chorus, Madagascar – Daan Hendriks

Soundscape 2) Common loon duet – Wounded Buffalo

Soundscape 3) Meercat babies, Kalahari Desert – Ellie Williams

Chapter 2) Hidden Conversations

Hippo calls – Daan Hendriks

Elephants at night – Daan Hendriks

Elephant vocalisations – Sebastian Dunn

Red faced jumping spider – Damian Octavio Elias, Dept of Environmental Science, Policy, and Management, University of California, Berkeley

Gibbon chorus, Borneo – Dr Reza Azmi, Wild Asia

Gorillas eating and humming – Eva Maria Luef, Charles University, Dept. of Linguistics Prague

Chimpanzee pant-hoots, Gabon – Freddie Claire

Lions roaring, Botswana – Daan Hendriks

Black-backed Jackal – Daan Hendriks

Leopard sawing, Tanzania – Dr Jonathan Growcott

Chapter 3) The Forest Orchestra

Howler monkey – Wounded Buffalo

Amazon daytime cicadas, Peru – Freddie Claire

Leafcutter ants, Peru – Ellie Williams

Amazon forest after a rainstorm, Bolivia – Daan Hendriks

Brown-throated sloth calling – Wounded Buffalo

Club-winged manakin, Ecuador – Xeno Canto / Mitch Lysinger

Amazonian treehoppers – Rex Cocroft, Division of Biological Sciences, University of Missouri

Slender-legged treefrog – From Tiputini Research Station, Ecuador

Menwig or racing car frog, Bolivia – Steffen Reichle

Rosenberg's gladiator frog, Columbia – Xeno Canto / Fabrice Schmitt

Coqui frog chorus, Puerto Rico – Ellie Williams

Titi monkeys – From Tiputini Research Station, Ecuador

Chapter 4) From Earth and Beyond

Deep sea earthquake off Japan, recorded by microphones in Alaska – National Oceanic and Atmospheric Administration PMEL Acoustics Program

Stromboli volcanic eruption, Italy – Freddie Claire

Earwitness, Hunga Tonga eruption – Kai 'Uto. https://www.youtube.com/watch?v=owlRuul5Tk4

Hunga Tonga explosion captured in Idaho – Zachary Hoppinen and Jeffrey B. Johnson, Dept of Geosciences, Boise State University

Auroral chorus – Stephen P. McGreevy

Auroral sounds – Professor Emeritus in Acoustics Unto K. Laine, Aalto University, Finland

Sounds of Ngozumpa Glacier – Art We There Yet Project https://www.youtube.com/@ArtWeThereYet

Glacier calving, Greenland – Wounded Buffalo

Chapter 5) Voices of the Deep

Minke whale vocalisations – Arnold Mangott, James Cook University, Minke Whale Project

Blue whale call – Macaulay Library, Donald K. Ljungblad

Sperm whale clicks – Macaulay Library, Donald K. Ljungblad

Humpback whale song – Joe Stevens, Wounded Buffalo

Ambon damsel – Eric Parmentier, Université de Liège

Snapping shrimp – Aran Mooney, Woods Hole Oceanographic Institution

Bloop – National Oceanic and Atmospheric Administration PMEL Acoustics Program

52 Hertz whale – National Oceanic and Atmospheric Administration PMEL Acoustics Program

Upsweep – National Oceanic and Atmospheric Administration PMEL Acoustics Program

Narwhal calls, Greenland – Dr Evgeny Podolskiy, Hokkaido University Japan

Orca and boat noise – Dr Paul Spong, Orcalab

Chapter 6) Music from the Sun

UK dawn chorus – David Stripp, BBC Natural History Unit / Pro-Sound Effects

Cory's shearwater, Canary Islands – Xeno Canto / Ruben Barone

Musician wren, Brazil – Xeno Canto / Gabriel Leite

White bellbird, Brazil – Xeno Canto / Gabriel Leite

MacGregor's bowerbird, Papua New Guinea – Huw Cordey, Silverback films and Netflix

Striated antthrush, Peru – Macaulay Library / Ted Parker

Kaua'i 'ō'ō, Hawaii – Macaulay Library / C. Fred Zeillemaker

Skylark singing, UK – Dann Hendriks

Chapter 7) The Living Heartbeat

Night parrot, Australia – Xeno Canto / Nigel Jackett

Golden toad, Costa Rica – Macaulay Library / Arnoud B. van den Berg

Chapter 8) Silence and Storm

Polar bear cubs nursing in Dierenrijk zoo – Chad Van Gessel

Mother polar bear snoring in Dierenrijk zoo – Chad Van Gessel

Emperor penguin contact call, Antarctica – Tom Richards

Weddell seal song – Wounded Buffalo

Walrus haul out – Wounded Buffalo

Himalayan snowcock, Kazakhstan – Xeno Canto / Erik Hansson

Howling wolves – Wounded Buffalo

Himalayan village, Nepal – Freddie Claire

Yellow-billed chough, Nepal – Freddie Claire

Snow leopard chuffle, Ladakh – Khenrab Phuntsog and Smanla Tsering Hemis National Park

Acknowledgments

Eurasian blackcap, England – Xeno Canto / Shaun Micklewright

Acknowledgments

In writing this book, I have been lucky to have been supported by many friends and colleagues from the wildlife filmmaking industry here in Bristol. I am particularly indebted to the sound recordists who I have shared time with in the field. In particular I would like to thank Ellie Williams for her advice, loans of books, sound recordings and her reading of early drafts of the book. I must extend a big thanks too to Freddie Claire for looking after me on shoots, allowing me to access his wonderful sound library and the unexpected appearance of chocolate when I was flagging with my writing. Sebastian Dunn also lifted my spirits by sending me the gift of an inspiring sound recording of African birdlife, when the relentless rain of October in Bristol was dragging me down. It's true what they say – in television the nicest people are the sound recordists. The legendary natural history sound recordists Chris Watson and Martyn Stewart have always inspired my love for natural sound. Each has done much to teach me to listen to the world around me and for that I will always be grateful.

Wilderness Songs started out as a public lecture where I played sound recordings to a live audience and told the stories behind them. I would like to thank Kate Hopkins, Tim Owens, Tom Mercer and Clare Lawrence of Wounded Buffalo in Bristol for their help with this initial project and their ongoing support of the book that followed.

Over the years I have spoken to many dedicated and knowledgeable scientists who have replied to my questions with detail and patience. For their generosity I would particularly like to thank: Dr Rebecca Cliffe for her information on sloths; Professor Rex Cocroft for sharing the wonders of treehoppers; Diego Mosquera for inspiring me during my time in Tiputini; Dr Mark Bowler for his interpretations of howler monkey calls; Dr Koustubh Sharma for clarification on the calls of snow leopards; Dr Maria Maust-Mohl for her work on hippos; and Dr John Vandenberg and Dr Susan Jacobson for their memories of golden toads and helping me track down the last recordings of their calls. I would like to thank Ana Širović and John Ryan for their information on blue whale research and Dr Mary Stanley-Duke for kindly unlocking access to many key research papers. *Go raibh maith agat* to Eithne O'Mahony for her help with pronouncing the sounds of the Irish coastline.

All of the filming trips and close encounters with animals described in this book have been undertaken with the permission of the relevant authorities and guided by experts. In each case, I have been made very welcome by the hospitality of the local people who are custodians of the land. They have generously granted access and shared their knowledge. In particular, I would like to thank the wonderful people of Ladakh and the residents of Rumbak village. In Ecuador, the Waorani people, who are guardians of the rainforest. The Inuit people of Pond Inlet on Baffin Island, the Sherpa people of the Khumbu region of Nepal and the people of Botswana who take care of the Okavango Delta. Thanks to the wilderness locations featured in this book: Hemis National Park in Ladakh, India; Moremi Game Reserve, Botswana; Tiputini Research Centre, Yasuni National Park, Ecuador; Sagarmartha National Park, Nepal; the Nordauslandet and Søraust nature reserves in Svalbard; Barrier Reef Marine Park, Australia; and Sirmilik National Park on Baffin Island.

For all the adventures included in this book, I was reliant on an incredible team of facilitators, fixers, field assistants and filmmakers.

It all starts with a team in Bristol without whom any film crew would be simply lost. In particular I would like to thank Karen Le Huray, Loulla Charalambous, Katie Cuss, Kathryn Gilbert, Gemma Green, Anna Gol, Joe Stevens, Louise Emerson, Cleone Fox, Lexi Walling, Emma Brennand, Danielle Sykes, Mandy Knight, Linda Dale, Jonathan Smith, Alicia Decina, Rebecca Combes, Emily Guy, Jennie Collie, Nicola Melton, Natasha Filer, Emily Fellows, Claire Efergan, Jeanne Clennet, Kate Beacham, Carina Thomas, Yasmin White, Robin Dimbleby, Alice Marlow, Ralph Woollcombe, Steph Holt, Nardine Groch, Lucy Courtnall, Emma Dorman, Tom Packer, Jasmine Tapp, Melanie Guinee, Zoe Brandon, Sam Hodgson, Alex Williamson, Isla Williamson, Chloe Sarosh and Tom Hugh-Jones.

Without the support of local fixers and field assistants we would never get to be in the right place at the right time. Here I owe a debt of thanks to Jason Roberts, Arne Silvertson, Lasse Ostervold, Sven Are Johansen, Lorents Lorentsen, Kjell Arild Hansen, Grete Elin Eriksen, Sam Omik, Dave Reid, Hugo Hamel, Peter Duncan, Adarsh NC, Srihjarsha HK, Vydhehi Kadur, Wangchuk Kalon, Rinchen Kalon, Iswari Paudel, Becky Coles, Zac Poulton, Tsewang Morup, Tsering Norboo, Tsultim Sangay, Rigzen Norboo, Tashi Samstan, Stanzin Lakpa, Smanla Tsering, Jigmet Dadul, Tswewang Nurboo, Ngima Sherpa, Rajan Bhattarai, Manesh Rai, Kiran Rai, Tenji Sherpa, Bikram Rai, Ramesh Rai, Chare Rai, Makar Rai, Fudori Sherpa, Harish Maithani, Aditya Yadav, Nima Tashi, Hugo Cliff, Froilan Macanilla, Jose Macanilla, Jorge Anhalzer, Tomas David Espinosa, Ollie Laker, Yoya Landazuri, Joaquin Gamboa, Aldo Villaneuva, Guillermo Knell, Madume Matshemela, Tshupetso Rambao, Bata Mathinthi, Devon Jenkin, Mpho Johane, Thomas Semata, Patrick Simon, Liz Johnston, Grant Reed, Tania Jenkins, Caroline Lempadi, Reontse Pekenene, Rodney Nombekana, Neil Kendrick, Michael Watson, Kekgonne Kgosintwa, Matshwenyego Kgosiemany, Pelonste Mohara, Amos

Matoteny, Okwa Sarefo, Lucas Tshupo, Thabiso Molathlhegi, David Luck, Mhpo Ladick, Pula Juta, Itemogeng Ditoro, Guy Symons and Newman Chuma.

I have been lucky to have shared the film shoots in this book with some wonderful camera talent and friends. Many thanks to Martyn Colbeck, Warwick Sloss, Duncan Parker, John Shier, Mateo Willis, Nick Guy, Sue Gibson, Simon Werry, Sandesh Kadur, Dean Miller, Rory McGuiness, Mike Amos, Barrie Britton, Mike Holding, Stu Trowell, Rob Whitworth, David Seguardo and Zach Levi-Rogers. Writing about my adventures in Svalbard has rekindled memories of time spent with field guide Steinar Asknes, who sadly passed away a few years ago. As well as being a lovely chap, an incredible guide and expert finder of polar bears, he could also be relied on for a hot brew in a cold place. I now think of him every time I fire up a camp stove to make some tea.

In Ladakh I would like to thank Khenrab Phuntsog for his lasting friendship and boundless generosity and for getting me closer to the grey ghost of the mountains than I ever thought would be possible. *Julay* to you, my friend, until our next adventure.

Many generous sources have allowed me to use their sound recordings for the book. In particular I would like to thank Daan Hendriks for letting me use recordings from his incredible library. Also thanks to Dr Damian Octavio Elias, Eva Maria Luef, Dr Jonathan Growcott, Steffen Reiche, Zachary Hoppinen, Unto K. Laine, Arnold Mangott, Aran Mooney, Dr Evgeny Podolsky, Tom Richards, Stephen P. McGreevy, Eric Parmentier orcalab and the Art We There Yet project. I would like to thank Huw Cordey, Silverback Films and Netflix for allowing me to use their incredible sound recording of MacGregor's bowerbird as featured in their brilliant documentary *Dancing with the Birds*.

I would like to thank my agent Gill McLay and everyone at Batsford Press for their hard work on this book, particularly my editor Rebecca Armstrong. Thanks are also due to James Kellow, Nicola Newman, Lauren Whybrow, Ian Allen, Eoghan O'Brien and Mia Autumn Roe.

Thanks to my mum and dad and sister Rebecca for always being there for me. I owe the biggest thanks to my wife and children, Aoife, Cora and Padraig, who have had to put up with my growing book piles and my ever-spreading invasion of the kitchen table, where I wrote this book. Thanks for riding the wave of my enthusiasm for the stories and helping me through the wobbles.

This book is dedicated to my friend and nature writer Dan Eatherley – author of the amazing *Bushmaster* and *Invasive Aliens*. Dan's love for the natural world and telling its stories always shone through. He was so supportive of my attempts to follow in his footsteps and I am only sorry that he never got to read my finished book. The last time we met was on a summer walk in the woods, where we listened to a blackcap singing. Each time I hear this bird, Dan, I will remember you.

Scan to listen to a blackcap's song.

Bibliography

Chapter 1. Call of the Wild

Select Bibliography:

Liebenberg, Louis. *The Art of Tracking: The Origin of Science.* David Phillips, 1990.
Magan, Manchán. *Sea Tamagotchi: An Irish Sea Dictionary.* Red Fox Press, 2022.
Richardson, Miles. *Reconnection: Fixing Our Broken Relationship with Nature.* Pelagic, 2023.

A brief history of listening:

Hu, Isabel. 'Symbols of the Owl in Different Cultures', *John Moore Museum of Natural History journal*, https://www.johnmooremuseum.org/symbols-of-the-owl-in-different-cultures/#:~:text=In%20Asia%2C%20owls%20have%20various,to%20determine%20the%20baby's%20gender.
Kroeber, A. L. 'Indian Myths of South Central California'. *American Archaeology and Ethnology* 4 (1907): 169.
Quechua Realwords – an audio visual corpus of expressive Quechua ideophones. Janis B. Nuckolls, Prof of linguistics, Brigham Young University. https://quechuarealwords.byu.edu/.

Why natural sounds matter:

Gould van Praag, Cassandra D., Sarah N. Garfinkel, Oliver Sparasci, O. et al. 'Mind-wandering and Alterations to Default Mode Network Connectivity when Listening to Naturalistic Versus Artificial Sounds'. *Scientific Reports* 7, 45273 (2017).
'Research Finds Nature Sounds "Benefit Mental Health"', BBC, 23 March, 2022, https://www.bbc.co.uk/news/uk-england-devon-60840759.
Thoma Myriam. V., Ricarda Mewes and Urs M. Nater. 'Preliminary Evidence: The Stress-Reducing Effect of Listening to Water Sounds Depends on Somatic Complaints: A Randomized Trial'. *Medicine* 97(8): e9851 (2018).
Wood, Zoe. 'Thrush Hour: Study Suggests Birdsong can Ease Commuter Stress', *Guardian*, 29 August, 2024. https://www.theguardian.com/travel/article/2024/aug/29/study-birdsong-natural-sounds-ease-commuter-stress.
Yeo, K.-S., M.-S. Kim and M.-J. Bae. 'Acoustic Characteristics of Forest Sounds Inducing Sleep', *Information* (Koganei) 18, no. 10 (2015): 4407–4412.

Sounds of connection:

Cazalis, Victor, Michel Loreau and Gladys Barragan-Jason. 'A global synthesis of trends in human experience of nature'. *Frontiers in Ecology and the Environment* (2022). DOI: 10.1002/fee.2540.

Kesebir, Selin and Pelin Kesebir. 'A growing disconnection from nature is evident in cultural products'. *Perspectives on Phycological Science* 12(2) (2017): 258–269.

Mears, Meghann, Paul Brindley, Paul Barrows, Miles Richardson and Ravi Maheswaran. 'Mapping urban greenspace use from mobile phone GPS data'. PLOS One, 7 July, 2021. https://doi.org/10.1371/journal.pone.0248622.

O'Donoghue, Barry G., Anita Donaghy and Seán B. A. Kelly. 'National survey of breeding Eurasian Curlew *Numenius arquata* in the Republic of Ireland, 2015–2017'. *Wader Study* 126(1): doi:10.18194/ws.00130 (2019).

'The People and Nature Surveys for England: Monthly indicators with specific weight for April 2020 – March 2021'. GOV.UK.

Richardson, Miles, Michael Lengieza, Mathew P. White et al. 'Macro-level determinants of nature connectedness: An exploratory analysis of 61 countries'. *Ambio* 55, (2026): 80–100. https://doi.org/10.1007/s13280-025-02275-w.

Richardson, Miles. 'Modelling Nature Connectedness Within Environmental Systems: Human-Nature Relationships from 1800 to 2020 and Beyond'. *Earth* 6, no. 3 (2025): 82. https://doi.org/10.3390/earth6030082.

Straka, Tanja M., Carolin Glahe, Ulrike Dietrich et al. 'From nature experience to pro-conservation action: How generational amnesia and declining nature-relatedness shape behaviour intentions of adolescents and adults'. *Ambio* 54, (2025): 1165–1184. https://doi.org/10.1007/s13280-025-02135-7.

Twenge, Jean M., W. Keith Campbell and Brittany Gentile. 'Increases in individualistic words and phrases in American books, 1960–2008'. *PLOS One*, 7(7), e40181 (2012).

White, Mathew P., Ian Alcock, James Grellier et al. 'Spending at least 120 minutes a week in nature is associated with good health and wellbeing'. *Scientific Reports* 9, 7730 (2019). https://doi.org/10.1038/s41598-019-44097-3.

WWF. *Living Planet Report 2024 – A System in Peril*. WWF, 2024.

Excerpts from:

The Aberdeen Bestiary – MS 24. University of Aberdeen. View online at https://www.abdn.ac.uk/bestiary/.

Aristotle. *History of Animals, Volume 1: Books 1–3*. Translated by A. L. Peck. Loeb Classic Library 437, 1989.

Basho, Matsuo. *Basho – The Complete Haiku*. Translated by Jane Reichhold. Kodansha America inc., 2013.

Dickinson, Emily. *Emily Dickinson – The Complete Poems*. Faber and Faber, 2016.

Hoare, Phillip. Roger Payne Obituary. *Guardian*, 16 July, 2023.

Mustill, Tom. 'Afterword – Listen Carefully, Hello again, old friend'. https://www.tommustill.com/afterword-to-how-to-speak-whale.

Recordings of Ludwig Koch. BBC Sound archives. Excerpt taken from *Great Lives, Ludwig Koch* released on 29 August, 2023, and available on BBC Sounds. https://www.bbc.co.uk/sounds/play/m001q0sr.

Songs of the Humpback Whale (LP). Sleeve notes by Dr. Roger S. Payne. CRM Records SWR 11, 1970. Ocean Alliance.

Wordsworth, William. *The Book of Birds: Wordsworth's Poetry on Birds.* Ragged Hand – Read & Co., 2020.
Wordsworth, William. *The Book of Nature: Wordsworth's Poetry on Nature.* Ragged Hand – Read & Co., 2020.
Yeats, William Butler. 'He reproves the Curlew' from *Later Poems.* Macmillan, 1922.

Chapter 2. Hidden Conversations

Select Bibliography:

Butchhart, Duncan. *Wildlife of the Okavango.* Struik Nature, 2016.
Carnaby, Trevor. *Beat about the Bush: Mammals.* Jacana, 2006.
Estes, Richard Despard. *The Behaviour Guide to African Mammals.* University of California Press, 1991.
Kershenbaum, Arik. *Why Animals Talk: The New Science of Animal Communication.* Penguin, 2024.
Kingdon, Jonathan. *The Kingdon Field Guide to African Mammals.* Academic Press, 1997.
Mathevon, Nicolas. *The Voices of Nature: How and Why Animals Communicate.* Princeton University Press, 2023.
Mustill, Tom. *How to Speak Whale: A Voyage into the Future of Animal Communication.* William Collins, 2022.
Sukumar, Raman. *The Living Elephants: Evolutionary Ecology, Behaviour, and Conservation.* Oxford University Press, 2003.

Selected References:

Grunts, grumbles, hoots and honks:

William E. Barklow, 'Amphibious communication with sound in hippos, *Hippopotamus amphibius*', *Animal Behaviour* 68, issue 5 (2004): 1125 1132. ISSN 0003–3472. https://doi.org/10.1016/j.anbehav.2003.10.034.
Maust-Mohl, Maria, Joseph Soltis and Diana Reiss. 'Underwater click train production by the hippopotamus (Hippopotamus amphibius) suggests an echo-ranging function'. *Behaviour* 155 (2018). 10.1163/1568539X-00003484.
Maust-Mohl, Maria, Joseph Soltis and Diana Reiss. 'Acoustic and behavioral repertoires of the hippopotamus (*Hippopotamus amphibius*)'. *The Journal of the Acoustical Society of America* 138 (2015): 545–554. 10.1121/1.4923363.
Thévenet, Julie et al. 'Voice-mediated interactions in a megaherbivore (*Hippopotamus amphibius*)'. *Current Biology* 32, issue 2, R70–R71.

Nature bugged:

Devlin, Hannah. 'Grisly recordings reveal bat catching, killing and eating a robin mid-flight'. *Guardian*, 9 October, 2025. https://www.theguardian.com/science/2025/oct/09/grisly-recording-reveals-bat-catching-killing-and-eating-robin-mid-flight.

Stidsholt, L., E. Tena, I. Foskolos et al. 'Greater noctule bats prey on and consume passerines in flight'. *Science* 390, issue 6769 (2025): 178–181. DOI: 10.1126/science.adr2475.

Wild conversations:

Baotic, Anton and Angela S. Stoeger. 'Information content and acoustic structure of male African elephant (*Loxodonta africana*) social rumbles'. *Journal of the Acoustical Society of America* 139(6) (2016): 3330–3339.

Clarke, Esther, Ulrich H. Reichard and Klaus Zuberbühler. 'Context-specific close-range "hoo" calls in wild gibbons (*Hylobates lar*)'. *BMC Evolutionary Biology* 15, 56 (2015). https://doi.org/10.1186/s12862-015-0332-2.

Eleuteri, Vesta et al. 'Chimpanzee drumming shows rhythmicity and subspecies variation'. *Current Biology* 35, issue 10 (2025): 2448–2456. e4.

Elias, Damian O., Wayne P. Maddison, Christina Peckmezian, Madeline B. Girard and Andrew C. Mason. 'Orchestrating the score: complex multimodal courtship in the *Habronattus coecatus* group of *Habronattus* jumping spiders (Araneae: Salticidae)'. *Biological Journal of the Linnean Society* 105 (2012): 522–547.

Girard-Buttoz, Cédric, Christof Neumann, Tatiana Bortolato, et al. 'Versatile use of chimpanzee call combinations promotes meaning expansion'. *Science Advances* 11 (19) (2025). DOI: 10.1126/sciadv.adq2879.

Luef, Eva Marie, Thomas Breuer and Simone Pika. 'Food-Associated Calling in Gorillas (*Gorilla g. gorilla*) in the Wild'. *PLOS One* 11(2) (2016). e0144197. https://doi.org/10.1371/journal.pone.0144197.

O'Connell-Rodwell, Caitlin E., Jodie L. Berezin, Alessio Pignatelli and Timothy C. Rodwell. 'The use of vocal coordination in male African elephant group departures: evidence of active leadership and consensus'. *PeerJ* 12 (2024). e17767.

O'Connell-Rodwell, Caitlin E., B. Arnason and L. A. Hart. 'Seismic properties of Asian elephant (*Elephas maximus*) vocalizations and locomotion'. *Journal of the Acoustical Society of America* 108 (6) (2000): 3066–72.

Pardo Michael A., Kurt Fristrup, David S. Lolchuragi et al. 'African elephants address one another with individually specific name-like calls'. *Nature Ecology and Evolution* 8 (2024): 1353–1364.

King of the beasts:

American Institute of Physics – Inside Science News Service. 'The secret of a tiger's roar'. *ScienceDaily*, accessed 3 June, 2025. www.sciencedaily.com/releases/2000/12/001201152406.htm.

Wijers, M., P. Trethowan, B. Du Preez et al. 'Vocal discrimination of African lions and its potential for collar-free tracking'. *Bioacoustics* 30 (5) (2021): 575–593. https://doi.org/10.1080/09524622.2020.1829050.

Chasing shadows:

Fischer, Julia, Kurt Hammerschmidt, Dorothy L. Cheney and Robert M. Seyfarth. 'Acoustic Features of Female Chacma Baboon Barks'. Max-Planck Institute for Evolutionary Anthropology, Inselstr. 22, D-04103 Leipzig, Germany, 2008.

Growcott, J. et al. 'The secret acoustic world of leopards: A paired camera trap and bioacoustics survey facilitates the individual identification of leopards via their roars'. 2004. Preprint at https://doi.org/10.1002/rse2.429.

Kitchen Dawn. M., Thore J. Bergman, Dorothy L. Cheney, James R. Nicholson and Robert M. Seyfarth. 'Comparing responses of four ungulate species to playbacks of baboon alarm calls'. *Animal Cognition* 13 (6) (2010): 861–70. doi: 10.1007/s10071-010-0334-9. Epub 2010 Jul 4. PMID: 20607576.

Meise, Kristine, Franks, Daniel W. and Bro-Jørgensen, Jakob. 'Multiple adaptive and non-adaptive processes determine responsiveness to heterospecific alarm calls in African savannah herbivores'. *Proceedings of the Royal Society B: Biological Sciences* 285 (1882) (2018). 20172676.

Palmer, Meredith S. and Gross, Abby. 'Eavesdropping in an African large mammal community: antipredator responses vary according to signaller reliability'. *Animal Behaviour* 137 (2018): 1–9.

Price, Tabitha, Philip Wadewitz, Dorothy L. Cheney et al. 'Vervets revisited: A quantitative analysis of alarm call structure and context specificity'. *Scientific Reports* 5, 13220 (2015). https://doi.org/10.1038/srep13220.

Seyfarth, Robert M., Dorothy L. Cheney and Peter Marler. 'Vervet monkey alarm calls: Semantic communication in a free-ranging primate.' *Animal Behaviour* 28 (1980): 1070–1094.

Van Wyk, G. 'Aspects of the communication and feeding behaviour of captive leopards (*Panthera pardus*)'. Doctoral dissertation, University of the Free State, 2003.

Chapter 3. The Forest Orchestra

Select Bibliography:

Cliffe, Rebeccca and Suzi Esterhas. *Sloths: Life in the slow lane.* Sloth Conservation Foundation, 2017.

Hilty, Stephen and Mimi Hoppe Wolf. *Birds of Tropical America.* University of Texas Press, 2005.

Kowalewski, Martin M. and Mariana Rano. 'Howler Monkey (Alouatta)'. In *The International Encyclopedia of Primatology,* edited by Agustín Fuentes. John Wiley & Sons, Inc. 2017.

Krause, Bernie. *The Great Animal Orchestra: Finding the Origins of Music in the World's Wild Places.* Little, Brown and Co., 2012.

Oxford, Pete, Renee Bish and Kelly Swing. *Yasuni, Tiputini and the Web of Life.* USFQ Press, 2012.

Petter, Jean-Jacques and Francois Desbordes. *Primates of the World: An illustrated guide.* Princeton University Press, 2013.

Resh, Vincent H. and Ring T. Cardé. *Encyclopedia of Insects.* Academic Press, 2009.

Wilson, Edward and Bert Holldobler. *The Leafcutter Ants – Civilisation by Instinct.* W. W. Norton and Company, 2010.

Selected References:

When the jungle roars:

da Cunha, Rogério, Dilmar Oliveira, Ingrid Holzmann, and Dawn Kitchen. 'Production of Loud and Quiet Calls in Howler Monkeys'. (2015). 337-368. 10.1007/978-1-4939-1957-4_13.

Drubbel R. V. and J. P. Gautier. 'On the occurrence of nocturnal and diurnal loud calls, differing in structure and duration, in red howlers (*Alouatta seniculus*) of French Guyana'. *Folia Primatol (Basel)* 60 (4) (1993): 195–209. doi: 10.1159/000156693. PMID: 8300015.

Dunn, Jacob C., Lauren B. Halenar, Thomas G. Davies et al. 'Evolutionary trade-off between vocal tract and testes dimensions in howler monkeys'. *Current Biology* 25 (21) (2015): 2839–2844. doi: 10.1016/j.cub.2015.09.029. Epub 2015 Oct 22. PMID: 26592343; PMCID: PMC4635310.

Kitchen, Dawn, Rogério da Cunha, Ingrid Holzmann and Dilmar Oliveira. 'Function of Loud Calls in Howler Monkeys'. (2015): 369–399. 10.1007/978-1-4939-1957-4_14.

Ramsier, Marissa, Andrew Cunningham, May Patiño, Kenneth Glander and Nathaniel Dominy. 'Audiograms of howling monkeys: are extreme loud calls the result of runaway selection?' (2019). 10.1101/539023.

Schön Ybarra, M. A. 'Loud calls of adult male red howling monkeys (*Alouatta seniculus*)'. *Folia Primatol (Basel)* 47 (4) (1986): 204–16. doi: 10.1159/000156278. PMID: 3609972.

Sekulic, Ranka. 'Male Relationships and Infant Deaths in Red Howler Monkeys (*Alouatta seniculus*)'. *Zeitschrift für Tierpsychologie* 61 (2010): 185–202. 10.1111/j.1439-0310.1983.tb01337.x.

Sekulic, Ranka. 'The Function of Howling in Red Howler Monkeys (*Alouatta seniculus*).' *Behaviour* 81, no. 1 (1982): 38–54. http://www.jstor.org/stable/4534196.

Shearer, Brian, Lauren Halenar, Anthony Pagano and Jeffrey Laitman. 'New Insights into Howler Monkey Vocal Tract Anatomy via 3-Dimensional Imaging Technology'. *The FASEB Journal* 29 (2015). 10.1096/fasebj.29.1_supplement.867.8.

Van Belle, Sarie. 'Female participation in collective group defense in black howler monkeys (*Alouatta pigra*)'. *American Journal of Primatology* 77 (6) (2015): 595–604. doi: 10.1002/ajp.22380. Epub 2015 Feb 20. PMID: 25704874.

Van Belle, Sarie, Alejandro Estrada and Paul Garber. 'Spatial and Diurnal Distribution of Loud Calling in Black Howlers (*Alouatta pigra*)'. *International Journal of Primatology* 34 (2013). 10.1007/s10764-013-9734-4.

Conducting the forest orchestra:

Ellinger, Norbert and Walter Hodl. 'Habitat acoustics of a Neotropical lowland rainforest'. *Bioacoustics* 13 (2003): 297–321. 10.1080/09524622.2003.9753503.

Hart, Patrick and William Ray. 'Cicadas impact bird communication in a noisy tropical rainforest'. *Behavioral Ecology* 26 (2015). 10.1093/beheco/arv018.

Luther, David. 'The influence of the acoustic community on songs of birds in a neotropical rain forest'. *Behavioral Ecology* 20, issue 4 (2009): 864–871. https://doi.org/10.1093/beheco/arp074.

Monacchi, David. 'Fragments of Extinction: Acoustic Biodiversity of Primary Rainforest Ecosystems'. *Leonardo Music Journal*. The MIT Press, 2013.

Nemeth Erwin, Torben Dabelsteen, Simon Boel Pedersen and Hans Winkler. 'Rainforests as concert halls for birds: are reverberations improving sound transmission of long song elements?' *The Journal of the Acoustical Society of America* 119 (1) (2006): 620–6. doi: 10.1121/1.2139072. PMID: 16454315.

Roces, Flavio, Juergen Tautz and Bert Hölldobler. 'Stridulation in leaf-cutting ants'. *Naturwissenschaften* 80 (1993). 521–524. 10.1007/BF01140810.

Rodriguez, Alexandra, Amandine Gasc, Sandrine Pavoine, Philippe Grandcolas, Philippe Gaucher and Jérôme Sueur. 'Temporal and spatial dynamics of animal sound within a neotropical forest'. *Ecological Informatics* 21 (2013). 10.1016/j.ecoinf.2013.12.006.

Sánchez-Giraldo, Camilo, Carol L. Bedoya, Raúl A. Morán Vásquez, Claudia V. Isaza and Juan M. Daza. 'Ecoacoustics in the rain: understanding acoustic indices under the most common geophonic source in tropical rainforests'. *Remote Sensing in Ecology and Conservation* (2020). ZSL.

Wonders of the rainforest:

Bostwick, Kimberly S. 'Display Behaviours, Mechanical sounds, and evolutionary relationships of the club-winged manakin (*Machaeropterus deliciosus*)'. *The Auk*. 117 (2) (2000): 465–478.

Bostwick, Kimberly S., Damian O. Elias, Andrew Mason and Fernando Montealegre-Z. 'Resonating feathers produce courtship song'. *Proceedings. Biological Sciences* 277 (1683) (2010): 835–841. https://doi.org/10.1098/rspb.2009.1576.

Bostwick, Kimberly S. and Richard O. Prum. 'Courting Bird Sings with Stridulating Wing Feathers'. *Brevia Science Magazine* 309 (2005).

Bostwick, Kimberly S. and Richard O. Prum. 'High-speed video analysis of wing-snapping in two manakin clades (Pipridae: Aves)'. *Journal of Experimental Biology* 206 (20) (2003): 3693–3706.

Bostwick, Kimberly S., Mark L. Riccio and Julian M. Humphries. 'Massive, solidified bone in the wing of a volant courting bird'. *Biology Letters* 8 (5) (2012): 760–763. https://doi.org/10.1098/rsbl.2012.0382.

Cocroft, Reginald. 'Offspring-parent communication in a subsocial treehopper (Hemiptera: Membracidae: *Umbonia crassicornis*)'. *Behaviour* 136 (1999): 1–21. 10.1163/156853999500640.

Cocroft, Reginald B. and Jennifer A. Hamel. 'Vibrational communication in the "other insect societies": A diversity of ecology, signals and signal functions'. *The Use of Vibrations in Communication: properties, mechanisms and functions across taxa*. (2010).

Cocroft, Reginald B. and Rafael L. Rodríguez. 'The Behavioral Ecology of Insect Vibrational Communication'. *BioScience* 55, issue 4 (2005): 323–334. https://doi.org/10.1641/0006-3568(2005)055[0323:TBEOIV]2.0.CO;2.

Cossio-Rodriguez, Romina, Reginald B. Cocroft, Hermann M. Niemeyer and Carlos F. Pinto. 'Mate searching in *Ennya maculicornis* (Membracidae: Polyglyptini) initiated by females: behavioural and acoustic descriptions'. *Ecological Entomology*. (2019). https://doi.org/10.1111/een.12718.

Hamel, Jennifer A. and Reginald B. Cocroft. 'Maternal Vibrational Signals Reduce the Risk of Attracting Eavesdropping Predators'. *Frontiers in Ecology and Evolution* 7 (2019).

Hamel, Jennifer A. and Reginald B. Cocroft. 'Negative feedback from maternal signals reduces false alarms by collectively signalling offspring'. *Proceedings. Biological Sciences* 279 (1743) (2012): 3820–3826. https://doi.org/10.1098/rspb.2012.1181.

Joyce, Christopher and Bill McQuay. 'Good Vibrations Key to Insect Communication'. NPR online article and radio piece. 27 August, 2015.

Kui, Mackenzie. 'Differential maternal defence behaviour in three species of treehoppers (Hemiptera:Membracidae)'. Digital Commons @ University of South Florida. (2017).

Lin, Chung-Ping. 'Social behaviour and life history of membracine treehoppers'. *Journal of Natural History* 40 (2006): 1887–1907. 10.1080/00222930601046618.

Miles, Meredith C., Franz Goller and Matthew J. Fuxjager. 'Physiological constraint on acrobatic courtship behavior underlies rapid sympatric speciation in bearded manakins'. *eLife* 7 (2018). e40630.

Owens, Brian. 'Bats use ear trumpets for social calls'. *Nature* (2013). https://doi.org/10.1038/nature.2013.13960.

Pinto, Carlos, Daniel Torrico-Bazoberry, Luis Flores-Prado, Ramiro Bustamante and Hermann Niemeyer. 'Demographic and performance effects of alternative host use in a neotropical treehopper (Hemiptera: Membracidae)'. *Ecological Modelling* 416 (2019). 10.1016/j.ecolmodel.2019.108905.

Prum, Richard O. 'Sexual Selection and the evolution of mechanical sound production in manakins (Aves: Pirpridae)'. *Animal Behaviour* 55 (1998): 977–994.

Torrico-Bazoberry, Daniel, Caceres-Sanchez, Liliana, Flores-Prado, Luis et al. 'Kin recognition in a subsocial treehopper (Hemiptera: Membracidae)'. *Ecological Entomology* 43 (2018). 10.1111/een.12506.

Torrico-Bazoberry, Daniel, Liliana Caceres-Sanchez, Daniela Saavedra-Ulloa, Luis Flores-Prado, Hermann M. Niemeyer and Carlos F. Pinto. 'Biology and Ecology of *Alchisme grossa* in a Cloud Forest of the Bolivian Yungas'. *Journal of Insect Science* 14, issue 1 (2014): 169. https://doi.org/10.1093/jisesa/ieu031.

Torrico-Bazoberry, Daniel, Carlos Pinto, Luis Flores-Prado, Francisco Fontúrbel and Hermann Niemeyer. 'Natural selection in the tropical treehopper *Alchisme grossa* (Hemiptera: Membracidae) on two sympatric host-plants'. *Arthropod-Plant Interactions* 10 (2016). 10.1007/s11829-016-9427-y.

Urquizo, Omar, David Véliz, Daniel Torrico-Bazoberry et al. 'Reproductive and brood-rearing strategies in *Alchisme grossa* (Hemiptera: Membracidae): genetic analyses of kinship relationships'. *Insectes Sociaux* 67 (2020). 10.1007/s00040-020-00776-3.

Zolfagharifard, Ellie. 'The bats with hearing aids! Creatures discovered using rolled-up leaves as "ear trumpets" to hear far away calls'. *Daily Mail* online article. 17 October 2013.

Moonlit chorus:

Andreani, Tainã L., Rogerio Bastos, R. P., Tailise M. Dias, Cynthia P. A. Prado and Allesandro Morais. 'Acoustic variability among male gladiator frogs, *Boana goiana* (Lutz, 1968) (Anura: Hylidae): an 18-year analysis across several reproductive seasons'. *Amphibia-Reptilia* 42 (1) (2020): 43–57. https://doi.org/10.1163/15685381-bja10029.

Brunetti, Andrés E., et al. 'Extended Vocal Repertoire *in Hypsiboas punctatus* (Anura: Hylidae).' *Journal of Herpetology* 49, no. 1 (2015): 46–52, accessed 10 December, 2025. https://www.jstor.org/stable/44164531.

Feng, Albert S., Peter M. Narins, Chun-He Xu et al. 'Ultrasonic communication in frogs'. *Nature* 16 440(7082) (2006): 333–6. doi: 10.1038/nature04416. PMID: 16541072.

Goutte, Sandra, Matthew J. Mason, Jakob Christensen-Dalsgaard et al. 'Evidence of auditory insensitivity to vocalization frequencies in two frogs'. *Scientific Reports* Sep 21; 7 (1) (2017). 12121. doi: 10.1038/s41598-017-12145-5. PMID: 28935936; PMCID: PMC5608807.

Harris, James. 'Lungs like noise-cancelling headphones help frogs find suitors from the same species amid the noise of other frogs'. *The Standard Online*. 4 March, 2021.

Lee, Norman et al. 'Lung Mediated Auditory Contrast Enhancement Improves the Signal-to-Noise Ratio for Communication in Frogs'. *Current Biology* (2021). DOI: 10.1016/j.cub.2021.01.048.

Mayer, Michael, Lisa M. Schulte, Evan Twomey and Stefan Lötters. 'Do male poison frogs respond to modified calls of a Müllerian mimic?' *Animal Behaviour* 89 (2014): 45–51. ISSN 0003-3472, https://doi.org/10.1016/j.anbehav.2013.12.013.

McCracken, Shawn F. and Michael R. J. Forstner. 'Oil Road Effects on the Anuran Community of a High Canopy Tank Bromeliad (*Aechmea zebrina*) in the Upper Amazon Basin, Ecuador'. *PLOS One* 9 (1) (2014). e85470. https://doi.org/10.1371/journal.pone.0085470.

Morrison, Clare, Jean-Marc Hero and William P. Smith. 'Mate selection in *Litoria chloris* and *Litoria xanthomera*: Females prefer smaller males'. *Austral Ecology* 26, issue 3 (2001): 223–232.

Rojas, Bibiana and Andrius Pasukonis. 'From Habitat Use to Social Behavior: Natural History of a Voiceless Poison Frog, *Dendrobates tinctorius*'. (2019). 10.1101/515122.

Echoes of impact:

'Ecuador's new bill will privatize protected areas and ignores the existence of indigenous peoples'. Press release. Amazon Frontiers – July 2025.

Marsh, Laura. 'Primate species at the Tiputini Biodiversity Station, Ecuador'. *Neotropical Primates* 12 (1997). Biol. Conserv. Oryx Am. J. Primatol. Ecology and Behavior of Neotropical Primates World Wildlife Fund. 70-99192. 10.62015/np.2004.v12.575.

Müller, Alexandra and Gustl Anzenberger. 'Duetting in the Titi Monkey *Callicebus cupreus*: Structure, Pair Specificity and Development of Duets'. *Folia primatologica; international journal of primatology* 73 (2002): 104–15. 10.1159/000064788.

Wallis, Arthur Scott. 'Demand for oil is squeezing the life out of one of the world's wildest places'. *National Geographic Magazine*. January 2013.

Chapter 4. From Earth and Beyond

Select Bibliography:

Henderson, Caspar. *A Book of Noises. Notes on the Auraculous*. Granta, 2023.

MacDonald, John. *The Arctic Sky – Inuit Astronomy, Star Lore, and Legend*. Royal Ontario Museum and Nunavut Research Institute, 1998.

Sherpa, Ang Rita. *Climate Change in the Himalayas – a case from Solu Khumbu*. The Partners Nepal, 2020.

Winchester, Simon. *Krakatoa – The day the world exploded*. Viking Press, 2003.

Selected References:

The big bang:

'Earthquake booms, Seneca guns and other sounds'. https://www.usgs.gov/programs/earthquake-hazards/earthquake-booms-seneca-guns-and-other-sounds.

Lawson, Andrew C. *The California earthquake of April 18th 1906. Report of the State Earthquake investigation commission*. Carnegie Institute of Washington, 1908.

'Listen: Boise State researchers record world's loudest sound since 1883, Hunga Tonga eruption'. *Boise State News*, 31 January, 2022. https://www.boisestate.edu/news/2022/01/31/listen-boise-state-researchers-record-worlds-loudest-sound-since-1883-hunga-tonga-eruption/.

'Noise from underwater volcano eruption across the Pacific Heard in the Yukon'. *CBC News* online, 15 January, 2022. https://www.cbc.ca/news/canada/north/noise-from-underwater-volcanic-eruption-across-the-pacific-heard-in-the-yukon.

Tosi, Patrizia, Paola Sbarra and Valerio De Rubeis. 'Earthquake sound perception'. *Geophysical Research Letters* 39 (2012). L24301. doi:10.1029/2012GL054382.

Spirits' footsteps:

Laine, Unto K. 'Localization of sound sources in temperature inversion layer during a geomagnetic storm'. 24th International Congress on Sound and Vibration. London, July 2017.

Warnings from the ice:

Benn, D. I., S. Wiseman and K. A. Hands. 'Growth and drainage of supraglacial lakes on debris-mantled Ngozumpa Glacier, Khumbu Himal, Nepal'. *Journal of Glaciology* 47 (159) (2001): 626–638. doi:10.3189/172756501781831729.

Chand, Mohan and Teiji Watanabe. 'High-resolution inventory of glacial lakes in the Ngozumpa Glacier basin, Everest region, Nepal'. *Bulletin of the Nepal Hydrological Association* 5 (2020).

Dyurgerov, Mark and Mark Meier. 'Glaciers and the Changing Earth System: A 2004 Snapshot'. 58. (2004).

'Everest's Sherpas fear their homes could wash away'. BBC news online article, 20 August, 2024. https://www.bbc.co.uk/news/articles/c785nwq568zo.

Glowacki, Oskar and Grant B. Deane. 'Quantifying iceberg calving fluxes with underwater noise'. *The Cryosphere* 14 (2020): 1025–1042.

Horodyskyj, Ulyana Nadia. 'Thermal and Physical Investigations into Lake Deepening Processes on Spillway Lake, Ngozumpa Glacier, Nepal'. *Water* 9, no. 5 (2017): 362. https://doi.org/10.3390/w9050362.

International Centre for Integrated Mountain Development – Online press release,

18 August, 2024. 'GLOF from Thyanbo glacial lake sweeps away Thame Village'. https://www.icimod.org/press-release/glof-from-thyanbo-glacial-lake-sweeps-away-thame-village/.

Kapil, J. C. Sakshi Sharma, Karmjeet Singh, J. S. Shahi and Rama Arora. 'Acoustic emission monitoring and analyses for avalanche release and slab fracturing events observed in Great Himalaya'. *Nondestructive Testing and Evaluation* 39 2 (2024): 446–473.

'Nepali Government's National Disaster Risk Reduction & Management Authority – report into Thame GLOF'. https://www.youtube.com/watch?v=ZVL8vbe09rU.

Shea, Joseph, W. Immerzeel, P. Wagnon, C. Vincent and S. Bajracharya. 'Modelling glacier change in the Everest region, Nepal Himalaya'. *The Cryosphere* 9 (2015): 1105–1128.

Thakuri, S., F. Salerno, N. Guyennon et al. 'Glacier response to climate trend and climate variability in Mt. Everest region (Nepal)' May 2013, American Geophysical Union, Spring Meeting 2013, abstract id. C21B-01.

'The Thame Flood – a window into the Himalayan climate crisis'. Nepal Economic forum online article. https://nepaleconomicforum.org/the-thame-flood-a-window-into-the-himalayan-climate-crisis/.

Thompson, Sarah, Douglas Benn, Kathryn Hands and Adrian Luckman. 'A rapidly growing moraine-dammed glacial lake on Ngozumpa Glacier, Nepal'. *Geomorphology* 145 (2012). 10.1016/j.geomorph.2011.08.015.

Excerpts from:

'A tremendous rumble' quote from 'Portrush man describes devastation of Nepal earthquake'. BBC news online, 26 April, 2015. https://www.bbc.co.uk/news/uk-northern-ireland-32465338.

Family interview. https://www.youtube.com/watch?v=e5X2V5OlCzE.

Hawkes, Earnest W. *The Labrador Eskimo*. Ottawa Government Printing Bureau, 1916.

Hooper, W. H. *Ten months among the tents of the Tuski, with incidents of an Arctic boat expedition in search of Sir John Franklin*. John Murray, 1853.

'It came with a huge roar, the water and boulders just rushed down' – eyewitness accounts. Thame GLOF *The Katmandu Post* online link. https://kathmandupost.com/national/2024/08/16/flood-in-solukhumbu-destroys-12-houses.

Captain W.J Watson of the Charles Bal from Symons, quoted in The Krakatoa Committee of the Royal Society, *The Eruption of Krakatoa, and Subsequent Phenomena* (Trübner & Co, 1888), 20.

Captain O Sampson of the vessel Norham Castle from Simon Winchester, quoted in *Krakatoa: The Day the World Exploded* (HarperCollins, 2003), 234.

Quote from elder Mark Ijjangiaq. Original Source – The Igloolik Oral History Project. Mark Ijjangiaq: IE-081 - Jan 1990 / IE-138 March 1990 / IE-184 fEB 1991 / IE - 187 fEB 1991 / IE - 203 October 1991 *The Arctic Sky – Inuit Astronomy, star lore and legend* by John MacDonald, Royal Ontario Museum and Nunavut Research Institute 1998. P149.

Quote from elder Catherine Arnatsiaq. Original Source – The Igloolik Oral History Project. Catherine Arnatsiaq: IE - 077 Jan 1990 *The Arctic Sky – Inuit Astronomy, star lore and legend* by John MacDonald, Royal Ontario Museum and Nunavut Research Institute 1998, p 149-151.

Quote from elder George Kappianaq. Original Source – The Igloolik Oral History

Project. George Kappianaq : IE -071 Dec 1986 / IE - 096 Feb 1990 / IE -102 Feb 1990 / IE - 155 October 1990 / IE - 174 Jan 1991 / IE- 187 Feb 1991 / IE 253 Jan 1993 / IE - 256 Feb 1993 / IE- 267 1990 / IE- 273 March 1993 / IE - 329 Jan 1995 *The Arctic Sky – Inuit Astronomy, star lore and legend* by John MacDonald, Royal Ontario Museum and Nunavut Research Institute 1998 p152.

Quote from elder Niviattian Aqatsiaq. Original Source – The Igloolik Oral History Project. Niviattian Aqatsiaq: IE - 079 January 1990 / IE -149 June 1990 *The Arctic Sky – Inuit Astronomy, star lore and legend* by John MacDonald, Royal Ontario Museum and Nunavut Research Institute 1998 p151-152.

Unto K Laine, quoted in 'How one scientist decoded the mysterious sound of the Northern Lights,' Tom Metcalfe, archived October 12, 2016, at https://www.livescience.com/56457-scientist-decoded-mysterious-northern-lights-sounds.html.

Rasmussen, Knud. *Across Arctic America. Narrative of the Fifth Thule Expedition*. G. P. Putnam's Sons, 1927.

Sherpa, Mingma Rita – eyewitness accounts Thame GLOF. 'Devastation of Thame and How to Help Through the Thame Support Fund'. Foundation for the Preservation of the Mahayana Tradition. https://fpmt.org/charitable-activities/devastation-of-thame-and-how-to-help-through-the-thame-support-fund/.

Størmer, Carl. *The Polar Aurora*. Clarendon Press, 1955.

Von Humboldt, Alexander. *Cosmos, A sketch of a physical description of the Universe*. George Bell and Sons, 1893.

Chapter 5. Voices of the Deep

Select Bibliography:

Byatt, Andrew, Alastair Fothergill and Martha Holmes. *The Blue Planet – A Natural History of the Ocean*. BBC Books, 2001.

Carwardine, Mark. *Field Guide to Whales, Dolphins and Porpoises*. Bloomsbury, 2022.

Horowitz, Joshua. *War of the Whales*. Simon and Schuster, 2015.

Kingdon, Amorina. *Sing Like Fish*. Scribe Publications, 2024.

Martin, Dr. Anthony R. *Whales and Dolphins*. Salamander Books, 1990.

Mustill, Tom. *How to Speak Whale: A Voyage into the Future of Animal Communication*. William Collins, 2022.

Paine, Stefani. *The Nature of Arctic Whales: Belugas, Bowheads and Narwhals*. Greystone Nature, 1995.

Rothenberg, David. *Thousand Mile Song*. Basic Books, 2008.

Selected References:

Making friends with a whale:

Gedamke, Jason, Daniel Costa and Andy Dunstan. 'Localization and visual verification of a complex minke whale vocalization'. *The Journal of the Acoustical Society of America* 109 (2001): 3038–47. 10.1121/1.1371763.

The big one:

Clark, Christopher W. and David K. Mellinger. 'Application of Navy IUSS for whale research'. *The Journal of the Acoustical Society of America* 96 (5_supplement) (1994): 3315. https://doi.org/10.1121/1.410808.

Lewis, Leah A., John Calambokidis, Alison K. Stimpert et al. 'Context-dependent variability in blue whale acoustic behaviour'. *Royal Society Open Science* 5 (8) (2018): 5180241. http://doi.org/10.1098/rsos.180241.

Širović, Ana and Erin Oleson. 'The Bioacoustics of Blue Whales—Global Diversity and Behavioral Variability in a Foraging Specialist'. In *Ethology and Behavioral Ecology of Mysticetes*, edited by Christopher W. Clark and Ellen C. Garland. Springer, 2022.

Stafford, Kathleen M., Christopher G. Fox and David S. Clark. 'Long-range acoustic detection and localization of blue whale calls in the northeast Pacific Ocean'. *The Journal of the Acoustical Society of America* 104 (6) (1998): 3616–3625. https://doi.org/10.1121/1.423944.

The loudest of all:

Sharma, Pratyusha, Shane Gero, Roger Payne et al. 'Contextual and combinatorial structure in sperm whale vocalisations'. *Nature Communications* 15, 3617 (2024). https://doi.org/10.1038/s41467-024-47221-8.

Song of the seas:

Au, Whitlow. W. L, Adam A. Pack, Marc O. Lammers, Louis M. Herman, Mark H. Deakos and Kim Andrews. 'Acoustic properties of humpback whale songs'. *Journal of the Acoustical Society of America* 120, issue 2 (2006): 1103–1110.

Cholewiak, Danielle M., Salvatore Cerchio, Jeff K. Jacobsen, Jorge Urbán-R. and Christopher W. Clark. 'Songbird dynamics under the sea: acoustic interactions between humpback whales suggest song mediates male interactions'. *Royal Society Open Sciences* 5 (2) (2018). 171298. https://doi.org/10.1098/rsos.171298.

Copeland, Adrienne. M., Whitlow W. Au, Marc O. Lammers, Adam A. Pack and Julie N. Oswald. 'Characterizing and classifying humpback whale (*Megaptera novaenagliae*) song units'. *The Journal of the Acoustical Society of America* 129 (2011): 2639–2639.

Darling, James D. and Martine Bérubé. 'Interactions of singing humpback whales with other males' (2006). https://doi.org/10.1111/j.1748-7692.2001.tb01005.x.

Green, Sean R., Eduardo Mercado III, Adam A. Pack and Louis M. Herman. 'Recurring patterns in the songs of humpback whales (*Megaptera novaeangliae*)'. *Behavioural Processes* 86 (2011): 284–294.

Green, Sean R., Eduardo Mercado III, Adam A. Pack and Louis M. Herman. 'Characterizing patterns within humpback whale (*Megaptera novaeangliae*) songs'. *Aquatic Mammals* 33 (2007): 202–213.

Herman, Louis M. 'The multiple functions of male song within the humpback whale (*Megaptera novaeangliae*) mating system: review, evaluation, and synthesis'. https://onlinelibrary.wiley.com/doi/am-pdf/10.1111/brv.12309.

Herman, Louis M., Adam A. Pack, Scott S. Spitz et al. 'Humpback whale song: who sings?' *Behavioural Ecology and Sociobiology* 67 (2013): 1653–1663. https://doi.org/10.1007/s00265-013-1576-8.

Leighton, Timothy G., Simon D. Richards and Paul R. White. 'Trapped within a "wall of sound": A possible mechanism for the bubble nets of the humpback whales'. *Acoustics Bulletin* 29 (1) (2004): 24–29.

Leighton, Timothy G., Dan Finfer, Ed Grover and Paul R. White. 'An acoustical hypothesis for the spiral bubble nets of humpback whales and the implications for whale feeding'. *Acoustics Bulletin* 22 (1) (2007): 17–21.

Mercado III, Eduardo, Louis M. Herman and Adam A. Pack. 'Stereotypical sound patterns in humpback whale "songs": Usage and utility'. *Aquatic Mammals* 29 (2003): 37–52.

Mercado III, Eduardo, Louis M. Herman and Adam A. Pack. 'Song copying by humpback whales: Themes and variations'. *Animal Cognition* 8 (2005): 93–102.

Schulze, Josephine N., Judith Denkinger, Javier Oña, M. Michael Poole and Ellen C. Garland. 'Humpback whale song revolutions continue to spread from the central into the eastern South Pacific'. *Royal Society Open Science* 9 (8) (2022). 220158. https://doi.org/10.1098/rsos.220158.

Smith, Joshua N. et al. 'Songs of male humpback whales, *Megaptera novaeangliae*, are involved in intersexual interactions'. *Animal Behaviour* 76, issue 2 (2008): 467–477.

Szabo, A., L. Bejder, H. Warick et al. 'Solitary humpback whales manufacture bubble-nets as tools to increase prey intake'. *Royal Society Open Science* 11 (8) (2024). 240328. https://doi.org/10.1098/rsos.240328.

Au, Whitlow W. L., Adam A. Pack, Marc O. Lammers, Louis M. Herman, Mark H. Deakos and Kim Andrews. 'Acoustic properties of humpback whale songs'. *The Journal of the Acoustical Society of America* 120 (2) (2006): 1103–10. DOI: 10.1121/1.2211547.

Popping shrimp and squeaking fish:

Byrne, Maria, Alexander Waller, Matthew Clements et al. 'Catastrophic bleaching in protected reefs of the Southern Great Barrier Reef' *Luminology and Oceanography Letters*. 16 January, 2025. https://doi.org/10.1002/lol2.10456.

Colleye, Orphal and Eric Parmentier. 'Overview on the Diversity of Sounds Produced by Clownfishes (Pomacentridae): Importance of Acoustic Signals in Their Peculiar Way of Life'. *PLOS One* (2012). https://doi.org/10.1371/journal.pone.0049179.

González-Irusta, José. M. and Peter J. Wright. 'Spawning ground of Atlantic cod (*Gadus morhua*) in the North Sea'. *ICES Journal of Marine Science* 73 (2) (2016): 304–315.

Grabowski, T. B, V. Thorsteinsson and G. Marteinsdóttir. 'Assessing the lekking hypothesis for the mating system of Atlantic cod (Gadus morhua) using electronic data-storage tags'. (2009). ICES CM 2009/B:01.

Kingston, Alexandra C.N., Sarah A. Woodin, David S. Wethey and Daniel I. Speiser. 'Snapping shrimp have helmets that protect their brains by dampening shock waves'. *Current Biology* 32, issue 16 (2022): 3576–3583. e3. ISSN 0960-9822, https://doi.org/10.1016/j.cub.2022.06.042.

Koukouvinis, Phoevos, Christoph Bruecker and Manolis Gavaises. 'Unveiling the physical mechanism behind pistol shrimp cavitation'. *Scientific Reports* 7, 13994 (2017). https://doi.org/10.1038/s41598-017-14312-0.

Lowe, Jake. 'Young wrasse hit hard by cyclones and bleaching'. James Cook University featured news, 14 October 2020.

McGrath, Matt. 'Climate change: World's oceans suffer from record breaking year of heat'. BBC News online, 8 May, 2024.

Nordeide, J. T. and I. Folstad. 'Is cod lekking or a promiscuous group spawner?' *Fish and Fisheries* 1 (2000): 90–93.

Nordeide, Jarle Tryti, Christel Solberg, Lasse Willumsen and Stian Berge Amble. 'Seasonal variation and condition-dependence of the drumming muscle of cod, *Gadus morhua* L.? – An experimental approach'. *Journal of Experimental Marine Biology and Ecology* 363, issues 1–2 (2008): 66–74. ISSN 0022-0981, https://doi.org/10.1016/j.jembe.2008.06.019.

Oladipo, Gloria. 'Florida's mystery bass rumble may be sound of frisky fish mating'. *Guardian* online, 30 January, 2024.

Parmentier, Eric and Bruno Frédérich. Broadening of acoustic repertoire in Pomacentridae: tonal sounds in the Ambon damselfish *Pomacentrus amboinensis*. *Journal of Zoology* 300, issue 4 (2016): 241–246.

Parmentier, Eric, David Lecchini, Bruno Frédérich, Christophe Brié and David Mann. 'Sound production in four damselfish (Dascyllus) species: phyletic relationships?' *Biological Journal of the Linnean Society* 97 (2009): 928–940.

Russel, Mark. 'Mating fish keep Florida residents awake at night'. *Dive Magazine*, 3 February, 2024.

Slabbekoorn, Hans, Niels Bouten, Ilse van Opzeeland, Aukje Coers, Carel ten Cate and Arthur N. Popper. 'A noisy spring: the impact of globally rising underwater sound levels on fish'. *Trends in Ecology and Evolution* 25 (2010): 419–427.

Steinhoff, Nane. 'Coral bleaching on Great Barrier Reef reaches catastrophic levels'. *Oceanographic Magazine*, 22 January, 2025.

Drowning in noise:

Erbe, Christine, Sarah A. Marley, Renée P. Schoeman, Joshua N. Smith, Leah E. Trigg and Clare Beth Embling. 'The Effects of Ship Noise on Marine Mammals – A Review'. *Frontiers in Marine Science* 6 (2019). 606. doi:10.3389/fmars.2019.00606.

'The Heard Island Experiment'. American Philosophical Society podcast. https://www.amphilsoc.org/heard-island-experiment.

Jones, Joshua M., John A. Hildebrand, Bruce J. Thayre et al. 'The influence of sea ice on the detection of bowhead whale calls'. *Scientific Reports* 12, 8553 (2022). https://doi.org/10.1038/s41598-022-12186-5.

Kavanagh, Ailbhe, Kylie Owen, Michael Williamson et al. 'Evidence for the functions of surface-active behaviors in humpback whales (*Megaptera novaeangliae*). *Marine Mammal Science* 33 (2016). 10.1111/mms.12374.

Matthews, Leanna P. and Susan E. Parks. 'An overview of North Atlantic right whale acoustic behavior, hearing capabilities, and responses to sound'. *Marine Pollution Bulletin* 173, part B (2021). 113043. ISSN 0025-326X, https://doi.org/10.1016/j.marpolbul.2021.113043.

Marotte, Emmaline, Andrew J. Wright, Heather Breeze et al. 'Recommended metrics for quantifying underwater noise impacts on North Atlantic right whales'. *Marine Pollution Bulletin* 175 (2022). 113361. ISSN 0025-326X, https://doi.org/10.1016/j.marpolbul.2022.113361.

Nowacek, Douglas P., Mark P. Johnson and Peter L. Tyack. 'North Atlantic right whales (*Eubalaena glacialis*) ignore ships but respond to alerting stimuli'. *Proceedings. Biological Sciences* 271 (1536) (2004): 227–231. https://doi.org/10.1098/rspb.2003.2570.

Tervo, Outi M., Susanna B. Blackwell, Susanne Ditlevsen et al. 'Narwhals react to ship noise and airgun pulses embedded in background noise'. *Biology Letters* 17 (11) (2021). 20210220. https://doi.org/10.1098/rsbl.2021.0220.

Podolskiy, Evgeny A. and Shin Sugiyama. 'Soundscape of a narwhal summering ground in a glacier fjord (Inglefield Bredning, Greenland)'. *Journal of Geophysical Research: Oceans* 125 (2020). e2020JC016116. https://doi.org/10.1029/2020JC016116.

Podolskiy, Evgeny A., Monica Ogawa, Mayuko Otsuki et al. 'Repeated narwhal interactions with moorings challenge safety assumptions of passive acoustic monitoring in the Arctic'. *Communications Biology* 8, 1557 (2025). https://doi.org/10.1038/s42003-025-09106-4.

'Review of maritime transport 2023. Towards a green and just transition'. UNCTAD. Division on Technology and Logistics. Trade Logistics Branch.

Rolland, Rosalind M., Susan E. Parks, Kathleen E. Hunt et al. 'Evidence that ship noise increases stress in right whales'. *Proceedings. Biological Sciences* 279 (1737) (2012): 2363–8. doi: 10.1098/rspb.2011.2429. Epub 2012 Feb 8. PMID: 22319129; PMCID: PMC3350670.

Segre, P. S., J. Potvin, D. E. Cade et al. 'Energetic and physical limitations on the breaching performance of large whales'. *eLife* (2020). e51760. doi: 10.7554/eLife.51760. PMID: 32159511; PMCID: PMC7065846.

Williams, Terrie M., Susanna B. Blackwell, Outi Tervo et al. 'Physiological responses of narwhals to anthropogenic noise: A case study with seismic airguns and vessel traffic in the Arctic'. *Functional Ecology* 36, issue 9 (2022). P 2251-2266.

Chapter 6. Music from the Sun

Select Bibliography:

Carson, Rachel. *Silent Spring*. Houghton and Mifflin, 1962.

Couzens, Dominic. *A Year of Birdsong*. Batsford, 2022.

Lewis-Stempel, John. *The Soaring Life of the Lark*. Doubleday, 2021.

Lockhart, James MacDonald. *Wild Air: In Search of Bird Song*. Fourth Estate, 2023.

Oxford, Pete, Renee Bish and Kelly Swing. *Yasuni Tiputini and the Web of Life*. USFQ Press, 2012.

Thomas, Adrian. *RSPB Guide to Birdsong*. Bloomsbury, 2019.

Selected References:

Courtship and conflict:

Colombelli-Négrel, Diane, Andrew C. Katsis, Lauren K. Common and Sonia Kleindorfer. 'Personality predicts song complexity in superb fairy-wrens'. *Royal Society Open Science* 12 (4) (2025).

Gonzalo-Tarodo, A., R. J. Facey and J. O. Vafidis. 'Bioacoustic variation in Wren *Troglodytes troglodytes* populations on Welsh islands'. *Bird Study* 67 (2) (2020): 173–180.

Odom, Karan J., Michelle L. Hall, Katharina Riebel, Kevin E. Omland and Naomi E. Langmore. 'Female song is common and ancestral in songbirds'. *Nature Communications* 5, article 3379 (2014).

Zipple, Matthew N., Susan Peters, William A. Searcy and Stephen Nowicki. 'Sounds of senescence: male swamp sparrows respond less aggressively to the songs of older individuals', *Behavioral Ecology* 31, issue 2, (2020): 533–539.

Learning the notes:

Derryberry, Elizabth P., Jennifer N. Phillips, Graham E. Derryberry, Michael J. Blum and David Luther. 'Singing in a silent spring: Birds respond to a half-century soundscape reversion during the COVID-19 shutdown'. *Science* 370 (6516) (2020): 575–579. doi: 10.1126/science.abd5777. Epub 2020 Sep 24. PMID: 32972991.

'Natural England's People and Nature Survey'. 2020. https://www.ons.gov.uk/economy/environmentalaccounts/articles/howhaslockdownchangedourrelationshipwithnature/2021-04-26.

Tropical troubadours:

Blake, John G. and Bette A. Loiselle. 'Sharp declines in observation and capture rates of Amazon birds in absence of human disturbance'. *Global Ecology and Conservation* 51 (2024). e02902. ISSN 2351-9894, https://doi.org/10.1016/j.gecco.2024.e02902.

Doolittle, Emily and Henrik Brumm. 'O Canto do Uirapuru: Consonant intervals and patterns in the song of the musician wren'. *Journal of Interdisciplinary Music Studies* (2013).

Max Planck Institute for Ornithology. 'I'm singing in the rainforest: Researchers find striking similarities between bird song and human music.' *ScienceDaily*, 16 October 2013. www.sciencedaily.com/releases/2013/10/131016100307.html.

Podos, Jeffrey and Mario Cohn-Haft. 'Extremely loud mating songs at close range in white bellbirds'. *Current Biology* 29 (2019). R1068-R1069. 10.1016/j.cub.2019.09.028.

Pollock, Henry S., Judith D. Toms, Corey E. Tarwater, Thomas J. Benson, James R. Karr and Jeffrey D. Brawn. 'Long-term monitoring reveals widespread and severe declines of understory birds in a protected Neotropical forest'. *PNAS* 119 (16) (2022). e2108731119, https://doi.org/10.1073/pnas.2108731119.

Lost songs:

Bird Life International. *State of the World's Birds 2022*. https://www.birdlife.org/wp-content/uploads/2022/09/SOWB2022_EN_compressed.pdf.

Joy ascending:

Cresswell, Will. 'Song as a pursuit-deterrant signal, and its occurance relative to other anti-predation behaviours of skylark (*Alauda arvensis*) on attack by merlins (*Falco columbarius*)'. *Behavioural Ecology and Sociobiology* 34 (1994): 217–24.

Hammoud, Ryan, Stefania Tognin, Lucie Burgess et al. 'Smartphone-based ecological momentary assessment reveals mental health benefits of birdlife'. *Scientific Reports* 12, 17589 (2022). https://doi.org/10.1038/s41598-022-20207-6.

Stevenson, Sharon A., Alice Piepenburg, Jeremy A. Spool et al. 'Endogenous opioids facilitate intrinsically-rewarded birdsong'. *Scientific Reports* 10, 11083 (2020). https://doi.org/10.1038/s41598-020-67684-1.

Excerpts from:

Coulson, Private Leslie. 'The Rainbow'. 1917.
Darwin, Charles. *On the Origin of Species*. John Murray, 1859.
Hughes, Ted. 'Skylarks'. 1966.
Meredith, George. 'The Lark Ascending'. 1881.
Shakespeare, William. 'Sonnet 29, When in disgrace with fortune and men's eyes'. 1609.
Wordsworth, William. 'To the Skylark'. 1827.

Chapter 7. The Living Heartbeat

Select Bibliography:

Moore, Robin. *In Search of Lost Frogs*. Bloomsbury, 2014.
Ritland, Trevor and Kyle. *The Golden Toad*. Diversion Books, 2025.

Selected References:

Pulse of the planet:

Biller, David. 'An Amazon rainforest rite of passage in threatened territory'. *Morning Star*. Feature article, 16 June, 2023. https://morningstaronline.co.uk/article/f/amazon-rainforest-rite-passage-threatened-territory.

Ngururrpa Rangers, Clifford Sunfly, Andrew Schubert et al. 'Potential threats and habitat of the night parrot on the Ngururrpa Indigenous Protected Area'. *Wildlife Research* 51 (2024). WR24083. https://doi.org/10.1071/WR24083.

Topher White, quoted in Rolex Awards for Enterprise, "2019 Rolex Awards Associate Laureate Documentary: Topher White," YouTube, https://www.youtube.com/watch?v=7zOgF-7ewhE.

Elnaldo Tembé and Topher White, quoted in Google (@google), "Ep 2: Beneath the Canopy," YouTube, https://www.youtube.com/watch?v=Lbn6kVlFaSQ.

Ravi, Reethu. 'Rainforest connection – Saving the rainforest through cloud computing, AI and machine learning to detect threats'. *Lampoon*, online article, 30 September, 2022.

Rosen, Len. 'Rainforest Connection reminds us how connected we need to remain to our planet's shrinking biome'. 21st Century Tech Blog, online article, 11 July, 2020.

Finding frogs:

Garrido Sanchis, Adrian, Lorenzo Bertolelli, Anke Maria Hoefer, Marta Yebra Alvarez and Kumudu Munasinghe. 'The FrogPhone: A novel device for real-time frog call monitoring'. *Methods in Ecology and Evolution* 00 (2019): 1–7. https://doi.org/10.1111/2041-210X.13332.

Jacobson, Susan Kay. 'Short Season of the Golden Toad'. *International Wildlife* 13 (6) (1983): 25–27.

Jacobson, Susan K. and John J. Vandenburg. 'Reproductive Ecology of the Endangered Golden Toads'. *Journal of Herpetology* 25, no. 3 (1991): 321–327.

'Jerdon's Babbler rediscovered in Myanmar'. Oriental Bird Club news. Online article, 5 March, 2015. https://www.orientalbirdclub.org/club-news/2015/03/05/jerdons-babbler-rediscovered-in-myanmar.

Luedtke, J.A . et al. 'Ongoing declines for the world's amphibians in the face of emerging threats'. The IUCN Red List of Threatened Species: Amphibian Dataset. 2023.

Palus, Shannon. 'Rediscovering a lost Babbler – a small songbird from Myanmar hadn't been spotted for decades'. *Audubon Magazine*, 10 March, 2015.

Savage, Jay M. 'An Extraordinary New Toad (Bufo) from Costa Rica'. *Revista de Biologia Tropical* 50, no. 2 (1965).

Waddle, Anthony W., Simon Clulow, Amy Aquilina et al. 'Hotspot shelters stimulate frog resistance to chytridiomycosis'. *Nature* 631 (2024): 344–349. https://doi.org/10.1038/s41586-024-07582-y.

Walker, S. F., J. Bosch, T. Y. James et al. 'Invasive pathogens threaten species recovery programs.' *Current Biology* 18 (18) (2008). R853–R854. DOI: 10.1016/j.cub.2008.07.033.

The quietening of giants:

Goldbogen, J.A., D.E. Cade, J. Calambokidis et al. 'Extreme bradycardia and tachycardia in the world's largest animal'. *PNAS* 116 (50) (2019): 25329–25332. https://doi.org/10.1073/pnas.1914273116.

Gordon, Timothy A. C., Andrew N. Radford, Isla K. Davidson et al. 'Acoustic enrichment can enhance fish community development on degraded coral reef habitat'. *Nature Communications* 10 5414 (2019). https://doi.org/10.1038/s41467-019-13186-2.

Moan, André and Arne Bjørge. 'Pingers reduce harbour porpoise bycatch in Norwegian gillnet fisheries, with little impact on day-to-day fishing operations'. *Fisheries Research* 259 (2023). 106564. 10.1016/j.fishres.2022.106564.

Rockwood, R. Cotton, John Calambokidis and Jaime Jahncke. 'High Mortality of Blue, Humpback and Fin Whales from Modeling of Vessel Collisions on the U.S. West Coast Suggests Population Impacts and Insufficient Protection'. *PLOS One* 12 (8) 2017. e0183052. doi.org/10.1371/journal.pone.0183052.

Ryan, John P., William K. Oestreich, Kelly J. Benoit-Bird et al. 'Audible changes in marine trophic ecology: Baleen whale song tracks foraging conditions in the eastern North Pacific'. *PLOS One* 20 (2) (2025). e0318624. https://doi.org/10.1371/journal.pone.0318624.

Excerpts from:

Ana Sirovic, "Two studies tackle threat to whales from shipping," interview by Acoustics Bulletin, January/February, 2018, 36.

Ana Sirovic, "Watching Over the Whales," interview by Sonia Fernandez, *The Current*, University of California, September 17, 2020.

Chapter 8. Silence and Storm

Select Bibliography:

Aars, Jon, Magnus Anderson and Kit Kovacs. *Polar Bears in Svalbard*. Norwegian Polar Institute, 2005.
Cherry-Garrard, Apsley. *The Worst Journey in the World*. Constable and Co., 1922.
Lopez, Barry. *Arctic Dreams*. Vintage Books, 1986.
Parker, Steve. *Scott's Last Expedition*. Natural History Museum, 2011.
Phuntsog, Khenrab and Smanla Tsering. *Tales of the Snow Leopard*. Philomene Verlann, 2016.
Shawl, Tahir. *Field Guide to Mammals of Ladakh*. WWF India.
Polar Bears by Ian Stirling. Fitzhenry and Whiteside 1998.
Schaller George B. *Stones of Silence*. Viking Press 1980

Selected References:

The sea bear:

Cushing, Bruce S., Nancy L. Cushing and Charles Jonkel. 'Polar bear responses to the underwater vocalizations of ringed seals'. *Polar Biology* 9 (1988): 123–124. https://doi.org/10.1007/BF00442039.
Owen, Megan A. and Ann E. Bowles. 'In-Air Auditory Psychophysics and the Management of a Threatened Carnivore, the Polar Bear (*Ursus maritimus*)'. *International Journal of Comparative Psychology* 24, issue 3 (2011). https://doi.org/10.46867/ijcp.2011.24.03.05.
Sergiel, Agnieszka and Russ Van Horn. 'Bear Sensory Systems'. (2022). 10.1007/978-3-319-55065-7_1745.
Togunov, Ron R., Andrew E. Derocher and Nicholas J. Lunn. 'Windscapes and olfactory foraging in a large carnivore'. *Scientific Reports* 7, 46332 (2017). https://doi.org/10.1038/srep46332.
van Gessel, Chad. 'Polar bear mother-offspring interactions in maternity dens in captivity'. *Zoo Biology*. 34 (5) (2015): 453–9. doi: 10.1002/zoo.21232. Epub 2015 Aug 7. PMID: 26252623.
van Gessel, Chad. 'Decoding Polar Bear Vocalizations in the Den'. Polar Bears International, 15 October, 2013. https://polarbearsinternational.org/news-media/articles/decoding-polar-bear-vocalizations-den-behavior.

Emps:

Aubin, Thierry, Pierre Jouventin and Christophe Hildebrand. 'Penguins use the two-voice system to recognize each other'. *Proceedings. Biological Sciences* B 267 (2000): 1081–1087.
Gilbert, Caroline, Stéphane Blanc, Yvon Le Maho and André Ancel. 'Energy saving processes in huddling emperor penguins: from experiments to theory'. *The Journal of* Exp*erimental* Biol*ogy* 211 (1) (2008): 1–8.
Phillips, Kathryn. 'How huddles help penguins weather winter'. *The Journal of Experimental Biology* 211 (1) (2008): i.

Zitterbart, Daniel P., Barbara Wienecke, James P. Butler and Ben Fabry. 'Coordinated Movements Prevent Jamming in an Emperor Penguin Huddle'. *PLOS One* (2011). https://doi.org/10.1371/journal.pone.0020260.

Windy walruses and singing seals:

Kubny, Heiner. 'Hunting ban helped the walrus on Svalbard'. *Polar Journal* online article, 7 April, 2022.

Larsen, Ole N. and Colleen Reichmuth. 'Walruses produce intense impulse sounds by clap-induced cavitation during breeding displays'. *Royal Society Open Science* 30 8 (6) (2021). 210197. doi: 10.1098/rsos.210197. PMID: 34234955; PMCID: PMC8242830.

Stirling, Ian, Wendy Calvert and Cheryl Spencer. 'Evidence of stereotyped underwater vocalizations of male Atlantic walruses (*Odobenus rosmarus rosmarus*)'. *Canadian Journal of Zoology* 65 (1987): 2311–2321. DOI: 10.1139/z87-348.

The shattered stillness:

Anderson, Magnus. 'Short term behavioural responses of polar bears (*Ursus maritimus*) to snowmobile disturbance'. *Polar Biology*, March 2007.

Jones, Esther L., Gordon D. Hastie, Sophie Smout et al. 'Seals and shipping: quantifying population risk and individual exposure to vessel noise'. *Journal of Applied Ecology* 54, issue 6 (2017): 1930–1940.

Owen, Megan A., Ann E. Bowles, Sheyna Wisdom and Anthony M. Pagano. 'Estimating the Audibility of Industrial Noise to Denning Polar Bears'. *Journal of Wildlife Management* 85, issue 2 (2020): 384–396.

Lunn, Nick J., Ian Stirling, Dennis Andriashek and Evan Richardson. 'Selection of maternity dens by female polar bears in western Hudson Bay, Canada and the effects of human disturbance'. *Polar Biology* 27 (2004): 350–356. 10.1007/s00300-004-0604-6.

Molnár, Péter K., Cecilia M. Bitz, Marika M. Holland et al. 'Fasting season length sets temporal limits for global polar bear persistence'. *Nature Climate Change* 10 (2020): 732–738. https://doi.org/10.1038/s41558-020-0818-9.

Quigley, Gwendolyn , Todd J. Brinkman, Ryan Wilson and Aaron Christ. 'Behavioral response of polar bears to aircraft activity on the northern coast of Alaska'. *Wildlife Management* 88, issue 3 (2024). E22554.

Stroeve, Julienne, Alex Crawford, Steve Ferguson et al. 'Ice-free period too long for Southern and Western Hudson Bay polar bear populations if global warming exceeds 1.6 to 2.6 °C'. *Communications Earth and Environment* 5, 296 (2024). https://doi.org/10.1038/s43247-024-01430-7.

The grey ghost:

Blomqvist, Leif. *International Pedigree Book of Snow Leopards,* Panthera uncia. Helsinki Zoo, 1982.

Brown, Janine L. 'Female reproductive cycles of wild female felids'. *Animal Reproduction Science*. Special Issue: Reproductive Cycles of Animals. 124 (3) (2011): 155–162. doi:10.1016/j.anireprosci.2010.08.024. ISSN 0378-4320.

Madhu Chetri, Morten Odden, Koustubh Sharma, Øystein Flagstad and Per Wegge. 'Estimating snow leopard density using fecal DNA in a large landscape in north-central Nepal'. *Global Ecology and Conservation* 17 (2019). e00548, ISSN 2351-9894. https://doi.org/10.1016/j.gecco.2019.e00548.

Jean-Louis, Uranie. 'Effect of sensory enrichments on the behaviour of captive Northern lynx (*Lynx lynx lynx*) and assessment of automated behaviour monitoring technologies'. Linköping University, Department of Physics, Chemistry and Biology, thesis (2019).

Kershenbaum, Arik, Holly Root-Gutteridge, Bilal Habib et al. 'Disentangling canid howls across multiple species and subspecies: Structure in a complex communication channel'. *Behavioural Processes* 124 (2016): 149–157. ISSN 0376-6357. https://doi.org/10.1016/j.beproc.2016.01.006.

Larsen, Hanne Lyngholm, Cino Pertoldi, Niels Madsen et al. 'Bioacoustic Detection of Wolves: Identifying Subspecies and Individuals by Howls'. *Animals* 12 (5) (2022): 631. https://doi.org/10.3390/ani12050631.

McCarthy, T., D. Mallon, R. Jackson, P. Zahler and K. McCarthy. 'Snow leopard (*Panthera uncia*)' (errata version 2017). The IUCN Red List of Threatened Species (2017). e.T22732A115174017.

Peters, Gustav and Barbara A. Tonkin-Leyhausen. 'Evolution of Acoustic Communication Signals of Mammals: Friendly Close-Range Vocalizations in Felidae (Carnivora)'. *Journal of Mammalian Evolution* 6 (1999): 129–159. https://doi.org/10.1023/A:1020620121416.

Raina, Pankaj, Ninad Avinash Mungi, Ujjwal Kumar et al. 'Comprehensive assessment of snow leopard distribution and population in the Indian Trans-Himalaya, Ladakh: Standardizing methods for evidence-based conservation'. *PLOS One* (2025). https://doi.org/10.1371/journal.pone.0322136.

Rose, Shanna J., Drew Allen, Dan Noble and Jennifer A. Clarke. 'Quantitative analysis of vocalizations of captive Sumatran tigers (*Panthera tigris sumatrae*)'. *Bioacoustics* 27 (1) (2018): 13–26.

Ryckeley, Meghan. 'Evaluating the Social Behavior and Activity Patterns of Clouded Leopards (*Neofelis nebulosa*) at the Nashville Zoo: Research and Literature Review'. Honors College Capstone Experience, Thesis Projects (2017).

Saloni, Bhatia, Suryawanshi Kulbhushansingh, Redpath Stephen Mark, Namgail Stanzin and Mishra Charudutt. 'Understanding People's Relationship With Wildlife in Trans-Himalayan Folklore Frontiers'. *Environmental Science* 9 (2021). DOI=10.3389/fenvs.2021.595169, ISSN=2296-665X.

Titze, Ingo R., W. Tecumseh Fitch, Eric J. Hunter et al. 'Vocal power and pressure-flow relationships in excised tiger larynges'. *Journal of Experimental Biology* 213 (22) (2010): 3866–3873. DOI: 10.1242/jeb.044982. ISSN 0022-0949.